The Nature of Childhood

The Nature of Childhood

An Environmental History of Growing Up
in America since 1865

PAMELA RINEY-KEHRBERG

UNIVERSITY PRESS OF KANSAS

Published by the
University Press of
Kansas (Lawrence,
Kansas 66045), which
was organized by the
Kansas Board of Regents
and is operated and
funded by Emporia State
University, Fort Hays
State University, Kansas
State University, Pittsburg
State University, the
University of Kansas, and
Wichita State University

Library of Congress Cataloging-in-Publication Data

Riney-Kehrberg, Pamela.
The nature of childhood : an environmental
history of growing up in America since 1865 /
Pamela Riney-Kehrberg.
pages cm
Includes bibliographical references and index.
ISBN 978-0-7006-1958-0 (hardback)
1. Children—United States—History.
2. Families—United States—History. 3. Children
and the environment—United States. 4. Children—
United States—Social conditions. 5. Human
ecology—United States. 6. Nature—Effect of human
beings on—United States. 7. United States—Social
conditions. 8. United States—Environmental
conditions. I. Title.
HQ792.U5R57 2014
305.230973—dc23
2013044561

British Library Cataloguing-in-Publication Data is
available.

Printed in the United States of America
10 9 8 7 6 5 4 3 2 1

The paper used in this publication is recycled and
contains 30 percent postconsumer waste. It is acid
free and meets the minimum requirements of the
American National Standard for Permanence of
Paper for Printed Library Materials z39.48–1992.

For Scott Riney, my brother
and
Rachel Myron, my sister-by-choice,
my companions in many childhood adventures

Rachel Myron with the author, Tomahawk Ranch Girl Scout Camp, Colorado, June 1975. Photograph by permission of Mary Thompson Riney.

CONTENTS

This book is the product of having grown up in a particular time and a particular place. Although I have memories of my early childhood in Houston, my strongest recollections really begin in 1969, when I was six, and my family moved to the suburbs of Denver. I would roam (more or less freely) through my neighborhood until 1981 when I left home to go to college. It was a good era and a good place in which to be a kid. Parents told their children to "never talk to strangers," but there was very little fear of child snatching and molestation by unknown others. Adults were comfortable allowing children almost unfettered access to the streets, the playgrounds and the suburban wild places that still abounded. Sometimes children had to stay within calling distance of a mother's voice; sometimes mothers and fathers allowed them to go where and when they wanted, as long as they were home for dinner, or at bedtime. Playing unsupervised in the dark was also within the realm of possibility, as long as my friends and I promised to stay out of the street. In a lot of ways, my brother and I were "free range" kids, allowed to come and go as we pleased, as long as we knew the rules (like never talking to strangers) and exercised a modicum of good sense (which might include not telling our parents about the stupid stunts we tried or the things that scared us).

My childhood was particularly blessed by location. I grew up directly across the street from the High Line Canal, an irrigation ditch that runs from the foothills through Denver's suburbs to the farms of the eastern plains. In 1969, my parents bought a house on the south side of South Marion Way, a street that curved along the canal. While there were houses on the south side of the street, there were none immediately across, along the canal. There was only a strip of weedy land between the street and the ditch. Later, some of the neighbors would buy up that land to guarantee that nothing would be built there.

The canal was part of a complex of "wild places" near our house. At the end of the block was an open field, as yet undeveloped. Across the canal were two very small farms, and just to the east was DeKoevend Park, which until 1973 remained undeveloped. There was even an old silo at its edge, a remnant of the not-so-distant agricultural past. The silo came down in the 1980s. The rumor was that "big kids" used the structure for various clandestine activities, such as smoking pot and making out. It always just looked dirty and littered to me. One by one, the wild places disappeared, with the little farms and open field gradually succumbing to development. Soccer fields, picnic shelters, and baseball diamonds eventually consumed the park. But the canal and its adjacent walking path remained.

The canal was always a magical place for me. My parents allowed almost completely free access. I had to stay away from the water when the canal was running full, but I could still play along the banks at those times. My father demonstrated the danger of the fast running water by sending our large golden retriever, Beau, into the water to fetch a retrieving dummy. Powerful, eighty-pound Beau struggled against the current, reinforcing the message that the water was too swift for us. When the canal was empty, which was most of the time, I could play anywhere I wanted, including climbing down into its depths to root around in the mud. There really weren't a lot of rules, other than to exercise good sense. Mostly I played down there with a friend or my brother.

The canal was a great place to play "pioneers going west." My inspiration must have been Laura Ingalls Wilder's *By the Banks of Plum Creek*. I don't remember the details, but lots of imagination was involved. We had to fight our way through the brush, prairie fires and blizzards. Sometimes I just walked and talked with friends, enjoying being out of the house. At other times, it was a place for adventure. Once, on the last day of school, my friend Rachel and I went walking in the undeveloped part of DeKoevend Park, below the canal. It was a dangerous thing to do, since on the last day of school, teenagers preyed on littler kids, doing things like grabbing them and "scrubbing" their faces with lipstick, or ruining their hair with Nair. A big kid followed us, hoping for a successful scrubbing. Little did he know that he'd chosen the wrong duo. We hit him, scratched him, knocked him down and sat on him. We never did succumb to a scrubbing.

Most of my visits to the canal were less dramatic. In late summer, various plants growing along the canal's banks yielded edible treats. The wild plums could be eaten out of hand, and were actually pretty good. My brother, mother and I picked them and took them home for mother to make into jam. The jam was good for a while, but got mighty old by winter's end. There were also chokecherry bushes in places, and again, my brother, mother and I picked them. These my mother made into jam—which refused to jell—yielding gallons of chokecherry syrup. It had a nice, deep, reddy-purple color, but the taste became tediously cloying with time.

I learned to skate on the canal. The boy next door got too big for his hockey skates, and they ended up at our house. One winter there was sufficient ice for an attempt at skating. The patch of ice wasn't big enough to be really satisfactory, but it was big enough for me to learn that this was something I'd like to pursue in more congenial environs. Another time, playing on less than solid ice, I fell and sent my arm through the surface, cutting my right wrist. I still have the scars. But not to worry, the water was not terribly deep. The Denver Water Board never left more than a foot in the canal over the winter. In most places, it was simply sandy or muddy.

My brother occupied himself with the canal more than I did. He and his friend Stacy spent days on end digging around in the mud, hunting crawdads and other forms of life. The crawdads they brought home to boil and eat. I was never tempted to try them. The frog that they found was awesome in size. From the tip of his nose to the tips of his toes, he had to have been more than a foot long. No one had ever seen such a creature in Colorado. He was so powerful that he pushed his way out from under the rock and board my brother was using to try to keep him in a bucket. I'd never seen a bigger frog before, and I've never seen one since.

Other types of wildlife lived along the canal too. There were ducks, of course, and I eagerly awaited the ducklings in the spring. There were raccoons. A den of foxes lived down in DeKoevend Park (I think they still live there today). An occasional coyote made its way down the trail. In the 1990s, people started thinking that they were seeing mountain lions, although I'm not sure anyone ever had definitive evidence of a sighting in our neighborhood. But by then, I was no longer a regular visitor.

What I think I valued most about the canal was the walking and talking. It was a place where you could build up a good head of steam, walk for miles, and pour out your heart to whomever your walking companion might be. I walked there with friends, boyfriends, my brother, and both my parents, but mostly my father. When he was out of the house and walking, he relaxed a bit and was easier to talk to. We had some of our best father-daughter moments walking along the canal.

I also had one of my less happy moments along the canal, one that cured me forever of walking there, or any other secluded place, alone. Sometimes I went down to the canal when I was blue and sat and watched the water. It was a tranquil place, good for thinking and dreaming. I was having one of those blue moments in the summer I was fifteen, and was sitting on the stump of a cottonwood tree, watching the green-brown water flow past. I have forgotten what it was that bothered me that afternoon, although I have forgotten few of the other details. As I sat there, I noticed a young man, probably in his late teens or early twenties, wearing only a pair of shorts and riding by slowly on his bicycle. I was a little disturbed to see him riding by a second time, even more slowly yet. The third time he rode by, his shorts were gone. Scared and furious, I stomped up out of the canal's banks onto the path, and stormed my way home. Nobody was there when I arrived, so I closed all the windows and doors and locked myself inside. I should have called the police, but I was too shocked and embarrassed. I didn't tell my parents. I don't think I told anyone until many years later. But for me, the canal as a place of refuge and solitary contemplation was gone. It disappeared with a naked man on a bike. When I went walking along the canal again, it would be with a big dog or a companion.

And that is why, in good measure, this topic of environments and children interests me. In my lifetime, a historical transformation I deeply regret has taken place. In the last thirty years, American children have lost the opportunity to explore their neighborhoods independently. The United States is no longer populated by children who are free to enjoy the out-of-doors in an unsupervised manner. Instead, they spend their leisure time at soccer matches, watching television, or looking at their computers, cell phones and video games. If they spend time in parks and playgrounds, it is generally within the confines of a parent's gaze, on a plastic play structure, designed with their protection in mind. Even though I live in a fairly safe small city, I very rarely see an unsupervised child in an outdoor public place. It would not be fair to begin this book without telling you this—that I regret the passing of a certain kind of childhood. I grew up with an abundance of wild space, and I was able to use it largely without supervision. That experience gave me time to think, developed my creativity and nurtured my independence.

But I understand the flip side of the coin as well: parents want to protect their children from dangers that—real or not—seem so much more pressing than they did thirty and forty years ago. My own independent experience of the High Line Canal ended abruptly and unpleasantly. Thankfully, the damage was minimal. I understand the qualifications parents place on their children's freedom, even if they disturb me. My own son's autism precludes independent play in public places, so my regret does not have to be tested against the reality of what I will allow my child to experience. Independent, unsupervised play in the out-of-doors has never been on his personal radar screen, so I do not have to feel any angst about what I do and do not allow my son to do with his free time. I come to this topic as an interested observer, who feels great nostalgia for a kind of childhood that seems to have vanished.

Pamela Riney-Kehrberg
Ames, Iowa

ACKNOWLEDGMENTS

Two of the leading figures in the history of childhood deserve credit first and foremost for my decision to write this book. Ray Hiner and Joe Hawes asked me to write a chapter on environment for volume six of Berg's *Cultural History of Childhood and Family*. In the course of writing that chapter, I discovered that while many authors had dealt with bits and pieces of the environmental history of childhood, no one had really tried to bring together the big picture. Great thanks go to Ray Hiner and Joe Hawes for pointing me in this direction. Additionally, I want to thank the History Department at Texas Tech University, which invited me to give their Charles L. Wood Memorial Lecture in Agricultural History in February 2006. They wanted, they said, a talk examining both environmental history and the history of children on farms. The result was "Childhood on the Farm: A Natural History," which formed the basis of my first chapter.

Numerous individuals helped with the research and writing of this book. Anne Spurgeon deserves extra thanks for inviting me to stay in her home while I was in Madison, Wisconsin, as well as the time she spent helping me at the Wisconsin Historical Society. Don't worry, Anne—I will get back to researching Campo Fiesta for Girls sometime in the future, even if it's not in this book. Three Iowa State University undergraduates, Teri Schnelle, Abbie Sipfl and Sydney Marshall, were particularly helpful in gathering research materials. My long-suffering graduate students deserve great credit for allowing me to ramble at length about my topic and the writing process. I also owe a great deal to the History Department secretary, Jennifer Rivera, who has put up with my edginess over this project (and others) for many long years. Roberta Trites, Scott Riney, Julie Courtwright and Jay Taylor did early readings of some materials for me, and I greatly appreciated their insights. My heartfelt and enormous thanks go to Elliott West and Fred Woodward, who provided excellent guidance in the revision process. The librarians and archivists at the State Historical Society of Iowa, Iowa Women's Archives, the Parks Library at Iowa State University, Minnesota Historical Society, Kansas State Historical Society, Illinois State Historical Library, Nebraska Historical Society and Wisconsin Historical Society all deserve special thanks for pointing me in the direction of many useful sources and illustrations. The Library of Congress, Ames Historical Society, the University of Chicago, the U.S. Forest Service and the Museum of the City of New York have also provided access to wonderful materials for illustrations.

Other individuals have rendered much more personal aid in the development of this book. My husband, Rick Kehrberg, is an Eagle Scout, and has regaled me with many tales from his camping and counseling days at Wisconsin's Camp Phillips. This, no doubt, has influenced the way in which I think and write about scouting. I greatly appreciate both him and his stories, and the care he took of our son while I was researching and writing. My son, Ricky, has never been much interested in outdoor exploration, but I deeply appreciate the walks along the Skunk River he has shared with me and the opportunity those walks have afforded me to observe the absence of other children in the out-of-doors.

I doubt it would have occurred to me to be interested in this topic were it not for the way in which my parents raised me. My father was a fisherman and hunter, and my mother was a longtime Girl Scout and camp counselor. They regularly enforced the idea of getting children out of the house to entertain themselves. One of the reasons my parents bought the house I grew up in was because of its proximity to urban wild places. In addition to letting my brother and me roam relatively freely and taking us to the mountains, they got me involved in the Girl Scouts, the organization I credit for most of my camping experiences. They also created a lifelong friendship with our next-door neighbors, Marilyn and Marvin Shrout. I wish Marvin Shrout was still with us, so I could thank him (a Boy Scout leader and camp administrator) for the many times he led us on fishing and camping expeditions. The friends of my childhood were my companions in exploring the world. Whenever I think about summer evenings spent out-of-doors, or winter afternoons spent building snow forts and sledding, I cannot help but think about time spent with the Norton children, Debbie, Stacy, Parker and Susan. I also think of my brother, Scott Riney, and my oldest friend, Rachel Myron. Those two were my companions in many, many adventures over the years, and it is to them I dedicate this book.

INTRODUCTION

THE ENVIRONMENTAL CHILD

It is more than a little trite, but entirely true, to say that the world we live in today is not the world that existed 150 years ago. It looks different, sounds different and definitely smells different. The way in which we experience our world is different, mediated by layers of technology that either did not exist, or were in their infancy, in the years immediately following the Civil War. In the United States, the late years of the nineteenth century and the beginning of the twentieth were marked by a dramatic increase in industrialization and urbanization, changes that would completely alter the human experience of the world. The nation that had been born in the country was moving to the city, with the result that its citizens were living at an ever-increasing distance from the rhythms, wonders and perils of the natural world. Ever larger numbers of people, young and old, worked long hours in factories, greatly diminishing their contact with the out-of-doors. The housing in which the poor lived stretched upward into tenements, and many families lived in rooms essentially without windows, and without access to natural light or fresh air. Inner-city children played in an urban jungle, surrounded by brick, concrete and grime, rather than grass, trees and earth. Middle- and upper-class families became less aware of winter's discomforts as central heating and indoor plumbing became more common. Motorized transportation further diminished the degree to which families suffered with the cold. One of the consequences of urbanization and industrialization, at some level, was a growing distance from the elements, in all of their forms.

Children did not simply experience these changes, they played an active part in this national transformation. They, like their parents, had to accustom themselves to new places and new circumstances and adapt themselves to a changing landscape. Children, as much as any other Americans, lived immersed in their physical settings. Perhaps, I could argue, children lived in their environments even more than adults did, since they generally had more free time to explore their surroundings and even to wallow in them. The world was their workplace, their school, and their playground. In 1900, many Americans believed that children had more at stake in their surroundings than their elders. The environment shaped the child, for good or for ill, and, in turn, the child would shape the nation. If the environment within which the nation reared its young changed significantly, then perhaps those children would be shaped in new and significant ways as well. Thinkers and reformers agreed that this was a precarious moment in the nation's history.

Children, like all people, live in interaction with the environment around them. It is important, however, to understand what is meant by terms such as *environment* and *nature*. Environment, as a term, encompasses the physical features and characteristics of a particular place. Is it urban, rural or suburban? Is it developed or undeveloped? The features may be predominantly naturally occurring, such as trees, grasses and rivers, or they may be predominantly human-made, such as sidewalks, buildings and playgrounds. Of course, some "naturally occurring" environments appear to be more natural than others. An open field may seem to be completely natural, but be filled with invasive plant species, not native to its location, transported there by humans and domestic animals. A cultivated wheat field may seem less-than-completely natural, but may at the same time be home to many native plants, insects, rodents and other forms of animal life. And either one seems more natural than an asphalt-paved schoolyard, in spite of the weeds and anthills making their way up through the cracks.[1]

Nature is a more loaded term, generally applied to naturally occurring environments, preferably untouched or minimally touched by human hands. The way the term is used often implies the superiority of such environments over any other. The term *nature* reveals a real tension between the opinions and experiences of adults and children. While adults often drew fine distinctions about the superiority of one type of environment over another and generally preferred the "naturally occurring," children made the best of whatever environment presented itself, naturally occurring or otherwise. Some even preferred constructed environments to those derived from nature. Historian Bernard Mergen captured this reality beautifully, as he explained the way in which children evaluated the environments in which they lived:

> Some places are valued because of the uses children put them to in play, such as ball fields, homemade forts and houses, climbing trees, sliding places, brooks and woods. Other places are valued because of some person who works or lives there. Some places are valued for what can be bought there, such as supermarkets, ice cream shops, and service stations. Still others are valued because of how they look or feel, such as

intersections where the traffic light changes colors. And finally, some places are valued because they are dangerous—streets, quarries, rivers, abandoned buildings and graveyards.[2]

What a child made of a place was often quite different than what adults made of it, based on an entirely different set of criteria. While adults often believed that children should prefer open fields and trees to urban environments, and playgrounds to city streets, children had their own priorities.

Children's experiences of the places in their lives were mediated by a number of factors—geography, class, gender, race and ethnicity, to name a few. The influence of geography is perhaps the most obvious. In the simplest sense, farm children in Minnesota would have had a far different experience of winter than children in Texas, Mississippi or Alabama. Working outside in January would have been a much more uncomfortable experience for the child living in the upper Midwest, whereas working outside in June would have been less comfortable for children in the South. Class shaped children's experiences, too. It had a direct effect on the amount of space in which families lived. In the late nineteenth and early twentieth centuries, the conditions in small, crowded homes encouraged poor and working-class children to go outside and explore their surroundings, while middle-class children, who lived in larger homes, may have had more places and opportunities to play indoors. In the late years of the twentieth century, the situation was somewhat reversed. Deteriorating conditions in America's inner cities encouraged poor parents to keep their children indoors, while children living in higher-income neighborhoods were able to spend more time outside, because their parents perceived their environments as relatively safe. The influence of gender most clearly manifested itself in limitations on the activities of girls; parents were reluctant to allow their daughters the same access to the outdoors as their sons, for fear of whom and what they might encounter while unsupervised. Ethnicity complicated this further, with some groups, such as Italian immigrants, placing even greater restrictions on daughters than others. Ethnicity and race also served to delineate the boundaries of children's explorations, making some environments less safe for certain groups. Children did not experience their worlds on a level playing field.

Before going further, this is the place to explain what this book is and is not about. My geographic focus is largely the Midwest and Great Plains, with some attention to the major cities of the east. The South, which gets a very limited treatment, certainly deserves a book of its own. I have not spent a great deal of time with the Mountain West, given Elliott West's excellent treatment of this region in *Growing Up with the Country: Childhood on the Far Western Frontier*. The Far West (not to mention Hawaii and Alaska) deserves separate treatment. I also will not be spending much time on environmental health. Other historians have ably tackled the larger topic of children's health, and smaller topics under this umbrella, such as the perils of lead paint, and threats to health and safety in remote western communities.[3] In some areas, I have provided limited coverage of topics that I believe merit far greater discussion. I hope that readers find a number of subjects for further research. The outdoor education activities of settlement houses would seem to be one of these topics, as would Smokey Bear, Woodsy Owl and other mid- to late twentieth-century attempts at environmental education.

In this book, I have several goals. The first is to construct a narrative following the environmental history of American childhood from the end of the Civil War through the opening years of the twenty-first century. In order to do this, I bring together analysis of primary source materials, as well as synthesis of important secondary materials on this topic. For the most part, historians have not set out to write environmental histories of American childhood. One early exception was West's *Growing Up with the Country*. In this book, West examined the relationship of children's lives to the place in which they lived and made important observations that have shaped the way in which I view children and environment. In his analysis, West emphasized that children made the new places and circumstances they encountered on the frontier their own. They did not see that world through the same eyes as their parents and other adults. The grown-ups around them often saw the deficiencies of the western environment as a place to raise children; the children, on the other hand, saw the possibilities in that world. It was their home, and it was not strange to them. As West commented in the introduction to his book,

> The westering experience meant one thing to older pioneers and quite another to the younger. The youngest emigrants had little of the East to remember, and those born in the new country had none whatsoever. For the young, in a sense, this was not a frontier at all—not, that is, a line between the familiar and the new. Rather, it was the original measure for the rest of their lives, and that measure was not the one their parents had known.[4]

I believe that historians can more broadly apply West's analysis to child-life beyond the frontier. When the way in which children interacted with the world around them changed over time, or the world with which they interacted changed, adults often reacted with dismay, concern or even horror. The children were generally less concerned by the situation.

Most treatments of children's relationship with the world in which they lived are less overtly concerned with environment. There are recent exceptions, such as Susan A. Miller's *Growing Girls: The Natural Origins of Girls' Organizations in America*, Leslie Paris's *Children's Nature: The Rise of the American Summer Camp*, and Kevin Armitage's *The Nature Study Movement: The Forgotten Popularizer of America's Conservation Ethic*. On the whole, the environmental history of childhood has been written in bits and pieces, and is embedded in social, policy and cultural histories, such as David Nasaw's fine 1985 work, *Children of the City: At Work and at Play*. Nasaw's work, as well as Viviana Zelizer's 1985 study *Pricing the Priceless Child: The Changing Social Value of Children*, and several more recent books, such as Jeff Wiltse's *Contested Waters: A Social History of Swimming Pools in America*, and Howard Chudacoff's *Children at Play: An American History*, are full of the environmental history of American children. At the center of each of these analyses is a fascinating story of conflict over who would control children's access to their preferred environments, with the adults more often than not winning.

My second goal in this book is to follow this conflict across the decades and to help to explain why and how we have reached a point in this country where children have to be cajoled to go outside and play by parents, panicky about their children's seeming lack of interest in the world immediately outside of their doors. These same parents, too, are panicky about the state of the outdoors, worried that their children will encounter unacceptable perils outside the home, often in the shape of dangerous adults who wish them ill. Slowly but surely, children's focus has, for the most part, moved indoors, and away from the naturally occurring and constructed landscapes beyond their homes. As such, this book is also an attempt to explain how and why children were "islanded" in the United States, progressively separated from adult space, and moved into their own spaces, designed specifically for children. As historian John R. Gillis has written:

Children have been systematically excluded from the former mainlands of urban and suburban existence, especially the streets and other public spaces. What has been described as a 'sanitized childhood, without skinned knees or the occasional C in history' is evident both in the United States and Western Europe. . . . Parks and playgrounds, once the free space of childhood, are increasingly supervised. Even the suburban neighborhood, once a territory of spontaneous encounter, is now a series of oases, connected by caravans of SUVs.[5]

Unlike the seemingly "free range" children of earlier generations, today's children have considerably less freedom than their grandparents to roam and less opportunities to make themselves comfortable in the public spaces of their communities.

This is not as it always was. In the middle of the nineteenth century, most children in the United States were residents of rural locations, living with a combination of human-made (homes, barns and schools) and naturally occurring (open fields, trees, streams) environments. As more and more families moved to urban, and later suburban, locations, the preponderance of children's interactions with environments would be with human-made, or strongly human-influenced environments, such as houses, streets, yards and parks. In the transition, their surroundings changed considerably.

At the time, observers argued that children had lost something significant in this transition. Children, they argued, had lost contact with nature. They were not simply arguing that children had lost contact with trees, grass and rocks, however: they were arguing that children had lost contact with a better, more valuable environment. But they were also arguing for a domesticated and gentle nature, not the natural world that farm youngsters might face in the form of brutal cold, rabid animals and prairie fires. As the nation industrialized, urbanized and moved progressively farther from its agricultural roots, reformers came to promote an idealized nature as the most important environment within which to nurture children's characters. Children, however, did not always have the same preferences as adults, and could find much to admire and enjoy in environments that had little of the natural left in them.[6]

But this story is not entirely about change. This book will begin with an examination of children in farming communities. At the close of the Civil War, many Americans continued to live on farms and raise their families in rural settings. Millions of farm children lived in very close proximity to the joys and perils of natural landscapes. Those landscapes and their features influenced every aspect of a child's life, be it work, play or school, and many children faced environmental dangers largely unknown in the twenty-first century. In a letter written to the children's page of the *Nebraska Farmer*, young Helena Karella, of Madison County, Nebraska, reflected on the beauties and pleasures of child life on the farm. "The spring has said goodbye and beautiful summer is here. The birds, bees, and ants are always busy. So are the happy boys and girls that live on a farm. They always have plenty to do and always have plenty of time for play. I would lots rather live on a farm than in a city, for on a farm you can skate in winter and pick flowers in summer and always have a good time."[7] Focusing her attention on the positive aspects of her relationship to the surrounding world, the young farm girl's words reinforced a common perception in late nineteenth and early twentieth-century America: that farms were the best possible place to raise children. Chapter One explores the world of the rural child, and the degree to which the natural world shaped all aspects of child life, for good or for ill, in this essentially premodern environment. It also treats the ways in which organizations for rural youth attempted to help youngsters to see their environment in the "right" way. Even 4-H, that quintessentially rural organization for farm youth, reoriented itself to provide greater conservation programming for its members.[8]

Increasingly, however, cities attracted residents from the countryside and abroad, and growing numbers of children would find their place in urban America. Covering the years from the late nineteenth century to the middle of the twentieth, Chapter Two follows America's children to the cities and examines the different ways in which children related to this novel environment. Many children, but particularly the children of the poor and the working classes, would make the city streets and empty lots their own, of necessity redefining what could have been hostile space into an environment for play and other activities. Inevitably, this created some tension, as children competed with adults for space and used and remade spaces in ways that did not please adult observers.[9] The move to the cities subjected children to new environmental perils, a concern that will also be treated in this chapter. Among the middle classes, however, there was a retreat from the city and its real and perceived dangers. Although the middle class continued to make their homes in urban and suburban environments, parents focused upon creating a haven for their children within a potentially hostile landscape. Parents made use of larger homes, sculpted back yards, and purpose-built playgrounds to direct their children's play away from the dangers of the street to the comfort and safety of the home.[10]

Chapter Three explores the dilemmas adults faced when contemplating the economic and social transformations taking place in the late nineteenth and early twentieth centuries and their implications for the lives of children. These transformations posed serious intellectual problems for a nation long wedded to agrarianism and challenged adult notions about the importance and value of nature. Thomas Jefferson's oft-quoted commentary on the value of agriculture and agriculturalists emphasized repeatedly the importance of laboring in the earth, and a relationship with the land, to genuine human virtue. It was not just producing the most basic of human needs that made farmers virtuous, but their contact with the splendors of nature and God's creation that made them more honest, more moral and generally of more use to a young nation.[11] Even as urbanization overtook the United States, and maybe because of it, these notions persisted, with the result that parents and educators would develop substitute measures to provide urban children adequate experiences with nature. These experiences, however, would not be the raw, unmediated experiences of farm children on their parents' land. Summer camps, scouting and nature education would take the place of unstructured experiences with natural and constructed environments.

Not only did children require experiences in nature, they needed new ways to think about nature as well. Chapter Four examines the midcentury tug-of-war between the lure of the indoors and adult desires to get children outdoors. Radio and television were helping to create a more sedentary experience of youth, but the society as a whole continued to value the relationship between children and the wider world. Youth organizations continued to take children into the wild, and parents loaded their children into station wagons to introduce them to Yellowstone. Popular culture also introduced the nation's children to a whole range of animal characters created to cultivate environmental awareness, such as Smokey Bear, Ranger Rick, Woodsy Owl and Bambi. While Walt Disney Studios appropriated Bambi to sell movie tickets, other familiar characters such as Smokey Bear existed to sell a particular environmental message to the nation's youth. From Smokey Bear's "Only YOU can prevent forest fires" to Woodsy Owl's "Give a hoot, don't pollute," the U.S. Forest Service developed a whole curriculum intended to promote environmental consciousness in the young. Additionally, private organizations, such as the National Wildlife Federation, often used characters such as Ranger Rick, a conservation-minded raccoon, to market their messages. This chapter will examine how images of nature, and particularly images of animals, have been used to create a love of the wild and environmental consciousness in children who may never have seen a deer, bear, owl or even a raccoon outside of the confines of a zoo.

Not all urban and suburban children, however, formed their dominant perceptions of nature in relation to movies, television and the printed word. Throughout America, wild spaces persisted in spite of the urban and suburban development. Chapter Five focuses on one of these urban wild spaces, metropolitan Denver's High Line Canal. This seventy-one-mile-long canal, constructed in the late nineteenth century as an irrigation ditch for farmers on Colorado's eastern plains, also became a playground for generations of children and youth. For youngsters who lived out of range of open farm and ranch land, the canal and its adjacent access road offered a welcome location for bicycle riding, crawdad hunting, tubing and all manner of outdoor activities. It was also a welcome place in which to escape the gaze of prying adults. In the 1950s, 1960s and 1970s, before worries about "stranger danger" overwhelmed suburban and urban parents, the High Line's children wandered freely, largely without supervision, and in relative safety. The High Line Canal was one of many places nationwide where postwar youngsters sought out and found their own spot in the "natural world," even though its nature had been created and heavily modified by human action.

The days of such open and unfettered use of the outdoor world, however, were numbered. Chapter Six examines the late twentieth-century child, who had more or less completely moved indoors in response to technological and social change, as well as parental fears. As the twentieth century progressed, children increasingly abandoned the out-of-doors in favor of the family room and the shopping mall. For most middle-class children, this movement reflected changes in technology and perceived, rather than real, dangers. Increasingly, playtime outside meant either supervised play on a plastic playground or organized team sports on a carefully delineated field. In impoverished inner-city neighborhoods, on the other hand, this movement reflected rising crime and the increasing degradation of the urban environment, so ably documented by writers such as Alex Kotlowitz, author of *There Are No Children Here*.[12] In the case of both the middle-class and the inner-city child, a sea-change had transpired. The day of the free-roaming child, exploring urban, suburban or wild space seemed to be over, the result of a complex mixture of social and cultural forces.

The final chapter will consider the reaction, beginning in the 1990s and becoming ever more vocal in the new century, against the migration of children indoors. In the 1990s, naturalists such as Robert M. Pyle lamented the dramatic reduction in the number of children independently and intimately experiencing wild spaces, as he had done as a child along the Denver metropolitan area's High Line Canal.[13] In the twenty-first century, these concerns have blossomed into an organized call for action. The "No Child Left Inside," or "Leave No Child Inside," movement has popularized the idea of reintroducing children to nature and curing their "nature deficit disorder" through various forms of familiarization with the wild.[14] A national movement is building to change the way in which children play and interact with the world around them. Whether twenty-first century children (and parents) will respond positively to this movement, however, remains to be seen. The complex interaction among parental fears, children's preferences and pervasive cultural change make it highly unlikely that children will ever again interact as freely with the outdoor environment as their parents and grandparents once did.

Who has won the battle over children's interactions with the world surrounding them? While children might have once chafed at the restrictions imposed by cautious parents and urban and suburban development, the parents of today seem more distressed about the current situation than their children. Had the indoor environment of the 1950s and 1960s persisted, featuring relatively limited personal space, poor climate control and only three television channels, the youngsters might be in rebellion. Given the revolution in home amenities and electronic devices, the children seem to have won the battle. They are exactly where they want to be.

CHAPTER ONE

THE ENVIRONMENT AND
THE FARM CHILD

In the summer the children play,
They swing and jump and hide all day,
The hot sun beats the earth so dry,
And when it rains the children say "My,
I'll go bare-foot in the water."
And then they go, pitter patter.
And when the flowers get in bloom,
Everyone run and pick them soon.
There's daisies, poppies and sweet peas,
And that is where you see the bees.
The bees they buzz and buzz all day,
to get the honey
While the children play
On the summer day.
In the winter the children go,
Through piles of leaves and heaps of snow.
To school they walk and sun so swift,
And in the school-house they do lift,
Their feet so softly as on a cliff.
All the children say, "Teacher, look,"
They shake the snow from head to foot.
They throw snow balls and the snow does fall,
The boys throw hard clear cross the yard,
The girls catch them when they're thrown,
And in their faces snow is blown.
Now they're having fun, but the teacher says "It's done."
And then she says "Now dear children
school will start,
I hope it doesn't break your heart."

—Louise Fassacht, age 12[1]

Louise Fassacht's poem celebrated the interaction with the world outdoors that was a part of farm children's daily lives. Fresh air, sunshine and open space in abundance surrounded children on America's farms. In a time when cities were characterized by soot, overcrowding and filth of many varieties, farm children would seem to have had a distinct advantage when it came to the virtues of the environment in which they lived. Indeed, rural children had a greater chance of living to adulthood than their urban peers.[2] Children in rural communities, however, were not just living in an agricultural paradise of sunny skies and green fields, communing with the animals in the fields and the birds in the air. They were immersed in their environments in a way virtually unknown in the twenty-first century. They lived with nature in all of its moods, whether fair or foul. Farm children's relationships with nature were complex; the land could be a friend and ally, but also an adversary.

It was impossible for farm children to avoid regular interactions with the natural environment. Mamie Griswold, who grew up in Greene County, Illinois, kept a diary throughout her adolescent years. Her reflections and experience were much like those of most other girls and young women who did the majority of their work within the confines of the household, barnyard and garden, but were also involved in some field work as their families required. In the late 1870s and early 1880s, her writings were replete with references to the natural world. At the most basic level, she was acutely aware of the weather, commenting upon it nearly every day, whether it was "clear and cold," as it was on January 1, 1878, or whether it "look[ed] like snow," as it did later that month on the 22nd. While snowy conditions forced her to travel to school by sled in the winter, she and the other female students celebrated the first day of the spring term by going "down in the woods west of the schoolhouse to gather flowers." The naturally occurring environment organized other spring and summer activities, with fishing and berry picking figuring prominently. In the fall, the family went to the woods to gather hickory and other nuts. The arrival of cold weather did not preclude outdoor entertainment. Although in the depths of winter indoor activities such as dances, candy pulls and parties seem to have been preferred forms of entertainment, skating drew Mamie and other youngsters outdoors again.[3]

Although she was not particularly attuned to or curious about the natural world (if she was, it does not appear in her diary), Mamie Griswold's writings show that even young people who were not what we would call "outdoorsy" were of necessity immersed in nature. The weather shaped her family's working life, as well as her ability to attend school, so she could not help but be concerned about it on a daily basis. Because her family fed itself largely through its own subsistence efforts, Mamie, her siblings and her parents combined work with play in gathering bounty from the surrounding countryside. Families' fortunes rose and fell on the environmental conditions of any given year. Intimate experiences with the natural world could hardly be avoided, even by a young woman who was far more interested in dancing than observing the habits of plants and animals and the changing of the seasons.

Young men were sometimes better positioned to live closely with the natural landscape and observe and experience it on a regular basis. While many girls and young women spent most of their time working next to their mothers in the household, the vast majority of boys and young men did field work and other outside chores with their fathers. Such was the case of Hermann Benke, who grew up in central Kansas in the late 1800s. His diary is a testimony to the degree to which many farm boys lived with the out-of-doors, both in their work and play. In the winter in particular the elements shaped his days. The icy early days of January 1886 found him struggling with the cold. Benke confided to his diary, "Perhaps the most blistering day in the winter. I and mother rise in the morn and build a fire. The stables are covered with snow. . . . Had to thaw snow in order to water the cattle . . . we had to dig out Bossy. At times we could not open our eyes." The cold followed him into the house, and he noted, "Set up far into the night to keep the room warm." Winter was a round of working to keep the well free of ice and snow, shoveling out the stables, and hauling food and fuel for humans and beasts.[4] Spring, summer and fall also took Hermann outside, although under somewhat less dramatic conditions. Plowing, planting, harvesting and myriad other chores meant that Hermann spent the vast majority of his time out-of-doors, sometimes even working by moonlight.[5]

Where boys may have had the greatest latitude to investigate their environments was in hunting, fishing and trapping, which were, for most farming males, dual-purpose activities. On the one hand, they could be justified as work. Hunting, fishing and trapping involved killing animals that could be used for food, the pelts of which could be sold, or that could be defined as pests. On the other hand it is also clear from the way in which many youngsters discussed these outdoor activities that they were important elements of leisure as well. Hunting, from the point of view of many boys, was more fun than work. A commentator in a children's column in the *Atchison* (Kansas) *Daily Globe* illuminated the betwixt and between nature of hunting: "Boys are occasionally willing to tramp the woods all night, over hill and valley, and wade creeks 'possum hunting, when it almost kills them to work mildly in the cornfield half a day."[6] Many a boy's activities illustrated this principle, and Hermann Benke's certainly did. Even on the coldest days, he took to the fields, hunting rabbits and other animals. Although he described January 3,

1886, as "the most blistering day in winter" and complained about the difficulty of even keeping his eyes open against the cold, conditions did not keep him from venturing into the fields with his gun. He wrote, "I was out on a hunt but did not meet with any success at all."[7] Benke limited his efforts to fairly small game, including mice, gophers, rabbits and ducks.

Although Benke's interest in hunting was usual among boys, another one of his hobbies, drawing, was less common. As he explored the land surrounding his family's home, he was also observing its contours and inhabitants and putting pencil to paper. In February 1886, he traveled to Cheyenne Bottoms to hunt. While he apparently was unsuccessful with his hunting, he did observe ducks and other waterfowl in their natural habitat and committed their images to the pages of his diary. His are probably some of the earliest sketches of the marshes at Cheyenne Bottoms and their feathered inhabitants.[8] Benke was, in some ways, a young naturalist. He was not the only youngster with these interests. Historian Elliott West's examination of childhood on the far western frontier described many a child with a deep interest in the plants, animals and terrain that surrounded them.[9]

Mamie Griswold and Hermann Benke had what could be viewed as fairly typical experiences for youngsters in their time and place. The natural environment and the round of seasons organized their every move. Their working lives were bound inextricably to the growing season, with family activities defined by the stage and state of the crops in the field. Although girls might not spend as much time in the fields as their brothers, their work, too, was defined by the seasons. Activities such as gardening, canning, caring for chickens and making butter all moved with a seasonal rhythm, and cleaning, mending and sewing ebbed and flowed with the farm's other demands as well. Play, too, might be defined by nature, with each season having its proper activities. Even an activity such as dancing, which we may think of as appropriate at any time, was related to the seasons. Very few dances happened in the summertime, when men and boys were far too busy with the crops to have strength to spare for dancing. Dances generally occurred in the winter, when they did not have to compete with the crops for male energy. Dancing also generated heat, welcome in the winter but less comfortable in the summer, a serious consideration in a world without central heating and cooling.

When the editors of the children's pages of agricultural newspapers asked their young readers about their reactions to the world in which they lived, and those parts of agricultural life they particularly liked, children's love of the outdoor world—especially in its relationship to leisure—poured

Sledding, even without hills, was a favorite winter pastime. Descartes L. Pascal Papers, by permission of Special Collections Department / Iowa State University Library.

out. When the editor of the *Prairie Farmer*'s children's page asked his readers why they liked the month of June, all of the answers foregrounded youngsters' preference for being outside. Ross Winkler, of Newman, Illinois, wrote, "The cattle stand under the trees or in the small streams, enjoying themselves to the fullest extent. All the day we stay close to nature out in the fields turning up the rich soil, and after supper we can go down to the old 'swimmin' hole,' which is one of our best pastimes." He also appreciated the relative dryness of June, as compared to the winter and spring. "The farmer can spin to town in his automobile because June has made the roads like pavement." His compatriot, Willie Woodruff, of Sadorus, Illinois, appreciated the fresh grass and green leaves and the opportunity to dig up a can of worms before "slipping away to the river." Water was on everyone's mind. Pearl Welden, of Cumberland, Wisconsin, wanted to head for Vermillion Lake, "one of two quite large lakes near my home here."[10]

At other times, winter outdoor activities got their share of attention (and also featured water, in its many forms). Making snowmen and snow forts regularly entertained youngsters, but sledding, also called coasting, was by far the preferred activity. As Martin Olsen of De Kalb County, Illinois wrote, "Sometimes when it starts to get dark, I put some water on my coasting place so it will be slippery and make the sled go fast."[11] While it is rather unlikely that the editors would have printed letters expressing a distaste for the out-of-doors, or for farm life in general, children's comments reflected a real, daily familiarity with their environment and an appreciation for what it had to offer them in terms of entertainment and diversion.

Children's education, too, had a very strong relationship to seasonal demands for labor, which often took children out of classrooms, and into fields. Hermann Benke, who was a country schoolteacher in addition to being a farmer's son, wrote in his diary on a March day, "The effect of the working season is clearly visible in the low att[endance]."[12] Other seasonal influences led to low attendance as well. Students generally walked long distances to school, and weather that was too wet, or too cold, could keep them home for days at a time. On the other hand, a pleasant day's walk provided children the opportunity to observe seasonal changes, with birds and plant life appearing in their prescribed time throughout the year. Children's understandings of distance would also be affected by the weather. In response to a research survey, a schoolboy wrote, "A _____ is only twelve miles from our school. It seems further when you have to go in the mud about up to your head."[13] The building of all-weather roads and the purchase of school buses by consolidated districts would reduce the frustrations posed by mud but would also limit early morning and late afternoon examinations of the landscape.

It is no wonder that rural diary writers, both children and adults, generally noted the weather in each entry and gave it a place of prominence, just below the date. At the most basic of levels, it defined the content of a family's days. The elements organized farm people's lives, from season to season, from infancy through adulthood, and it was impossible to escape their influence. An anonymous boy in a late nineteenth-century essay describing "Life on the Farm" captured this succinctly: "One must adapt himself to outdoor life and surroundings in order to enjoy farm life."[14]

For other children at other times, the environment was a difficult and sometimes disorganizing and disruptive force. The environments with which farm children lived were not an idealized and gentle nature, but instead could pose serious dangers to life and limb. It is not enough to say that the seasons defined farm people's work. The reality was that farm work in some seasons could be painful and hazardous. The chores had to be accomplished in all weathers, including winter. Families depended upon animals and crops for survival, and work continued in even the worst of weather. One frigid December, a Nebraska father wrote of his children's work to harvest the corn crop. They picked and husked in the cold and wind, and his son "stood it first rate made no complaint and he, too, was bare handed."[15] Winter's cold could cause even more serious problems than chapped hands and frostbitten toes. Those who did not understand and heed the threat that prairie and plains blizzards posed might perish. A Nebraska father, writing to his family back east, noted the fate of neighbor child. "Last Tuesdy a Bohemian boy 9 yrs old went out in the storm to a neighbors to borrow flour. Got the flour and on his return was lost and of course froze to death in a very short time. The neighbors turned out and hunted for him several days as he was undoubtedly covered up in the snow."[16] The father's tone was matter of fact: "of course," the boy died, and no doubt he ended his life buried in a snow drift. A March 1886 blizzard trapped hundreds of Iowa children in their schoolhouses, largely unprepared for the experience. In one schoolhouse, the teacher rationed the food, and she and an older student stayed up all night, stoking the stove with coal. Fortunately the supply was adequate. The same was not true of other schools. Some had inadequate fuel for the night, and children suffered serious frostbite injuries or died of hypothermia. Other teachers tried to lead their young charges to safety, with equally disastrous results. As one woman later remembered, "Tragedy stalked the land for miles and miles, and very few escaped entirely."[17] In winter, injury and death might await the unwary.

Winter posed its problems, but summer did as well. The heat could make young laborers ill. Agnes Schulz, shocking wheat on an August day, worked hard enough to cause herself physical distress. Her father wrote in his diary, "harvesting upon Morrell's farm, Agnes prepairing [sic] dinner there & helping in the field, her nose bleeding several times, caused from the hot weather."[18] Perhaps only fall, with its milder weather and drier conditions, was a truly comfortable time in which to do field work.

Encounters with wild creatures complicated children's labors, too. Young Emily Culek, hunting in the dark for a hen's nest, found a rattlesnake instead. She reacted wisely and later wrote, "You may be sure I did not stay there longer to hunt for eggs."[19] Other children did not have the option of simply avoiding such dangerous creatures. Charles Turner grew up in frontier Nebraska, and while his father broke prairie, Charles was supposed to plant the garden. The garden plot, however, was infested with rattlesnakes. At first, he coped by having his father kill the snakes. He wrote, "every little while I would call my father to come and kill a rattlesnake. He was killing one very often by stamping them to death with his heavy high topped boots." Charles's father, however, believed that this was a job that his son should be doing, commenting that "if I was a boy ten years old and had an axe I'd never call any one to come and kill a rattlesnake for me. Well the next one I met I very carefully reached and killed him and before we finished breaking that little patch I had killed 10 rattlesnakes and he must have killed over fifteen on about an acre of land."[20] Fortunately, Turner survived his experience unscathed.

Play, too, exposed children to the vagaries of the wild. Because of the danger of wolves on Minnesota's Red Lake Indian Reservation, Maude Baumann's mother restricted her children's berry picking. As Baumann wrote, "Ma says we musent go alone any more."[21] John Ise in *Sod and Stubble*, his autobiographical account of growing up in north-central Kansas, related the sad tale of Nebraska Stevens, a neighbor boy who in the summer of 1871 ran afoul of a wolf, mad with rabies. The community gathered to tend to his needs, and he died after days of agony. Because of an outbreak of rabies among the wild and domestic animals in the area, mothers kept their children close that summer.[22]

Wild animals were a dramatic threat to life and limb, not common to every day. Water, however, was another matter. Children, impatient to play, were perpetually falling through the ice covering ponds, lakes and streams. After an afternoon of sledding, a group of siblings decided to go sliding on a frozen pond. One wrote "When I started to turn around the ice broke and we went in the water up to our waists. We were almost in the middle of the pond. The next time we go down to the pond we will see if the ice is safe before we go upon it."[23] While these children ended their adventure merely wet and cold, other children in similar situations drowned or became hypothermic. Water in all forms was, in fact, a hazard.

Simple observation of the natural world could also lead to experimentation and misadventure. Young Walker Wyman, growing up in rural Illinois, found the crows, blackbirds, buzzards and sparrows inhabiting the family's acres an intriguing mystery. He wondered: "Could I fly away just as the buzzards seem to do so easily?" The answer was no, but he discovered this only after an experiment that included jumping off the roof of the henhouse with shingles attached to his forearms. Fortunately, one try was enough, and after hitting the ground with a thud, Wyman found that he had "lost [his] desire to test theories by jumping off the hen house again."[24]

Children's playful encounters with the natural world were particularly dangerous because they were so often unsupervised. While parents admonished their children to take care, they generally were too busy with their own work to observe and supervise carefully their children's activities. In fact, children could easily be completely out of sight and earshot of their elders. Sometimes the hazard was as simple, and as potentially deadly, as becoming lost. Tall prairie grasses could obscure small children, making them invisible to their parents and older siblings, just as winter blizzards could.[25]

Life itself was a precarious proposition for many farm families. They faced a whole host of environmental challenges, based on issues such as climate and topography. Every location had its own share of environmental hazards and challenges. Time, knowledge and resources would only slowly diminish the weight of environmental hazards in children's lives. Some hazards were so small, they were barely visible, or were invisible, to the human eye. In the South, the warm climate not only allowed a long growing season and a wide variety of crops, but also encouraged the growth of other, more problematic forms of life. In this region, the ground rarely froze, which encouraged parasites and other disease-carrying organisms. Throughout the south, children suffered in particular from two environmental diseases, malaria and hookworm. Infected mosquitoes spread malaria, and before World War II progress against the disease was slow. Only changing the environment, by way of ditching, draining ponds and spraying insecticides would dramatically reduce the prevalence of the disease. Hookworm, caused by an intestinal parasite, also afflicted children, and the disease was common to those who went barefoot, stepping in infected feces or soil. The lack of privies both at home and at school exacerbated the problem. Only modern privies and increased shoe wearing would eradicate the disease. These changes would largely come after World War II.[26] Mosquitoes and hookworms as an environmental influence on childhood might seem to have been far less dramatic in their impact than other forces, such as blizzards and prairie fires. Their effects, however, should not be underestimated; continued exposure left children tired, listless and unable to learn their lessons in school. Ultimately, the effects of diseases borne by these pests could be deadly.[27]

Residents of some locales faced perennial problems. On the Great Plains, droughts, grasshoppers and dust storms threatened families' survival. In 1894, much of the Great Plains was in the grip of a terrible drought. As a result, the Gitchel family of Nebraska harvested only five and a half bushels of wheat. The parents enlisted their children in the difficult task of survival. "All the feed we have the children glean from the wheat field, where the wheat was too poor to cut."[28] Drought often went hand in hand with another scourge, the grasshopper plague. A woman who spent several years of her childhood in grasshopper-ridden Kansas remembered the lengths to which the voracious pests pushed some of her neighbors. "Then there was the drouth, hordes of grasshoppers and years of famine, when food and fuel were scarce. Neighbor . . . children were so hungry that they caught the hoppers and ate them."[29] While undoubtedly full of protein, it had to have been a desperate meal for those children.

The grasshopper threat even made its way into reading materials for children, as demonstrated by an 1877 poem, appearing in *American Young Folks*, a children's magazine published in Kansas. When the writer looked for a metaphor to illustrate the idea of small faults multiplying and overwhelming a person, a grasshopper motif seemed apt. One grasshopper was hardly a problem; a grasshopper plague, on the other hand, could destroy a farm, or even a community.

> The 'hoppers are coming, they're now in the west,
> They soon will be here; O, the terrible pest!
> Just look at their coming, like a cloud in the sky,
> Just look at their dropping, like snowflakes they fly.
> See, millions on millions now cover the ground;
> And millions on millions are flying around!
> Just look at our corn fields, the stalks eaten bare,
> Just look at our fruit trees,—no apple, no pear,
> Just look at our vineyards,—no grape to be seen,
> Just look at our gardens—they're all eaten clean
> Just look at our pasture, field, meadow and tree
> They've eaten them all, *desolation I see!*[30]

From a distance of more than a hundred years, it is sometimes difficult to remember that plagues of grasshoppers could mean starvation for the families whose "pasture, field, meadow and tree" had been decimated. In 1875, a Minnesota farmer wrote the state's governor to ask for aid. "No time since the grasshopper invasion have provisions been scarcer here than at present And for one I am at a loss to know what to do. My family consists of Eight persons, and ere this reaches you will be entirely out of provisions. . . . And then I know not what to do."[31] Children could not help but be aware of the desperate environmental conditions that challenged their parents' ability to make a farm and feed their families.[32]

Dry grass and high winds could lead to yet another scourge, the prairie fire. From a distance, prairie fires could be beautiful. What they destroyed, however, could be lives or a family's livelihood. Once started, a prairie fire might not just consume grass (which was valuable as pasturage for animals), but crops, houses, barns and anything else in its path.[33] When the grass was dry, and the wind blew, prairie fires always threatened. One woman remembered that as a five-year-old her parents and older siblings left her alone with two younger children, the youngest five or six months old, while they fought a prairie fire. "I don't know how many hours they were gone. But it was a long time for me. . . . It came quite near."[34] Older children, like Hermann Benke, might be recruited to help fight fires. On a March day in 1887 he noted "I helped at Ackermans where only by the greatest exertions we save the out buildings, hay, etc."[35] It could have been significantly worse. Prairie fires could take lives in addition to property.[36] Youngsters growing up on farms were well aware of the darker side of the natural world. Although their parents bore the ultimate responsibility of negotiating the family's difficult journey toward success or failure in the face of natural disasters, youngsters were often essential and knowing players in the family's struggles with the elements.

Sanora Babb's account of farming life in the early days of the twentieth century, *An Owl on Every Post*, illustrated the degree to which a father's unsuccessful encounters with the environment shaped every aspect of his children's lives. Babb's father moved his family west from Missouri, and gambled everything on the purchase of a dry land farm in far eastern Colorado, a very harsh, semi-arid landscape. Even in the early years of the twentieth century, settlement was sparse in this corner of the Great Plains. The days of the frontier had not yet passed. The family lived miles from any neighbors. The land was high and dry, questionably suitable for agriculture. Their only home was a hole in the ground, a basement dugout from whose ground-level window Sanora and her sister watched ants and beetles crawl. When a blizzard swept the plains, the snow trapped the family below ground for three days. On the third day, when the snow and wind finally stopped, their father dug out the door. Babb wrote, "Mama, Marcy, and I came out. Walking in the white corridor was a new delight. In order to see our winter world we must first find the woodpile and climb to its top. There we turned slowly around looking over the great circle of snow that for us began with our farm at the center and reached to the horizon. How tell its beauty? It lay white and silent, sparkling in the sun."[37] The days underground had been terrible; the snow-covered land above, however, was dazzling.

Ultimately, the land defeated Babb's father. Too little rain meant that the family could not grow a crop to sell. There was also far too little water for that other agricultural staple, a garden. Hardtack and pinto beans comprised the family's primary food supply, and they had little money to purchase these necessities. Only rarely did wild meat relieve the monotony of their diet. Rabbits were the primary game available, but many of them were diseased, and had to be destroyed, rather than eaten. The results were dire. As Babb bluntly put it, "There was a time to come seven days long when we had no food at all."[38] Eastern Colorado, ultimately, was too harsh a place for this family. The land offered no room for error on the part of a Midwestern baker-turned-farmer. He took his half-starved children to cities and small towns, leaving agriculture behind forever.

Although more extreme than the average, conditions such as these caused youngsters to carefully consider their own futures. Experiences with the land weighed heavily in young people's assessments of farms as a place upon which to make their lives. Around 1900, Liberty Hyde Bailey, a professor of agriculture at Cornell University and member of President Theodore Roosevelt's Country Life Commission, surveyed his students, both farm and city raised, to find out why they did or did not intend to become farmers after college graduation. One of Bailey's concerns, like Theodore Roosevelt's, was that the movement from farm to city would weaken the character of the American people. Bailey wrote, "farmers constitute the chief nature-bred class of men now remaining to us, and this fact cannot help having a far-reaching effect on the character of future populations."[39] Bailey found that among those who were farm raised but planned to leave the farm after graduation, the primary objections to a life in agriculture focused upon economic concerns and the difficulty of the physical labor involved. The farmer's problematic relationship to the forces of nature, however, figured into the equation as well. One student wrote that although he loved working outdoors, he did not enjoy the isolation that situation implied. "I love farming, I love the farm. I like to go out in the fields and work under the clear open sky; but man is a social being, and is not destined to live an isolated life." Thinking along the same lines, another commented that farm life was "pleasant enough in summer, but the cold and snow of winter and the deep mud of spring virtually shut out many farmers' families from social intercourse with their friends, and tend to make them narrow-minded." Another claimed that the drudgery of agriculture dulled the senses, blinding farm people to the beauty of nature. The farmer's "finer sensibilities are deadened by toil, and he becomes entirely unconscious of the many interesting and beautiful things around him. It is the man who was not born there who really sees and appreciates the beautiful things in the country."[40] For these students, the beauties of nature were tempered by the isolation and toil inherent in agricultural life and were not valuable enough to offset the cost of the economic and physical hardships that came with farming. A study

A goat cart took this boy on outdoor adventures. WHS Image ID 47194. By permission of the Wisconsin Historical Society, Madison, Wisconsin.

done with Iowa farm children in the 1920s would seem to bear out this observation. Although the researchers found that youngsters had myriad daily contacts with the land, they noted that "seldom in conversation with field workers did they show any appreciation of the natural world."[41]

Others, however, managed to enjoy their contact with the land in spite of themselves. Among farm-raised young people who planned to return to the farm after college, nature played a prominent role. Nearly two hundred of Bailey's students claimed that they were returning to farms after graduation, and one of the chief reasons was the close relationship of farmers to the land. While seventy-seven said that the independence of farm life was their chief concern, the second largest group, fifty-five, claimed that they wanted to pursue agriculture because of their "love of the out-of-doors and of nature." Along the same lines, forty-one claimed that farms provided a more healthful life, and twenty stated that farms were the "ideal place for home and rearing of children."[42] One young person explained his reasons in this way. "I intend to stick to farm life, for I see nothing in the turmoil of city life to tempt me to leave the quiet, calm, and nearness to nature with which we, as farmers, are surrounded." Another wrote "I love nature, and may be brought into more intimate relations with it by this profession than any other." As yet another put it, "I can not feel the sympathy which makes me a part of nature, unless I can be nearer to it than office or university life allows." Some clearly drew a distinction between the healthfulness of the countryside and the corruption of the cities. One respondent commented that he wished to return to the country to raise poultry and fruit "because of the false standards set up in the modern city; namely, hurry, worry, and selfishness."[43]

Perhaps not surprisingly, when sixty-eight town- and city-raised students told Bailey that they planned to move to the country to take up farming after graduation, love of nature was the reason most often given. In one of the more creative letters Bailey received, a student wrote "I want to go on a farm because I love the independent life, because I see business there, because I have a good, strong opponent (nature) on which to grind my knowledge, and because I want to demonstrate the feasibility of some social and economic problems in which I am interested."[44] A desire to grapple with the land and the elements as worthy adversaries was perhaps a minority opinion, and one that was unlikely to be expressed by many city-raised youngsters. Without having been raised on a farm, these students may not have thought of the elements as adversaries at all, a situation that was likely to be remedied within their first few months, or at most their first year, in residence on a farm.

No matter what young people believed about life on the farm, it is clear that many adults believed that farms were the best place—and perhaps the only place—to raise healthy, happy, moral children. This belief was visible in the efforts of Charles Loring Brace, founder of New York's Children's Aid Society, a man who deplored the effects of city life on impoverished children. As one of the nineteenth century's most prominent child welfare advocates (child savers, in the nineteenth-century parlance), he sought to mitigate the effects of the urban environment on children. He referred to the lightless, airless slum neighborhoods, awash with neglected children, as "fever nests" and breeding grounds for "ignorance, crime, and poverty."[45] The Children's Aid Society sponsored day trips, taking children from its industrial schools on summer picnic excursions on the Hudson River or to Staten Island, in order to escape the summer's oppressive heat.[46] Brace, however, did not believe that this was an adequate or long-term solution to the problem. His course of action was, for the day, a novel one: remove the child from the city permanently and send him or her to the countryside to live and work with virtuous farm people. The plan, called placing out, would allow children "an opportunity for self-improvement in a more healthful environment."[47] Many state and private charities would come to embrace his model of child saving.

Brace's efforts came to be popularly known as the "orphan trains." While some of the children riding the orphan trains were actually without parents, many were simply neglected or poor. Brace and his agents persuaded parents to give up their children, and to allow the Children's Aid Society to find homes for them in rural communities. Brace's efforts began in 1853, and his organization continued the program into the 1920s. Roughly 90 percent of the relocated children went to states in the Midwest—Michigan, Ohio, Indiana, Illinois, Iowa, Missouri and Kansas.[48] Farmers in these areas desperately needed agricultural laborers, and the Children's Aid Society expected children to work for the families that welcomed them into their homes.[49] Ultimately, the Children's Aid Society and other organizations that placed out youngsters believed that the exchange would provide benefits for all parties. Farmers would obtain workers, and children would live with (presumably) moral, upright farming families, reaping the rewards of a wholesome natural environment. Sometimes the programs met these goals; often they did not.[50] As many as 200,000 children may have been placed out by various organizations in the years between 1853 and 1929, forced to exchange the urban environment they knew for a rural environment they did not. Some refused this forced transplantation. As historian Marilyn Holt has noted, "there were those . . . who made their way back to the eastern cities or the new urban centers of the west. These placed out would not be tied to a rural life. Adjustment did not always come easy, and for some the familiar, however squalid, was preferable to the unknown."[51] Children, like adults, had preferences for certain environments, and not everyone found the countryside to his or her liking.

Working with the land, day in and day out, made a deep impression on farm-raised youngsters, even if it was not an impression that always led to appreciation and enjoyment of the earth and its wonders. While the farm and its relationship to natural environments exerted a powerful pull on the national psyche, the relationship between young people and the land was problematic. As a late nineteenth-century newspaper columnist exhorted, "A boyhood or girlhood in the bright, sweet country, where the sun shines, is worth a thousand years of city life." At the same time, the author acknowledged that many country activities, like gardening, which should in the best of all worlds be pleasing, wore on children. "There is no fun at all in just dull hoeing and back-breaking weeding."[52] Life in the countryside could cut both ways, and there seems to have been little predicting whether constant immersion in the environment would drive youngsters toward the land or away from it, although the experience of the harshest of natural disasters soured many on a life in farming.

An additional question remains. How did individuals raised on farms assess their experiences with natural environments, looking back on them as adults? Did an appreciation for the land persist, in spite of the years, or did individuals reflect on their youthful experiences with regret for the hardships that they imposed? In their memoirs and reminiscences, nearly every farm-raised adult remembered and commented upon the relationship they had forged with the grasslands or forests surrounding their homes. Anna Stanley, whose family made a farm in Dane County, Wisconsin, reminisced about the play houses she and her sisters made in the roots of toppled pine trees. Hours of play in their forest homes insured that the girls "were never lonely, bored, or longed for other playmates. Each day was brim full of interest and fun."[53]

For some, it was the memory of the simple thrill of exploring the land that remained, long after childhood was gone. George B. Thompson, remembering his childhood in Howard County, Nebraska, believed that he had experienced pleasures about which urban youngsters could not even dream.

> Boys of today, provided with modern schools and playgrounds and all of the conveniences and pleasures of present day living, will wonder how, under such a primitive way of living as then existed, any one could get much pleasure out of life. . . . The wide expanse of vision across the broad prairies made me realize how big and grand the world was. It excited my imagination. I thought of the big herds of buffalo and the wild tribes of Indians that had so recently roamed the land.[54]

The west and its possibilities thrilled many a young imagination. Frank Engles, whose family settled in Hitchcock County, Nebraska, wrote that he "just couldn't wait" until his family left Illinois for the plains. "I had just read a book . . . called *Heroes of the Plains* it was the life of Wild Bill Hickock [sic] Buffalo Bill and other great plainsmen which made me all the more eager to be there and be a part of the old west." This imagination led him to a greater appreciation for the wildflowers and wild animals of the plains, even those that were long gone. He reminisced "Buffalo paths crisscrossed the prairie in every direction. . . . I followed them miles on end grieving . . . I picked up over two hundred horns that first summer. . . . I spent countless hours scraping and polishing them."[55] Thompson and Engles saw within their environments an untamed and romantic past, one that helped them to appreciate the endless grasslands around them.

Others, however, found within their experiences of the agricultural environment a dose of harsh reality. Instead of the romance conjured up by buffalo bones, what they remembered were the freezing cold, the scorching sun, the destroying grasshoppers or the pain of hunger. What Curtis Harnack remembered, reflecting on his Iowa childhood, was the presence, always, of death. In his memoirs he commented that "there wasn't a day in summer one didn't kill what was happily alive, out of the farmer's rationale of necessity: weeds choking vegetables, rats eating corn; potato bugs not snatched by the yearly visit of a flock of grosbeaks we'd capture by hand and drop into kerosene cans." And while the farmer and his children attempted to subdue the land, the land "could subdue us at any moment with storms, crop blights, drought, and so our conscience over slaughtered animals, plants, insects, and birds were salved, our guilt expiated by Nature's random authority over us." The rhythms of daily life reminded farm-raised youth that they, too, were the environment's subjects. Harnack remembered, "My eleven year-old cousin Lloyd, playing beside me with the Erector set one day, became sick in the night and was dead the next day of appendicitis. We bore the shocks and sorrows of our lives as other creatures did theirs, all afflicted with natural and unnatural enemies."[56] What the land gave could also be taken away, with a vengeance.

One of the most thorough discussions of farm children's encounters with the natural environment, as seen through the lens of reminiscence, can be found in Laura Ingalls Wilder's eight-volume *Little House* series. Wilder wrote her books in the 1930s, when the path from farm to city was well established and fewer and fewer youngsters had first-hand experiences with life on farms. Wilder turned her own rather rugged childhood, experienced in locations all across the Midwest and Great Plains, into a much-loved series of children's books. Read with an eye toward the environment, Wilder described a natural world that was both dangerous and beautiful. Wilder's discussion of environmental challenges was fairly frank, but because Wilder wrote the books for a young audience, none of the Ingalls children's environmental encounters were fatal, or even left long-term scars. Dangerous possibilities, however, were always lurking. Although blizzards never killed anyone first-hand in Wilder's books, her young protagonists knew by way of hearsay that it was possible for children to be stranded alone in a blizzard, burn all the furniture and still "freeze stark stiff."[57]

Each of the seven books about Wilder's own childhood catalogued environmental hazards awaiting frontier children and their families. (The eighth, *Farmer Boy*, told the story of her husband's early years in relatively sedate upstate New York.) Her big woods of Wisconsin were a snug place, largely bounded by the family's warm, comfortable cabin and its immediate environs. Outside, however, dangers lurked in the form of wild creatures: bears, panthers and even swarms of angry yellow jackets. In *Little House on the Prairie*, set in Kansas Territory, the home was considerably less snug, and the dangers loomed larger: howling wolves, rising rivers and mosquitoes carrying near-fatal malaria. Space, too, was an environmental threat, with the nearest neighbors miles and miles distant. The banks of Plum Creek, in Minnesota, seemed no less scary, with their hissing badgers, floods, prairie fires and blizzards. Grasshopper plagues literally threatened the family with starvation. On Silver Lake in Dakota Territory, there were wolves. Once settled on their homestead claim near De Smet, South Dakota, a sea of grass quite nearly swallowed the family's youngest child, Grace, who was briefly lost on the prairie. Always, there was the threat of blizzards and bone-chilling cold. Wilder's descriptions are of an environment she both feared and loved. The power of natural forces was to be respected. Those forces could starve, dispossess, freeze and sicken even the best-prepared family. They even had the power to kill.[58]

But they were also forces to be overcome. This was most apparent in Wilder's grimmest tale, *The Long Winter*. Faced with blizzards that lasted from October to April, which completely isolated the tiny town of De Smet, in Dakota Territory, the town's residents had to find a way to endure without the railroad. It would not be until May that the lines would be clear, and the town would again have access to vital supplies from the outside. Wilder described in great detail her family's near starvation (never calling it that), but she focused on survival and their grim determination to see the winter to its end. The winds, snow and ice became peculiarly human foes, bent on invading their home. "Sometimes in the night, half-awake and cold, Laura half-dreamed that the roof was scoured thin. Horribly the great blizzard, large as the sky, bent over it and scoured with an enormous invisible cloth, round and round on the paper-thin roof, till a hole wore through and squealing, chuckling, laughing a deep Ha! Ha! the blizzard whirled in. Barely in time to save herself, Laura jumped awake."[59] In a winter when more than eleven feet of snow fell, the fictionalized Laura quite understandably perceived the elements as malevolent and directly attacking the household.[60] The blizzards might try to defeat them, but the Ingalls family, both chil-

Any place could be a good place to play, even an improvised teeter-totter in the farm yard. WHS Image ID 56730. By permission of the Wisconsin Historical Society, Madison, Wisconsin.

dren and adults, was more enduring than the hostile environment. A little food, warmth and sunshine put the winter to rest. A belated Christmas, celebrated in May, reassured them that their trials were finally over: "And as they sang, the fear and the suffering of that long winter seemed to rise like a dark cloud and float away on the music. Spring had come. The sun was shining warm, the winds were soft, and the green grass growing."[61] To paraphrase Friedrich Nietzsche, the blizzards that had not killed them had made them stronger.

Wilder's descriptions of the beauty of the land and its creatures, too, were every bit as powerful as her descriptions of its dangers. Particularly moving were Wilder's descriptions of the wilds of Dakota Territory, on the eve of set-tlement. She described a nighttime venture with her sister onto Silver Lake. "It was so beautiful that they hardly breathed. The great round moon hung in the sky and its radiance poured over a silvery world. Far, far away in every direction stretched motionless flatness, softly shining as if it were made of soft light. In the midst lay the dark, smooth lake, and a glittering moonpath stretched across it."[62] Feeling adventurous, the girls followed the glow across the lake, right into the path of a wolf. The wolf must not have been hungry or bored, because he let them retreat without following. Although Charles Ingalls went in search of the wolf in the morning, he was nowhere to be seen. The young Laura was glad; she did not want the wolf to be found or harmed. She said, "He didn't chase us, Pa, and he could have caught us."[63] Having met the challenge and survived, Laura was willing to live and let live. In these and other passages, Wilder painted a picture of a child drawing her strength from the land and its challenges, rather than being defeated by them.[64] In spite of constant struggles, it was the beauty and enchantment of the land that prevailed in Wilder's books, and presumably her memory.

It would be instructive to know if young Helena Karella, who as a child had written "I would lots rather live on a farm than in a city, for on a farm you can skate in winter and pick flowers in summer and always have a good time," still believed these words as an adult.[65] Did she still believe that what life in an agricultural setting had to offer farm children was essentially positive, or had she been influenced by wind, weather, animals, and other natural forces in ways that might have tempered her enthusiasm for the outdoors? Unfortunately, that is something that we cannot know. What we do know is that as the nineteenth century progressed and the twentieth century began, thousands of Americans, often as young adults, made their way from farm to city, away from a life steeped in naturally occurring environments, toward one increasingly mediated and moderated by technological adaptations. In spite of the abstract and concrete joys of a life lived close to the earth, those joys often could not compete against the economic and social realities of farm life.

Children, however, did not have to leave the farm for their situation in relation to the environment to change. In the early to middle years of the twentieth century, the conditions of life in rural and urban communities increasingly converged. Rural life and farm childhood was in the process of transformation as the countryside's residents increasingly adopted technologies previously known only to the cities. It is important, however, to put these changes in the appropriate time-frame and to understand that on the farm, much of this change came quite gradually. School buses and consolidated schools came at different times, in different communities and states. In some places, these innovations dated to the very early years of the twentieth century. In other places, like Iowa, these changes would arrive decades later. Household technology, such as electric lighting, central heating and indoor plumbing, which would increasingly hold the cold and dark at a distance in urban areas, would also come gradually to farm families, and many first experienced these luxuries in the period following World War II.

At the same time, changes in agricultural technology, such as combines, would increasingly take children out of the fields and reduce their exposure to the vagaries of the natural world. Gone was picking corn in the winter chill. Gone was eating grasshoppers, because the grasshoppers had eaten the crops. The number of days and weeks of schooling lost to muddy roads and inclement weather fell over time.

But even so, the weather would continue to dictate farm families' fortunes. Natural disasters reinforced the message that environmental forces, rather than human will, were in charge. One of the most dramatic of these disasters would be the Dust Bowl of the 1930s, which severely affected farm families on the Great Plains. Ten years of drought and the accompanying dust storms affected children's lives in myriad ways; for example, dust pneumonia, caused in part by inhalation of dust particles, killed scores of children, especially those with already-weakened immune systems.[66] The environmental conditions of the decade also forced many families into migrant farm labor. Their children would spend months, and sometimes years, living in very close proximity to the elements, camping in the open, following the harvest up and down the west coast. As was often the case, hard times had a way of lessening the distance between families and the hazards of the environment.

By the post–World War II era, much of the immediacy and urgency of the earlier relationship between farm children and the natural world would be diminished. The immersion of youngsters in natural environments, for better or for worse, would be reserved to smaller and smaller groups of children, until virtually all would have access to central heating, school buses, indoor bathrooms and other weather-mediating technologies. Even in rural areas, children would have increasing access to new indoor entertainments, such as radio and television. Children everywhere would spend more of the year in school, and considerably less time in and around their parents' farms. In the course of this transformation, there would be gains and losses. Hopefully, what would be left would be an appreciation of and a familiarity with the natural world beyond that which could be achieved in a mere occasional relationship with the wild, but without some if its harsher elements. But reformers no longer counted on this deep and abiding relationship existing between youngsters and the land.

The first half of the twentieth century saw attempts by several organizations to deepen and reinforce the relationship between farm youth and the natural world surrounding them. Reformers who worked with rural youth saw the need for an increased emphasis on nature education and attention to environmental issues. By the beginning of the twentieth century, the countryside was very clearly suffering from a rural youth "problem." Sometimes cast as a "boy problem" and at other times a "girl problem," agrarian reformers and some (but not all) rural parents lamented the steady outward migration of rural youth from the countryside to America's growing cities and towns. Youngsters, feeling the pinch of the confines of rural life, increasingly chose paths that led out of agriculture and toward urban locations. Even more distressingly, it appeared that it was the best and the brightest, the most ambitious of rural youth, who were abandoning the countryside at an alarming rate.[67]

Suggestions about how to stem the tide flooded in from numerous directions. Educational reformers and members of President Theodore Roosevelt's Country Life Commission suggested that the solution to the problem lay in the improvement of rural schools. In fact, the commissioners held rural schools "to be largely responsible for ineffective farming, lack of ideals, and the drift to town." They argued that "teaching should be visual, direct, and applicable" and address the issues of agricultural life. Improved education, and an education that emphasized rural subjects and practices, would impress youngsters with the beauties of the countryside and the importance of their continuing role in rural communities.[68] Nature education was part and parcel of this attempt to stem the loss of rural children to towns and cities.

At the center of the effort was Cornell University, arguably the nation's leading agricultural university. Led by Liberty Hyde Bailey, Cornell professors produced a series of nature study materials for teachers, which in 1907 became known as the *Cornell Rural School Leaflet*. The university distributed these materials far and wide. Conservation and the farmer's dependence on nature were at the center of the curriculum. When the materials proved successful in New York, educators around the country adopted Cornell's model, including George Washington Carver at Tuskegee Institution.[69] In the same vein, during the winter of 1922–1923, the Vocational Education Department at Iowa State College surveyed rural schools to determine the degree to which the state's rural youth were abandoning the farm for the city. The study concluded that the rate of outmigration was increasing and that the rural school curriculum, in part, was to blame. Responding to this problem, graduate students in Vocational Education at ISC trumpeted the cause of nature study in the state's rural schools.[70] Graduate student Melvin Strong wrote, "Education should begin with the physical features of the country in which the child lives—with brooks and lakes and fields and hills."[71] His thesis, among others, provided practical ways for country school teachers to incorporate the natural phenomena children encountered every day into their curricula. Educational reformers believed that nature study was good for the child, but that it was also good for the society, in that it promised to keep the best and the brightest of rural youth actively interested in the rural communities they called home.

Reaching children by way of nature education in the schools, however, was not enough. Leaders of youth programs outside of the classroom also sought to inspire youngsters with a love of the land. The World War I years saw the creation of the Farm Boy Cavaliers of America, as a rural alternative to the Boy Scouts. Dwight D. Mayne, principal of the School of Agriculture, University Farm, in St. Paul, Minnesota, created the organization to meet the needs of rural youth. Although the organization lasted only into the late 1920s, boys and girls organized chapters in approximately thirty states.[72]

Mayne argued explicitly that in the case of rural boys, the Farm Boy Cavaliers were a more suitable alternative to the Boy Scouts. And, in the early twentieth century, the Boy Scouts, as an organization, were not much interested in farm boys. On the whole, the leadership believed that farm boys had little need for their "character building" organization. Farm boys, presumably, were involved in all sorts of activities in their work and family lives that built character. Additionally, the Boy Scouts' leadership felt little interest in directing their program toward vocational training in agriculture, which they believed would introduce an unnecessary element of toil into what was supposed to be a leisure-time pursuit for boys. As historian David MacLeod put it, "They did not want to beat paddles into plowshares." The organization did attempt to promote country Boy Scouting by way of farm publications, but the effort was weak at best. In 1925, more than a quarter of American boys lived in the countryside, but only 6 percent of them (or perhaps less) were involved in Boy Scouting.[73]

The Boy Scouts' program was ill adapted to the countryside, something that little worried its leadership. Mayne, therefore, adapted his program to the conditions of life of rural youth. Mayne argued an interesting point. He believed that many of the activities that attracted city boys to scouting held little appeal for country boys. "Hiking through the country has no such attraction for a boy familiar with rural scenery, as for a boy living in a city home; neither does he feel, like the city boy, the lure of the woods, or the attractions of a camp by the side of a pretty lake—a lake which may be just like the one on the shore of which his father's house is built."[74] Steeped in country life, farm boys had little need or desire to be introduced to it through their leisure activities. Whether this was true or not is difficult to tell. Observers of farm youth have noted that, given the preponderance of rural scenery in their lives, rural youngsters often showed very little appreciation for the wonders of the landscape around them.[75] Even so, there is no lack of evidence of rural youth making enthusiastic use of the landscape around them, as they hunted, explored and immersed themselves in the possibilities available in the countryside.[76]

The reduced emphasis on hiking and camping, however, did not equate to a lessened concern about the relationship between youth and nature. One of the foremost principles of the organization was kindness—a quality not just extended to other humans, but also to animals. A Farm Boy Cavalier "is kind . . . to his horses, and to other dumb animals. He protects the birds, and destroys animal life only when necessary to human welfare."[77] Although the vast majority of Farm Boy Cavalier activities leading to badges centered upon agricultural activities, such as barnyard sanitation, bee culture and milk production, the organization also promoted an aesthetic appreciation of nature. Mayne's vision for the organization included an admixture of activities we would consider traditional to scouting into the agricultural formula. Boys could easily work on these nature-based activities as they worked on their daily chores. Farm Boy Cavaliers could pursue a Bird Study badge by naming and identifying a wide variety of birds, feeding birds in winter and constructing nesting boxes. Those earning a Forestry badge needed to successfully plant and cultivate evergreens and woodland trees, as well as learn to fight forest fires. The Photography badge required a mastery of nature photography, as well as photography of general subjects.[78] The organization encouraged boys to go "hunting with a camera," instead of a gun, in accordance with the emphasis on kindness to all living creatures.[79]

Oddly enough, given Mayne's comments about redundancy of camping for farm boys, the Cavaliers' program did include a camping element: the pilgrimage. Although the handbook did not describe the pilgrimage, the *Farm Boy Cavalier News* did. It included a trip to a secluded location on a "trusty steed," cooking outdoors, mounted exploration of the countryside and "discussion around the pilgrimage fire." There was no mention of this being an overnight activity. Rather, it was a form of day-camping.[80] Given the prevalence of daily chores in farm children's lives, staying away from home overnight was probably unrealistic. Parents would more likely permit activities that allowed youngsters to be at home or in the barn at the beginning and the end of the day. The Farm Boy Cavaliers incorporated love and appreciation of nature into their program but kept their focus firmly upon the farm youth's responsibility to his or her parents' farm, and the farming community.

Mayne's Farm Boy Cavaliers, however, were quite short lived, lasting only into the late 1920s. They were also probably not what educational and child-life reformers had in mind when they sought to improve the condition and environmental awareness of rural youth. In rural areas, reformers alleged, large numbers of children lacked "the right kind of play life, of intelligent contact with nature and of well-directed energy."[81] Others argued that farm children, because of their isolation and devotion to chores, would require instruction in leisure, "Because he does not have the one big thing in a young child's life, the knowledge of how to play."[82] Reformers with an urban orientation wanted rural children to focus their recreational activities; that is, on directed, supervised play as opposed to a continuation of their farm-based responsibilities. In urban areas, teachers and schools often had an important role in creating the proper play environment. This seemed unlikely in rural areas. The "tiny school" lacked a "suitable playing ground" and worse yet, the teacher generally had "no special training in the subject of play supervision." As one play reformer commented, "it is obvious that such a condition in the rural school is in need of immediate correction if there is to be a healthy development of the child body."[83] Just going outside to run, play crack the whip, or to throw the ball over the schoolhouse was no longer enough. The child out-of-doors was a child in need of direction.

Consequently, the members of the 1930 White House Conference on Child Health and Protection took as dim a view of the prospects of rural youth as it did of the urban. While rural youngsters were surrounded on all sides by the wonders of nature, their experiences out-of-doors, thought reformers, were entirely of the wrong sort: "There is tragedy for many country children in the emptiness of life, the absence of adequate companionship, the need for stimulation and for fostering ambition. They lack opportunities for self-expression in the arts and for developing muscular skills." Farm work, even though it provided an "abundance of physical exercise in the open air," did not properly build muscles. Instead, argued physician Henry S. Curtis, it made them awkward and caused uneven physical development. What they needed instead was play and recreational programs to make them graceful and strong. The conference recommended that the U.S. Department of Agriculture's youth program, 4-H, place more emphasis on its recreational program and that the Y.M.C.A., Boy Scouts, Girl Scouts, and Camp Fire organizations more thoroughly expand their reach into rural communities.[84]

It was 4-H that took the lead in the nation's rural communities. Because the agricultural extension service oversaw 4-H in each state, each state's experience with the program was different. However, within 4-H across the country, there was a growing interest in the relationship between youth and nature. In the teens, and particularly in the twenties, 4-H added camping to its repertoire. In 1919, West Virginia became the first state to incorporate camping into its 4-H program. Throughout the 1920s, other states added camps, and in 1927, the organization founded its national camp in Washington, D.C.[85] In addition to camping, 4-H leaders also developed their own experiments in nature education.

One of the most active of these extension nature educators was Wakelin McNeel, who was the conservation leader on the staff of the University of Wisconsin Extension Service.[86] Beginning in the 1920s, McNeel avidly supported environmental outreach work with Wisconsin's youth and strongly believed that Wisconsin's children, and in fact, all children, belonged out-of-doors. He opined "it is the birthright of every child to find that some of the best things in life are free, everywhere about them in the outdoors. . . . They should be out romping in the fresh air, getting that physical tiredness that invites sound sleep. It is a patent truth, taught in every forest and thicket, that all creatures need plenty of exercise and rest."[87] The way to achieve this goal was to send children into the woods. McNeel pursued this goal from a number of different angles—pursuit of forestry work within 4-H, the development of school forests and broadcasts for youth on topics related to nature.

The motto for the 4-H forestry program that McNeel designed was "have boys and trees grow up together."[88] 4-H materials indicated that the program was indeed designed for boys; there was little or no evidence that anyone thought that girls might want to join the program. In its forestry work, 4-H promoted a strong conservationist ethic for youth. The creed of the forestry program was:

> It shall be my purpose; to learn the ways of tree, forest and wild life that I may be of service in protecting and propagating these natural resources; to learn to love the things of outdoor life worth preserving, and to understand nature's method that I may be strong of body, courageous and self-reliant in spirit, ready to take my place among men when time decrees; and in all ways to help restore, to enjoy and to pass on to posterity our state more beautiful, enjoyable and provident than it was passed on to me.[89]

The program's creators hoped to harness the efforts of the state's youth to improve Wisconsin's forests for the long-term benefit of all state residents.

In order to join the program, a boy had to have access to land, private or public, upon which to plant trees. After consulting with the local 4-H leader or county extension agent, the boy would then begin the process of working through a four-stage program of increasingly more elaborate forestry projects. At the most basic level, boys planted and studied trees. The program, however, was far more elaborate than that. The final, most advanced level was that of the "cruiser." "A cruiser is one who estimates stands of timber. He is sometimes called a 'landlooker.' He was one of the most romantic characters of logging days. His experience developed a judgment and intuition that was uncanny."[90] The cruiser pursued advanced work, which required that a boy know how to fight forest fires, recruit other boys to join the 4-H forestry program, acquire knowledge of tree diseases and be able to calculate the board feet of lumber in a stand of trees or a woodlot. The successful cruiser would also develop an exhibit to demonstrate his prowess as a woodsman, just as other 4-H members demonstrated their crop, cooking or animal projects.[91] This was 4-H forestry at its most technically advanced level.

While the 4-H forestry program was for only the most dedicated young woodsmen, McNeel was also vital to the development of programs reaching a broader cross-section of Wisconsin's rural youth. He believed very strongly in the importance of farmers understanding conservation practices and incorporated the conservation message into the state's 4-H conservation camps. In 1945, he distributed several of naturalist Aldo Leopold's essays, including "The Farmer as a Conservationist," to the boys and girls attending the camp. He also invited Leopold to attend the camp and address the youngsters.[92] McNeel believed in bringing the latest in conservation expertise to his young charges. During fifteen years of conservation camps, the young 4-H members would learn from experts from the state conservation department and the Soil Conservation Service, as well as those from organizations such as Trees for Tomorrow. Hiking, camping and field trips existed side by side with intensive education in the conservation message.[93]

McNeel also directed Wisconsin's school forest program in his capacity as assistant state 4-H club leader. Begun in 1927, the school forests were just that—forty acres or more of land given over to a school district for the purpose of teaching children about forests and nature. Unlike the 4-H forestry program, the school forests were open to both boys and girls, and youngsters of any age. First and foremost, the school forests were to teach children to appreciate the out-of-doors, "especially trees." Children would learn "sympathy and understanding" for trees and all of the forest's living things. Interacting with the school forest, students would not just understand the aesthetics of forests; they would also understand the economics of forests, and the practical problems involved with developing a healthy stand of trees. They would also learn the state's wildlife laws, as they applied to game, fish and plants.[94] Ideally, teachers would incorporate the lessons learned in the forest into the classroom: "Not only would arithmetic correlate with forestry, but subjects such as home geography, nature study, agriculture and language would find numerous topics for projects, themes and debates."[95] In practical terms, the results were quite stunning. Every year throughout the 1930s, Wisconsin's school children planted approximately a million trees.[96] Wisconsin's school forests, still in existence today, provided a laboratory for many types of nature education.

McNeel carried his outreach further, for nearly twenty years broadcasting his conservation message to schools across Wisconsin. Beginning in 1932, "Afield with Ranger Mac" hit the airwaves on Mondays on Madison's WHA radio station, reaching children in small and large schools alike, although as many as 70 percent of his listeners may have come from single-teacher rural schools.[97] State law required the teaching of conservation in the public schools, but many teachers were unprepared to tackle the subject. Ranger Mac, broadcasting by way of Wisconsin's School of the Air, fulfilled that need.[98] It was a very successful program. In 1942, McNeel received a Peabody Award for outstanding educational radio programming.

McNeel called his listeners "Trailhitters" and encouraged them to get out into the woods on a regular basis. McNeel's interested listenership was visible in the stacks of correspondence he received from students and teachers throughout the state, asking for further information on topics of particular interest. The students of the Homiston School of Fond du Lac wanted to know how to play a game called "Leaves," very much like "The Farmer in the Dell." The fifth-grade students of the Washington School, in Marshfield, Wisconsin, listened to a broadcast on ice fishing and wanted a copy of the state's fishing laws, which Ranger Mac gladly provided. The youngsters in Wilson listened to his broadcast on birds and then decided to have a contest to see who could design and make the best birdhouse. When the students from the Gaston School, in Cottage Grove, wanted to know how to care for and feed the opossum at their school, Ranger Mac advised them of the animal's preference for fruit, but suggested that they not keep him for long, since "Like most wild animals it will not thrive in captivity, especially as an adult animal."[99] Ranger Mac became their personal advisor and information source for all matters pertaining to the natural world.

Ranger Mac, perhaps not surprisingly, also found himself answering questions on the subject of religion. Students at the rural Stone School in Omro wrote to tell him that he had mistakenly identified the fruit Eve fed Adam as an apple, since the third book of Genesis did not actually identify the type of fruit eaten. Ranger Mac hurriedly explained that Milton had identified the fruit as an apple in *Paradise Lost*. Mr. M. J. Bangert, a sixth- and seventh-grade teacher at St. Paul's Lutheran School in Sheboygan, wrote to express his concern that Ranger Mac was teaching evolution. "We do not expect you to teach religion," the teacher wrote, "however we would find the program more acceptable if no evolutionary theories were injected. We believe that the naturalist above all others, has opportunities to see God's handiwork in nature." Within a week, Ranger Mac wrote to the teacher, replying, "Your suggestion is sound, and no remark should creep in that might weaken the faith of young listeners. . . . Write me again both in helpful criticism and commendation."[100] Then, as now, nature educators had to find a way to deal with the conundrum of reconciling faith with scientific knowledge. McNeel did not comment on his own, personal position in the evolution versus biblical creation debate. Given his position as a leading 4-H educator in the state, he was unlikely to step into such controversial territory.

What reformers like McNeel hoped for, and what may or may not have been achieved, was a nation of farm youth attached to the land, not just as a place to earn a living, but as a place to love and nurture. They wanted youngsters to feel a personal attachment to the places in which they lived and worked. They wanted them to love the land, rather than view it as an adversary. A 1939 poem, written by Vincent Kuharic, a young farmer and participant in the agricultural short course at the University of Wisconsin–Madison, captured the best of what a working relationship with the land was supposed to bring to farm youth.

> Winter will not release its icy grip,
> Though the chilly blasts slowly cease.
> The wind whistles, the snow blows and piles—
> But in my world of the future, I open a door—
> My garden is in full bloom,—and on ahead
> The fruit hangs heavily on prolific trees and vines.
> I plough a straight black furrow.
> The rich dark soil heaves lightly away,
> And crumbles into a mellow seed bed.

My heart is light and carefree
As we slowly make the rounds.
The pungent odor of fresh turned soil is intoxicating
And makes me feel slightly giddy.
I lean on the plough and look ahead.
I watch the long straight rows of deep green corn,
Bending with the gentle summer wind.[101]

Reformers and teachers could only hope that as the twentieth century deepened, and as farm youngsters spent more time at school, less time in the fields and were increasingly distanced from the natural world, that some would still look to the fields, lean on the plow, and feel the intoxication of the land.

CHAPTER TWO

URBAN ENVIRONMENTS, URBAN CHILDREN

The last decades of the nineteenth century were a time of very rapid urbanization in the United States. Families and individuals moved from farm to town in unprecedented numbers, in search of the economic opportunities that cities represented. Immigrants from Europe also came to the United States in a great flood, settling largely (but not exclusively) in America's cities. By 1920, the Census Bureau would declare that the United States was now an urban nation, with at least half of the population living in cities and towns. It was a remarkable demographic shift, and one that had serious implications for the relationship between children and the world around them. On the farm, children had almost too much of the natural world with which to contend. As children moved from farm to town, and town to city, that contact would become more tenuous and difficult to maintain. Increasingly, children's interactions would be with a constructed and heavily altered environment, a situation that would distress adults (but not necessarily children), and challenge them to find new ways to connect children with the world around them.

At the close of the nineteenth century and the beginning of the twentieth, it was not always easy to define the differences between rural and urban childhood, particularly where small cities and suburbs were concerned. Even in town, many families lived without plumbing, electricity, central heating and sidewalks—some of the amenities that might seem to form a dividing line between urban and rural. Livestock was also common in urban areas, since horses were still the primary mode of transportation. Families in towns kept the occasional cow or pig, and often kept chickens. People usually knew their neighbors, and mothers were often home during the day, taking care of small children and attending to mountains of housework. Children were within shouting distance of an adult at most times. Although there were variations with age and gender, children generally had the run of the small communities within which they lived. Children under five had to stick more closely to their mothers, and girls (depending on the family) often had less

Children often explored their towns by bicycle. WHS Image ID 67864. By permission of the Wisconsin Historical Society, Madison, Wisconsin.

freedom than boys.[1] Helen Scheetz, who grew up in De Soto, Iowa, longed to have the freedom that her brothers had. "I adored my big brothers and looked up to them. I constantly wished that I had been born a boy so that I could join in their exploits. They had so much freedom and dared to do such exciting things."[2] Nevertheless, girls as well as boys ventured daily into the world beyond their homes. They showed a great familiarity with the natural environs around their homes, and also with the streets and businesses of their towns. Most children traversed their towns on foot, or sometimes by bicycle, and knew the places in which they lived quite intimately.

The distance between the city and the countryside could be quite small.

Charles Honce, who was born in 1895 and raised in Keokuk, Iowa, spent his childhood exploring the town and its periphery with a gang of boys. Summer was the time for running free. Town had its diversions, such as the local "haunted house," but "perhaps it didn't occur to us that we could avoid a long trip by playing in somebody's backyard." Their preferred destination was "'out in the country.'" Getting there "required a three mile hike, barefooted, of course, but there were cherries and red haws and papaws and other delicacies along the way to tempt the feet forward."[3] Once out into the country, they headed for "the crick," where they taught themselves to swim. The boys also built a cabin. "We always were trespassing but evidently there were no fences then and nobody cared."[4] Girls played in the woods, too, venturing there for games of "cops and robbers," or "cowboys and Indians," or perhaps the more sedate study of both birds and wildflowers. As one woman remembered, "We spent many hours with a bird book and pencil and paper to see who could find the most species."[5]

For Charles Honce and many others in the northern United States, winter was also a time for sallying forth with friends, but not before donning "long, heavy, fleece-lined underwear."[6] Once fitted with this and the other armor of a midwestern winter, local boys and girls ventured forth to tackle the town's hills. A late nineteenth-century poem captured the enthusiasm many children felt for sledding:

> I had rather go a-coasting
> Than sit by the fire a-roasting!
>   Won't you go?
> For I know how to steer,
> And can take you clear
>   Across the pond,
>   And way beyond,
> And that's not very near!
>   Wont' you go?
> And what if you do tip over?
> The snow is as soft as clover!
>   Won't you go?
> And never mind the bumps!
>   We coast and climb,
>   Have a jolly time!
> And who cares for the thumps!
>   Won't you go?[7]

Given the large number of steep hills in Keokuk, nearly everyone owned a sled. Honce noted, "Some hills were very steep and three or four blocks long. As street traffic was light the children and their sleds had the run of the hills. Seldom if ever was there an accident."[8] A ten-mile long canal that ran along the Mississippi also gave the children plenty of room for skating. Winter was not a time to retreat to the indoors, but to explore pleasures unavailable at other seasons.[9] In particular, ice and snow made the winter a time to go fast, propelled by blades down slopes and across frozen rivers and lakes. It was a time to freely enjoy sensations that required much more effort to achieve in the summer months.

Water was an essential element in many a childhood, not just Charles Honce's. Maxine Teele, who grew up in Council Bluffs, Iowa, made a telling comment. "I'd lived in a number of hamlets where Main Street began and ended in cornfields. This was pretty dull by comparison to the excitement and variety provided by the river. It gave to us all the pleasures afforded by any body of water—skating in the winter; swimming, fishing and boating in the summer."[10] Whenever children had access to water, the possibilities for adventure multiplied exponentially. Although parents must have been concerned about the possibility of drowning, there seemed to be no shortage of youngsters incorporating ponds, streams, canals and rivers into their adventures, winter and summer.

One of the more distinctive ways in which to know an environment was by smell. Ruth Barkley grew up in Odebolt, Iowa, where her father was a storekeeper. She became quite familiar with the town's main street and years later remembered it by referring to its many distinctive odors. She wrote that it was the "smells, mostly pleasant ones, that I associate with some business places on that street." She would pause in front of the town's two bakeries. "I don't remember that the odors that were wafted out of one were better than the other. I know it was always nice to be passing when someone opened one of the doors." Further on was the lumber yard and planing mill, with their distinctive woody odors. The meat market, curiously enough, also smelled of wood. The sawdust that covered the floor obscured other far less pleasant odors. The shoe store, of course, smelled like leather, and the printing office had the "sharp smell of ink." The smells of the dentist's office she associated with pain. "I never stood around waiting for that door to open to let that smell out to me." Some of the most compelling smells, however, came from her father's store: sauerkraut, pickles, coffee, cheese. "These are far from being all that went into that bouquet of smells in papa's grocery store."[11] Barkley did not mention many of the less pleasant odors that also must have defined her world, such as those emanating from manure piles, privies, coal-burning stoves and refuse. Since bathing was a once-a-week affair, the people most assuredly smelled as well. In a time before the air conditioning and sanitization that became common in the mid to late years of the twentieth century, all of a child's environments must have provided complex olfactory adventures.

These descriptions of an intense world of sight, smell and experience are common to small and medium-size cities in the late nineteenth and early twentieth centuries. This kind of freedom appeared in other locations as well. A study of Inwood, New York, which was at the beginning of the twentieth century a developing urban neighborhood at the northern tip of Manhattan, showed that children in that place had considerable freedom to explore their worlds. When the subway came to Inwood from New York City in 1906, the area began to develop rapidly, transforming Inwood from rural to urban, and many families with middling incomes found their way to the area.[12] Early on, it was entirely possible to forget that New York was just over the horizon. Dorothy Menkin loved the area around Inwood Park, where the daisies grew. "I used to lay among them and forget I was in New York. There were these Rose-of-Sharon trees along the topmost road, and to the west a small but beautiful patch of violets. It was all so exhilarating."[13] There were foxes, farms and traces of early Indian inhabitants to be found if children looked hard enough. There was also a creek for skating, canoeing and swimming.[14]

Children played vigorously in this community under construction. As Freddy Tarzian remembered, "We still had a lot of room to move around about. We ran up and down the buildings where the hills used to be. There were no locks on the doors downstairs, no locks on the doors to the roofs. You could go from roof to roof."[15] Abandoned barns and other remnants of the community's rural past offered play spaces for children as well. Children particularly enjoyed vacant lots. Recollecting his boyhood, Tarzian said that "since there were a lot of empty lots, we played there mostly. There was a lot of wood and old trees around, and we would make fires and cook potatoes."[16] Girls remembered building and furnishing playhouses using scraps of wood found on building sites. The Hudson and Harlem rivers offered opportunities for wading and swimming as well. The community had yet to build many playgrounds, and children made their own play places.[17] As historian Sanford Gaster has written, "Inwood . . . was not so much a stable, nurturing environment indulging children, as it was one that constantly *challenged* them. . . . children met their urban environment head-on; they were not presented with an array of pleasant alternatives, but rather derived much of their enjoyment through discriminating between what was to be enjoyed and what was to be avoided."[18] The children made excellent use of their environmental resources and adapted to the change that was happening so quickly around them.

Not far from Inwood, however, the differences between rural and urban childhood grew. Here was a stark urban environment, one that many Americans 100 years ago both loathed and feared. Urban America in the late nineteenth and early twentieth centuries was not a healthy place in which to live. Historian David Nasaw ably described the discomforts of the nation's large cities, particularly for the young:

> No matter where you lived or worked, you were assaulted daily by the smoke, soot, and dust in the air; the noise of clattering cobblestones, cable cars, trolleys, and the elevated; the smell of horse dung on the streets. In working-class and immigrant residential districts, these annoyances were intensified a hundredfold. It was in the city of the 'other half' that the sewers were always clogged and the streets and alleyways filled with garbage. It was here that dead horses lay for days, bloated and decaying, children poking at their eyes and pulling out their hair to weave into rings. . . . It was here that tuberculosis raged and babies died of exposure or cold or heat or spoiled milk, that pushcarts, streetcars, and horse-drawn wagons fought for space, and children were crushed to death in the duel.[19]

It was a crowded, filthy world, and one in which there was little room for children and their concerns.

In the 1950s, two urban planners interviewed individuals who had grown up in cities in the years from 1923 to 1937. Although there were many features of the urban landscape they enjoyed, there were also others that caused concern. Specifically, some surfaces, like brick, gravel and cobblestone, created difficulties for playing children. As one commented "I remember distinctly the brick sidewalks. I didn't like that at all. I was strictly for cement sidewalks, didn't like brick; they jibbled and jabbled all ways."[20] Others complained about the ubiquitous blacktop. "You couldn't dig . . . I like to dig. There weren't many places to dig because of the hard asphalt on the playground."[21] When cities surfaced streets, playgrounds and city lots, they generally did not consider the alternative uses to which children might want to put those surfaces. Adults proceeded with urban development; children then had to find their place within that landscape.

The news, however, was not all bad. As historian Howard Chudacoff described, the cities provided children an informal playground as well. Urban planners and builders may not have meant this world for the express use of children, but children found many ways to adapt the city to their use. "The advent of asphalt pavement and better street lighting; the planting of telephone poles, hydrants, and fences; the erection of walls and stoops; and the construction of other new edifices—all fueled youthful imaginations. Balls bounced higher on pavement than on dirt, nighttime no longer halted outdoor activity, new hiding places and bases could be found for old games, and inanimate objects could be appropriated as play partners."[22] There were new dangers in this world, but also enormous opportunities.[23] As two observers of early twentieth-century city children noted, "The street does not drive the child: it leads him on—to discovery, conquest, amusement, self-expression. . . . adventure offers boundless opportunities,— from tumbling into the Frog Pond to actually getting arrested."[24]

The oral histories taken of individuals who grew up in New York City in the late nineteenth and early twentieth centuries reveal a portrait of child-life spent in very close contact with a potentially harsh but engaging environment, one that cried out for exploration. Descriptions of urban childhood are gritty, filled with the rough texture of their world. Nasaw was not exaggerating when he described urban children playing with and around dead horses in the street. Indeed, Danish photographer Jacob Riis captured children doing just that in his graphic and groundbreaking slum photography. From the perspective of the twenty-first century, one could easily imagine that he had staged the pictures, for effect. After all, what child would want to play around and on a dead, decaying animal? But the testimony of those raised in urban slum neighborhoods confirmed the practice. Blanche Lasky grew up on New York's Lower East Side and commented, "There was a stable right next to me. I used to play on the dead horses. They'd just leave 'em layin' on the street, and then we'd play king of the hill on them. After a while, the smell didn't bother us."[25] Marty Cohen, also from the Lower East Side, shared similar memories. "When the horse would die, they would have to lie in the street until the SPCA came by with this big hearse. . . . Before they came, the horse would be lying here for days, and to kids, what the hell, if they played around a dead horse or a live horse, it didn't make any difference."[26] Ed McGee, who grew up in Hell's Kitchen, made the rotting carcasses a part of his active play. "When the horse died, they'd put him out in the street for a day or two. We liked to run and jump on dead horses. Once, the bladder broke on 'im—oh boy, the smell."[27] Children's activities

Dead horses provided children with hours of entertainment. Reproduced from the collections of the Library of Congress.

tell us that the opportunity for creative play was more compelling than the powerful smell of death and decay was offensive.

City life bred street culture among poor and working-class children. During waking hours, there was little room for children in the homes of the poor. An early twentieth-century observer of Boston's children commented, "The tenement home has neither nursery nor playroom. The space cannot be spared. Birth and death alike claim the privilege of privacy for but a moment."[28] As David Nasaw has noted, adults could make room for sleeping children, and infants and toddlers could be tucked into corners, but big kids had to make themselves scarce during the day. "Indoors was for adults; children only got in the way: of mother and her chores, of father trying to relax after a long day at work, of boarders who worked the night shift and had to sleep during the day. . . . The children required no special encouragement to go outside to play. That is where they belonged."[29]

Compared to the world outside their doors, children often found their homes uninteresting and uncomfortable places anyway. Robert Leslie's family lived in a five- or six-room flat on the Lower East Side that was short on windows, which meant it was dark at all times and uncomfortably hot in summer. "We slept on the fire escape or in the yard where the toilets were."[30] Joe Henry's experience in a flat on the Upper East Side was very similar. "There was no privacy, and in the summertime it was wicked."[31] In the winter, his family's apartment could be terribly cold, inadequately heated and ventilated.[32] In the absence of good alternatives, children migrated out onto the fire escapes and roofs and down into the streets. This did not mean, however, that the youngsters were entirely out of adult reach. In Mary Thompson's Chelsea neighborhood, "The low-rise buildings meant that everybody had access to the street, so that most of the children were watched not only by their own parents, but everyone else's parents. . . . There was a lot of hanging out in the streets."[33] Most tenements were only three to five stories tall, and parents in their apartments were not too far removed from children in the streets. Neighbors, too, watched each other's children.

Children had a strong sense of territory, based on neighborhood, geography, ethnicity and race. Although David Nasaw argued that race and ethnicity were not a factor in children's division of streets into territories, there is some evidence that they did, indeed, matter.[34] Anna Murphy, who grew up in Harlem, watched her brother sparring over territory. Her family was African American and clashed regularly with the Irish American youngsters who lived on the other side of Eighth Avenue. "Many times I would see my brother come in and get the broomstick in order to go out and fight. The Irish kids wouldn't let the black kids cross St. Nicholas to go into the park and sleigh-ride."[35] The most common unit of organization, however, was the block. Children played with children from their block, and considered their block their territory. Those who went adventuring off of their home turf knew that they might have to defend themselves against others who sought to protect their own block from interlopers.[36]

Gender was an important determinant of the ways in which children interacted with their environments. Girls faced more restrictions than boys. Some parents barred girls from swimming in the rivers, sending them instead to local pools, if they were available.[37] Presumably, the presence of strange boys in a state of undress was the primary consideration in parents' prohibitions. Parents might allow girls to go sledding in the winter, but regulated the way in which they did it. Olga Marx loved to go sledding in Central Park, but she had to play carefully. "I remember some girls did the belly flop, but our mother thought that was déclassé, so we would sit on the sled with our legs out on the side for brakes."[38] In the Italian American community, the restrictions were numerous. Some conservative parents barred their daughters from rowing, biking, skating, horseback riding and any number of other activities, although girls did not always obey.[39] In a study of children's activities on New York's Lower West Side, a largely Italian American area, researchers found that several factors restricted the boundaries of girls' worlds. Boys had far more leisure time than girls, whose parents expected them to spend long hours on housekeeping and child-care. Boys' work, such as it was, also allowed boys to escape into the out-side world, gathering firewood and running errands. Additionally, parents simply allowed boys more freedom.[40] Observers in Boston found the same gender-driven division of space among children in that city. "Girls spend their vacations nearer home than boys. They are more useful in the house and cooperate better with their mothers. The boys are therefore turned out of the homes into the street to play; and the girls are kept inside with dish-washing, sweeping, dusting and cleaning windows. . . . Many girls spend the greater part of the summer on the sidewalk 'minding' the baby."[41] The geography of the street favored big boys. Girls owned the stoops and spent a good deal of their time there working and visiting. Smaller children also occupied the stoops and sidewalks. But boys owned the whole street, as least as far as the traffic would let them.[42] This may explain why, in the early part of the twentieth century, New York City's boys had a far higher death rate from street accidents than girls.[43]

There were, of course, exceptions to the rule. Some parents allowed their daughters just as much leeway to explore the world as their sons. Una Hunt grew up in Cincinnati and remembered a remarkable range of activities, well beyond the range of many girls. Her preferred companions were boys with their more physical play. "The children I knew and played with during the eight years I lived in Cincinnati were nearly all boys. There were a few girls—I remember them in the background—but boys cared for the things I liked . . . So I spent most of my time with Harry [a neighbor boy] and his friends, and together we climbed every tree and shed in the neighborhood." Hunt's mother showed a great deal of forbearance, accepting and encourag-ing her daughter's explorations. She commented, "I have always admired my mother's courage in allowing it for I was often badly hurt, but after each fall, when vinegar and brown paper had been applied, her only comment was 'You must learn to climb better,' and I did. Soon I could get to almost any roof by way of the waterspout and gutters."[44] Hunt owned the neighbor-hood as thoroughly as any of her male companions.

It was the absence of other workable options that sent turn-of-the-century children into the streets, and they incorporated their features into their

The streets could be dangerous. This Washington, D.C., boy lost his leg to a trolley. FSA photograph collection. Reproduced from the collections of the Library of Congress.

games. Peter Pascale's description of playing stickball in East Harlem neatly encapsulates many of the features of street play in urban locations.

> We also played a lotta boxball and stickball. We used to have the teams go out and challenge the different blocks. Over here used to be the trolley cars, and we had a tough time playin' because of them. If the ball hit the tracks, tough luck, what happened happened. It was like hittin' the wall. If they catch it off the wall, you're out. Ya learned to play the track. Ya had to move over so that if it hit the crack of the track, it could jump by ya. If it hit the side, it would come straight at ya. We had the Second Avenue El. You hit on top of the El, it was a home run, because by the time ya found the ball, the guy was gone.[45]

Children made use of whatever spaces they had for play. If that was the street, then so be it. Each feature of the street had its own part in the game, even transient features, such as delivery wagons and ice trucks.[46] In spite of the dangers, railroad tracks became a part of children's territory as well. As Ed McGee commented, "We all liked to go down to Eleventh Avenue and jump on the sides of the trains and climb on top. Quite a few kids got killed or lost their limbs. That's why they called it Death Avenue."[47]

The children were not exaggerating. The streets had always been dangerous, but the addition of trains, trolleys and automobiles made the situation considerably worse. By 1910, accidents were becoming the leading cause of death for American children, and particularly those involving moving vehicles. In the years from 1910 to 1914, between 40 and 60 percent of traffic accident victims in New York were under the age of fourteen. Most were killed or injured a block or two from their homes, while they played, worked or ran errands for their parents.[48] On November 1, 1908, 500 children marched down "Death Avenue," demanding that the New York Central Railroad remove their tracks and make the street safe for play. They were, however, unsuccessful.[49] Commerce was the preeminent use of the street, not children's play.

Children made use of the streets for many purposes, some of them quite familiar to adults, such as stickball, baseball, tag and other common games. When children's urban pastimes became more creative, adults began to really worry. Children did not confine themselves to the easily understandable and respectable games that their elders wished. Progressive-era researchers made the disturbing discovery that children playing in city streets were not always amusing themselves innocently. On June 23, 1913, researchers in Cleveland made a census of children's behavior, observing 7,799 children, 5,241 boys and 2,558 girls. The observers found the vast majority of children in yards, vacant lots and alleys. While some children applied themselves diligently to working, housekeeping, minding a baby or gardening, most were playing. Some played baseball, flew kites or rode bicycles, but the vast majority engaged in "just fooling around" or "doing nothing." The category of "doing nothing" included "breaking windows, destroying houses, chalking suggestive words on buildings, throwing mud at street cars, touching girls, looking at pictures of women in tights . . . stealing, gambling and drinking."[50] The urban young were making themselves at home in their environment, and often in ways that disturbed and distressed adults.

The young also challenged adults for control of the streets. By incorporating local landmarks into their games and scampering throughout the neighborhood, oblivious to the adults, children were constantly in the way, annoying and inconveniencing the adults they encountered.[51] Only a very few adults were really sympathetic to their presence on the streets. Dr. Annie S. Daniel, who practiced medicine on New York City's East Side, championed the children. She wrote, "But they oughtn't to be kept off the streets!

Reformers feared the influence of the street, and especially on groups like this "Cleveland Boy Gang." Reproduced from the collections of the Library of Congress.

So long as the streets are their only playgrounds, they ought to be out there, in the open air, filling their lungs, exercising their bodies."[52] Her perspective was unusually tolerant.

Because of the dangers and because of the inconvenience that children caused to adults, city after city legislated children off the streets, demanding that they take their games elsewhere. Given the lack of playgrounds, however, many children had nowhere else to go. In 1906 in Cleveland, Ohio, this led to a small revolt. When the police ordered the children out of the streets, a group of boys and girls calling themselves the Courtland Street Liberty League went to call on Mayor Tom Johnson, blasting horns and carrying banners. After listening to the children's grievances, the mayor acknowledged the difficulty of their situation. "'If the children have no playgrounds,' said the Mayor, 'they should be permitted to play in the streets. Let 'em play to their hearts' content—any kind of games so they don't throw stones,' and then three rousing cheers were given for the Mayor."[53]

Most children, however, did not organize protests, and most cities continued to ban children from street play. The youngsters generally defied such orders, finding ways to hide their games from the police and maintain control of what they thought of as their own home turf. A 1917 Children's Bureau report noted that in Washington, D.C., 48.8 percent of boys and 37.5 percent of girls played in the streets, "which is both dangerous and contrary to law."[54] This resulted in arrests. In 1914, an investigator making a survey of children's street activities discovered that the police in New York City arrested approximately 12,000 children each year. He reported, "These are not exceptional children, and they are not a special problem. Rather, they are typical children. They are mere exhibits drawn from the mass of those children who live in the congested neighborhoods, a small proportion of the children who have done the same things and have not been caught."[55] An intensive study of 170 of these cases in the Hell's Kitchen neighborhood showed that the most common "crimes" for which children were arrested were "throwing various missiles," twenty-four instances; "baseball," twenty-two instances; and setting "bonfires," nineteen instances. As the investigator noted, "One offense is particularly singled out in the law to be prohibited on the streets. This offense is baseball. Baseball is no sin and the children know it. They merely know that they will be arrested if they play baseball. They know that if they are going to play ball they must send out pickets to announce the coming of the policeman."[56] And so children concealed their activities.

Children waged the same turf wars in other urban areas. A 1911 survey of immigrant neighborhoods in Milwaukee showed that the vast majority of the children played in the street, in spite of legislation against it. As historian Dominick Cavallo noted, the authorities had discovered that "the majority of the city's young people were breaking the law and getting away with it. This was hardly the best way to teach respect for American laws to the children of the foreign born."[57] A lack of play space was becoming a national concern, one with implications far beyond the problem of children playing where adults were trying to work. The time was coming when reformers would try to remake children's interactions with the environment in ways more pleasing and understandable to concerned adults.

Parks, interestingly enough, were not really a part of the poor urban child's world, in the sense of providing a usable outdoor space for play. In Washington, D.C., in spite of large amounts of public space, there was almost no place for children to play in many of the city's neighborhoods. In one of the most densely populated districts of the city, where more than 3,000 children lived, there was only one park, Franklin Park. As a Children's Bureau investigator noted, "It offers no play facilities . . . except a sand pile for the small children."[58] In New York City, the situation was much the same. Sometimes, when it was terribly hot, children might sleep in a park, like Central Park. Others went there to catch a breath of fresh air. Rarely did they go there to play.[59] Many crowded neighborhoods were not within easy distance of a park, and at the century's turn, parks, for the most part, were meant for the appreciation and leisure of adults. After the turn of the century, progressive reformers began advocating for children's playgrounds, but most of those would not be built within parks, at least not initially. Instead, they would be constructed in slum neighborhoods. The parks only gradually made adjustments for the city's children.

Central Park only tentatively welcomed children, with very gradual provision of playing fields and other amenities.[60] Children who tried to play in New York City's Gramercy Park found themselves at the mercy of the park's caretaker, a man named "Teck." As John Bainbridge, who grew up near the park, remembered, "If you violated his rules, such as stepping on the flower bed or fighting, you might have to sit by yourself on the west side of the park, where it wasn't very active, for half an hour, or you might have to walk around the park on the inside, maybe two, three, or four times, whatever he thought would be appropriate."[61] The idea of children running riot through the city's parks, exploring and playing imaginative games, was not acceptable to many adults. So children used instead whatever alternative urban spaces they could appropriate for their activities.

Like children in the countryside and smaller towns, those in New York City sought water in which to play. Rivers were accessible to many of the city's neighborhoods. As Stanley Marx, who grew up at the northern end of Manhattan put it, "If you live near a river, you have to be influenced by it. . . . It makes you more adventurous. There's just something about water that makes you want to cross it or be in it."[62] Unfortunately, crossing or being in one of New York City's rivers was a dubious proposition, at best. Like the rest of the city, the rivers were filthy, full of all manner of refuse, although at some times, the rivers were cleaner than at others. Swimming at high tide was safer than swimming at low tide, because the refuse was more diluted.[63] Robert Leslie and his friends headed for the East River, in spite of the waste that accumulated there. "The only recreation was to go down to the East River where the Barges were. The people would swim in it, but they also moved their bowels there."[64] It was not just isolated individuals who moved their bowels in the rivers, but the entire population. Prior to the development of city sewage systems, all of the city's waste emptied into its waterways. Peter Pascale lived in East Harlem, and swam at 114th Street, where the sewer emptied into the Harlem River.

Every once in a while the sewer stuff would come out. Gheeegh! Everything came out. 'Hey, it's comin' boys! Move out.' It was a riot. Ya got hit all over. Goddamn, we had to push that crap away when we went in there, otherwise ya caught it in the face. That stuff hit us left and right, but that was the only place we coulda swam, because in the other place there was a fence.[65]

Sewage was not the only worry; industrial waste fouled the water as well. Swimming near a slaughterhouse meant risking being covered in blood when the plant discharged its waste.[66] The Hudson River was no cleaner. Bill Bailey and his friends played there, and years later he shuddered at his memories. "We swam among the condoms, the garbage, and the filth, everything the Hudson was noted for. As a matter of fact, the first intestines I ever seen came floatin' down there once."[67] Children risked disease and infection by swimming in the city's open waters, but even so, could not resist the adventure.

As such descriptions might indicate the big city child, like those in smaller communities, lived in a world of smells, ranging from pleasant to highly offensive. For Bresci Thompson, who grew up in New York City's Chelsea neighborhood, it was the smells that dominated childhood memories. Sweet, chocolatey smells emanated from Runkle Brothers, which manufactured candy. More sweet smells drifted in from National Biscuit. Florence Willison remembered the enticing smells of a store that only sold pork and pork products, as well as the pickle factory that was right across from her school. Even the stables near her school, she thought, smelled good. They smelled of horses, "pungent but pleasant."[68] But there were the terrible smells, too, like the ones from the slaughterhouses, as well as the unpleasant everyday smells in the tenements of cat urine and human body odor.[69] Human feces were entirely unavoidable in a world of shared toilets, as Marty Cohen explained. "The toilets were out in the back. . . . There was a guy in the toilet, you couldn't get in, bang! They used to throw the stuff out of the windows. You'd get nailed with it. That was very common."[70]

For large number of poor and working-class children, and especially boys, the city streets were more than playgrounds; they were also workplaces. Children worked in what were called the "street trades," delivering and selling newspapers and magazines, shining shoes and boots, peddling, distributing handbills, and engaging in other occupations. In 1928, a Children's Bureau report estimated that there were upwards of 40,000 newsboys alone working in America's cities.[71] Their research showed that the average age of newsboys was twelve, but that many had begun selling papers at a much earlier age, some at six or seven. Given changes in mandatory education laws, most of them, by the 1920s, were also attending school. They sold their papers early in the morning, and from late afternoon to late at night. For the average newsboy, this meant sixteen hours a week on the city streets; many newsboys, however, worked thirty, forty, fifty hours a week or more.[72]

Interestingly enough, the Children's Bureau investigators did not believe that simply being on the street, per se, was harmful to the young workers. It might make their feet sore, and it might make them cold and uncomfortable, but the streets, as streets, offered "no special hazards" beyond those experienced by urban children playing in the same environment.[73] What could be dangerous, however, was the moral atmosphere and exposure to adults and their vices. Adults around whom newsboys worked might smoke, gamble and tell lewd stories, or worse. Because of this, legislators placed some strictures on boys' activities in street trades, but were much stricter with girls. In those states restricting street trading, the law generally required girls to be much older than boys in order to work.[74] Children, on the whole, were unconcerned about the issues that plagued lawmakers. Some worked because their parents needed the money. More often, though, children asserted that they worked because it was fun. They worked because it entertained them: as one commented, "'It's fun to hustle, and there's nothing to do at home.'"[75] These comments underscored David Nasaw's conclusions about city children's relationship to the environment in which they lived: "The streets bred a gritty self-reliance in its children. It was their frontier. In meeting its dangers and clearing a play and then a work space for themselves, they developed confidence in their strength of purpose and their powers to make their own way. The city held few mysteries for those who grew up with it."[76]

The cities, however, did not have universal appeal. While many youngsters found freedom and excitement in the transition from countryside to city, not everyone responded to the call of the nation's growing urban centers. In 1888, sixteen-year-old Frisby Rasp left his parents' Polk County, Nebraska, farm to attend Omaha Business College. His letters home are a litany of complaint against the deficiencies of the city. Some of his complaints were moral. Omaha was a godless place. "I saw three fellows drunk today the first I have seen. This is an awful wicked town the saloons run on sunday and most all work goes right on." Perhaps it was this wickedness that made Omaha's youth so unattractive to Rasp. "I havent seen a girl as pretty as our worst Hackberry girl. They are all . . . showy but pukey, and the boys are worse. I wouldnt give a fart for all of them."[77] Rasp could not see anything admirable or appealing in his urban peers.

Rasp's complaints, however, did not end with the moral; much of his critique was environmental. Like many observers before him, Rasp was discovering that American cities were dirty, crowded, uncomfortable places. As he wrote to his parents soon after his arrival, "Every thing here is Coal smoke and dirt and people."[78] Omaha was also muddy. Interesting for a farm boy, used to barn yards and pastures, the filth in the streets challenged his sense of order. "I don't like the city at all it is dusty just as soon as it quits raining and the dust here is worst dust I ever saw it is all stone and manure. streets that aint paved 2 feet deep of mud. I have been here one week and it seems more like a year."[79] The lack of fresh air and fresh water challenged his well-being. "I think this is the unhealthyest place I ever saw. The air is full of dirt and filth and the water is full of sewerage. I hav'nt drank a drop of water for a week. I dont drink anything but coffee. The coffee hides the filth in the water."[80] The noise pollution, too, was bothersome to someone accustomed to the relative stillness of rural Nebraska. "I am getting so I hate to hear an engine. there must be at least 50 at work beside the factories and they never stop night or day it is puff-puff-puff-puff-toot-toot-too-braw-braw-puff-uff-puffuff puff—"[81] The whole package of dirt and smell and noise was too much for Rasp. Not even a month into his urban experience, he rejected the cities: "I wouldn't live in the City always for anything. Get an Education there and a good start in life and then let me have a farm. If I had to live in the City always the very thought would kill me."[82] Indeed, that was how he lived the rest of his life.

Although Rasp may have been a bit more vehement than the average, the sentiments he penned were quite similar to those of many other Americans. Many adults, and especially those with a middle-class perspective and a reforming bent, tended to see the cities as dangerous and dirty places, unfit in their current state as habitation for the young. They were not comfortable with the ease children felt in their environments and wanted children to experience a world without urban ills. They wanted them to see the city through different eyes. By the beginning of the twentieth century, reformers were marshalling their forces to address the problems of urban America. Reformers, in particular, abhorred the terrible conditions in which children lived. Adults, to a certain extent, could be presumed to have some resources (either physical or emotional) with which to combat the conditions in which they lived. Many reformers also held adults responsible for their own poverty. A child's situation, however, was different. Children had no choice but to suffer with the environment in which their parents placed them. Child advocates observed the deplorable conditions in the nation's cities and searched for a solution that would, for at least part of the day, remove children from the muck and mire in which they lived. As historian James Marten has commented, "Child welfare became the issue that most Progressives could agree on."[83]

Notable among these Progressives were housing reformers, seeking to improve conditions in the nation's slums. In 1900, New York City's Tenement House Commission evaluated the conditions in slum habitation, and found that they ranged from poor to horrendous. This, the commissioners believed, had serious implications for the future of the nation's youth.

> The tenement districts of New York are places in which thousands of people are living in the smallest space in which it is possible for human beings to exist—crowded together in dark, ill-ventilated rooms, in many of which the sunlight never enters and in most of which fresh air is unknown. They are centers of disease, poverty, vice, and crime, where it is a marvel, not that some children grow up to be thieves, drunkards, and prostitutes, but that so many should ever grow up to be decent and self-respecting. All the conditions which surround childhood, youth, and womanhood in New York's crowded tenement quarters make for unrighteousness. They also make for disease.[84]

Poor housing, in the commissioner's estimation, incubated poverty, disease, crime and immorality. Although the commission argued that ideal conditions would only be achieved "when each family occupies its own separate house," the commissioners also recognized that such a goal was unlikely to be achieved by the mass of laboring families, with incomes too small and time too precious for long commutes from neighboring suburbs.[85] Given the unlikely movement of the poor to single-family homes in the suburbs, the reformers argued for the elimination of dangerous conditions, such as inadequate air shafts, crowded lots, dark hallways and filthy toilet facilities.[86] While reforms such as these would improve the quality of life for poor and working families in general, the commission made other recommendations specifically in the interests of children. One of these was to pave the streets in poorer districts, "so that they can more readily be kept clean. This is especially desirable in the crowded tenement parts of the city, where the street is constantly used by so large a part of the population, and particularly by the children."[87]

The commissioners went even further, embracing the development of parks and playgrounds. They reprinted the 1897 report of the Small Parks Committee, with its very telling opening:

In the original plan of the city of New York the children seem to have been forgotten. Doubtless this oversight was due to the extensive area of unoccupied land which was available for the games and sports in which the youth of that day were wont to indulge. But as the city has grown in population, and especially within the last thirty years, this unoccupied space has been covered by improvements which have left to the children no other opportunity for play but such as can be found in the streets.[88]

New York's forgotten children had no place to play. Conditions inside tenements were grim, but they were grim outside as well. Children in need of a place to play resorted to the filthy streets, or the equally filthy yards behind the tenements. C. A. Mohr, a tenement inspector, deplored the conditions in which children played. He described the yards: "No matter how much drought or how long there is no rain, this yard has the water plug in the centre, and is covered with a dirty slime. I have seen many children playing in this hideous slime, and sit down in it. . . . Many women do their washing in this yard, which adds to the slop. Besides being the playground of children, it is the gathering vestibule for gossip and exchange for profanity."[89] While there was probably nothing that could be done about children's exposure to adult sins such as gossip and profanity, the physical features of the places in which they played could be improved, and improved dramatically.

Lawrence Veiller, reporting for the commission, enlarged upon the concerns of the Small Parks Committee. He noted the incredible congestion with which many New Yorkers lived.

When it is borne in mind that the streets in our tenement house districts originally laid out for three-story dwelling houses, each house containing one family, or about five persons, are now occupied on both sides by tall tenement houses, usually five or more stories in height, contained from 22 to 26 families in each, with a population from two to three thousand persons in each block, with no back yards in which the children may play, it is evident that some method must be adopted of meeting the needs of this great and rapidly increasing population.[90]

Veiller discovered in his survey of the city's playground facilities that most children had little or no access to parks and playgrounds within four or five blocks of their homes, the maximum distance that he believed a child

These Boston girls had a playground for exercise. Note the hard surfaces under the jungle gym and the great height to which they could climb. Warren H. Manning Papers, by permission of Special Collections Department / Iowa State University Library.

should have to walk, or would be willing to walk, to play. Veiller argued that play facilities should include swings and sandboxes for small children, as well as gymnastics equipment for older children. Above all, a playground should be "a place where the children and young people of the neighborhood can play without restraint. In such playgrounds provision should be made for children of all ages."[91] The commission did not seem to be as concerned with providing children access to nature, in the form of trees and grass, as providing them a clean and less hazardous environment in which to run, jump and play. Perhaps it was easier to contemplate the construction of playgrounds than the radical transformation of urban spaces into park-like preserves.

New York's reformers were not the only ones deploring the impact of haphazard, high-density urbanization on the resident children. Graduate students at the University of Chicago's School of Social Service Administration spent most of the first thirty-five years of the twentieth century studying the problems of residents of tenement housing in their city and reported grave problems facing poor Chicagoans. Although conditions varied from location to location, and neighborhood to neighborhood, certain descriptions occurred again and again: houses in "disrepair," walks and stairs "broken," streets and alleys "untidy" and "trenches of filth."[92] The researchers found lots so crowded that children had only the smallest of spaces in which to play, such as corridors three by fourteen feet in size. Crowded lots meant that children had little access to fresh air and sunlight and no place to play but the streets.[93] Urban wildlife, in the form of rats, also complicated family life. The report noted, "In the Hull-House neighborhood, some of the families slept with guns under the beds to shoot the rats in the night. In the St. Stanislaus district one woman told our investigator she could not leave her baby outdoors in the baby carriage because she was afraid of the large rats. Food, in more than one house where tin boxes were scarce, was hung from the ceiling by strings to protect it from rats."[94] Undoubtedly, overcrowding exacerbated all of these ills in Chicago's poorer neighborhoods. In 1920, many parts of the city had population densities of 50,000 or more per square mile.[95]

The lack of playground facilities particularly appalled the University of Chicago researchers. They found that South Side neighborhoods had deteriorated significantly in the first thirty years of the new century and that the streets and alleys were filthy. "The investigators, in order to enter rear buildings, frequently had to walk along alleys that were almost impassable with mud and filth. . . . In some places the odor from decaying garbage, and sometimes dead rats, was almost insufferable." In the midst of this were the district's children, continuing their games in spite of their dangerous and dreary surroundings. "The streets and alleys swarm with children who have no other place to go." The children could play at the playgrounds of the public schools, but were otherwise forced onto their own resources.[96]

Ultimately, the researchers concluded that the only solution was better, less congested housing for the city's poor residents. Although housing had gradually improved since the beginning of the century, "slums remain slums," and children and their families continued to live in unhealthful surroundings. They argued for the improvement of family life through a combination of slum clearance, new building of low cost homes, enforcement of housing laws and reconditioning of existing premises.[97] Clean, airy open space, both at home and in the neighborhoods, would make the impoverished districts of Chicago habitable for all of their people.

By 1930, more than half of the nation's children were living in urban places, and "the old play-spaces are going or have gone for an increasingly

Privies such as these existed in Chicago's alleys into the 1940s. Photograph by Mildred Mead, Special Collections Research Center, University of Chicago Library. By permission of the University of Chicago Library.

large number of our children. And space is of course one of the first necessities for play." The open fields, attics, barns, cellars and woodsheds had disappeared, leaving behind a poor substitute, the streets, which James Edward Rogers, Director of the National Physical Education Service of the National Recreation Association, labeled a "playground" for children.[98] While apartments were sufficient for sedate indoor games, and the yards of suburban bungalows could accommodate the outdoor play of young children, there were few places where older youths could find enough room for vigorous team sports, let alone the outdoor resources necessary for fishing, swimming, hunting, sailing or paddling. In the long run, this constraint on children's bodies could only lead in one direction, toward a dramatic loss of health and vitality.[99] A large part of the answer, argued Rogers, lay in the development of school and community playgrounds. Those neighborhood institutions were the best option for providing youngsters wholesome and accessible recreational experiences.[100]

Boston constructed the first American playgrounds in 1886. They were an imitation of a European invention, the "sand garden," meant for preschool children living in slums. The sand gardens spread from Boston to Chicago and New York. Various children's charities began searching for vacant property for children's use. In 1893, New York City's Children's Aid Society began looking for empty lots that they could use free of charge for the summer months. The society pleaded, "This is an excellent opportunity for charitable lot owners to do good work for the children of the tenement houses, who have so few opportunities to escape from the miseries of city life during the heated term."[101] Reformers also demanded that play facilities be provided at schools for use during supervised summer programs. Into the 1890s, however, in response to the problem of children's street play, reformers demanded even more: facilities available year-round, and accessible to adolescents as well as small children.[102] At the heart of this idea, however, was child supervision: "children's play was too important to be left to children."[103] The Progressive Era saw the creation of a large, active children's rights movement, including a substantial number of activists concerned with children's play. In 1906, a number of influential reformers came together to form the Playground Association of America, an organization that intended to professionalize the planning and supervision of children's play.[104] Historian Bernard Mergen has commented that it was no coincidence that the movement to develop playgrounds coincided with other national efforts, such as those to create national parks and zoos. He wrote, "The feeling that it was necessary to preserve something of the past for future generations applied to play spaces as much as to the wilderness. In the minds of some late nineteenth-century reformers, the playground, like the zoo, was a place where an exotic and increasingly endangered species might be preserved."[105] Children's lives were at stake.

Playgrounds were to be the antidote for children's dangerous, illegal, and often (from an adult point of view) undesirable street play. According to the reformers, however, the actual *place* was not enough. Adults could not simply present swings, slides and teeter-totters to youngsters and wait to see what happened. Instead, children's activities on playgrounds had to be organized and directed along the proper lines. The street child, according to progressive reformers, was "a delinquent in the making." Those potential delinquents could not be trusted to "have the right ideas about play when left to themselves." The answer was supervision.[106] As historian Dominick Cavallo has argued, "Play organizers believed that structured and supervised play experiences strengthened the youth's moral fiber as much as they fortified his body."[107] Supervised games, administered by properly trained adults, could help the young deal with the overwhelming stimulus the cities provided. Organized playground games, and especially team sports, would help the child to respond on a moment's notice to ever-changing chaos surrounding him.[108] Of course, it was also a means of control. Supervised children were controlled children, no longer free to run in the streets or even on their newly constructed playgrounds. Reformers also hoped that this supervised, contained child would grow up to be an adult with greater self-restraint. As Luther H. Gulick, a prominent play reformer, opined, "When playgrounds for children are as convenient as saloons for men, perhaps when these same children grow up there will be less need of saloons."[109] Evidently, such arguments convinced many people. Before World War I, there were already nearly 4,000 playgrounds spread across 481 American cities, with 8,786 playground directors.[110]

Some cities, Cincinnati most notably, attempted to tame the streets for children, developing what was called the "play street." Beginning in 1920, Cincinnati's city officials began designating some city streets in poor neighborhoods as play streets, to be closed to traffic from roughly 6:30 p.m. until dark during the months of the children's summer vacation from school. In the beginning, volunteers managed the program; eventually, the city was able to hire trained play leaders. Play leaders registered participants and allowed them to use the street for the purpose of various kind of ball games (although baseball and softball were not permitted), singing games, circle games, storytelling, "jackstones, checkers, modified quoits, hopscotch, O'Leary, beanbag throw, and numerous other small group and individual games."[111] On a regular basis, the city brought in "gypsy storytellers" and a traveling theater. Probably even more enjoyable to the children was the provision made for water play: "Just before the street is closed on hot nights, specially constructed street showers are attached to the street hydrant and the children enjoy a shower."[112] A visitor recorded his observations in August of 1927. "When we arrived at the barricaded head of the street, the intense animation that greeted our eyes reminded us of one of the congested streets of New York's East Side—but with this great difference; the activities here were organized activities under the skillful direction of a young man and a young woman—trained members of the Public Recreation Commission staff."[113] As the visitors watched, small boys earnestly enjoyed a supervised game. Older boys and young men played a game of volleyball. Small children from age two to nine cooperated nicely with the play supervisors until they spotted the arriving gypsy storytellers, and rushed to hear their tales.[114]

To the casual observer, the play street left a happy impression of children and adults enjoying a hot summer evening outside of their normal cramped quarters. Contemporary reformers, however, pooh-poohed the effort, criticizing play streets for what they were not: a natural environment. "The best that can be said for play streets is poor indeed when we consider their inherent disadvantages. Concrete streets, brick walls, and a street shower are a far cry from the woods, the fields, and the crystal stream—the play areas of former generations in this country. It is depressing environment even when compared with a properly equipped and landscaped playground." Grudgingly, they acknowledged, "It is at least a place where children can play without danger of accident or death, and where, under trained supervision, such play, given a long enough period of time, may become a contributing means to improve public health and an educational factor for decency and order in all human fellowship relations."[115]

Youngsters, however, were not terribly happy to comply with the supervision, and seemed to prefer to make use of play spaces without any sort of adult supervision at all. On the whole, children were loath to make use of playgrounds. Surveys of children's play activities consistently showed that children avoided playgrounds, continuing to make use of unsupervised city streets and other more favored venues. As historian Howard Chudacoff has noted, children were notably absent from playgrounds in many major American cities. In Milwaukee and Cleveland, only about 4 percent of school-aged children made use of playgrounds, and only slightly more did in Chicago.[116] One disgruntled New York City homeowner discovered, much to her disgust, that local children would not go to their "play street," but insisted on playing directly in front of her home. In a frustrated article written for the *New York Times* she commented, "It's on the corners that they play in gangs their own peculiar games. For play in a 'play street' is not as other play."[117] Street children, and particularly working children with a little bit of money, also began migrating toward commercial amusements such as penny arcades.[118] When given the choice among the streets, the arcades and the playgrounds, the playgrounds generally lost out. This particular attempt at manipulating children's environments had very little effect on their actual use of the space in which they lived, and the movement to provide supervised playgrounds would largely disappear by the onset of World War II.[119]

Chudacoff, in part, blamed the demise of the supervised urban playground on the activities of middle-class families. Families whose incomes ranged from middling to wealthy increasingly found other ways to deal with the city's dangers. Some families moved to the suburbs, taking their offspring to what they assumed would be a more congenial environment. These new spaces "curbed the excesses of both cities and wilderness while preserving the advantages each had to offer."[120] There was no assumption, however, that simply moving to the suburbs was enough. At home, parents could direct their children's play inward, into the house and its immediate environs. Experts on child care encouraged parents to provide their children playrooms and backyard play spaces as a means of keeping their children both physically and emotionally close to home. Both the child and the family unit would be kept safe.[121] The Children's Bureau urged parents to devote all or most of a room to children's indoor play: "It is best to have the room in which he plays indoors so arranged that he can play freely all over it . . . and handle and touch everything within his reach. A playhouse or a porch that is fenced and screened but open to the sun is useful."[122] Accidentally, or perhaps on purpose, the suburban bungalow encouraged indoor play by its very design. Historian Clifford E. Clark, Jr., commented on the way in which designers laid out many early twentieth-century homes. "The alternative routes through the house created a circular pattern of use that delighted young children because they could run endlessly around the first floor."[123] In middle-class homes, floors provided smooth surfaces for games of marbles, furniture provided the structure for tents and canyons, and closets and cupboards contributed to games of hide-and-seek.[124]

But children needed to play outdoors, too. The bureau suggested not only a place to play in the backyard, but "some simple home-made play apparatus" for every backyard where small children played.[125] Parents were to provide a variety of boards for building and climbing, in addition to large blocks, meant to be pushed and climbed. Sandboxes were a must for small children. Wooden packing boxes would provide not only storage, but also places in which to play house or to enhance "other imaginative play." The bureau encouraged parents to provide large boxes for children to use as playhouses, boats or anything else they might imagine. A work table, a backyard pool, and various wheeled toys, such as tricycles, wagons and wheelbarrows would also provide hours of fun. Parents could also build climbing bars, seesaws and horizontal bars, while planning for the long run with swings, rings and bars.[126] Bureau publications provided supply lists and step-by-step instructions for home playground builders.

While none of this would seem too terribly outrageous or unusual from the perspective of the twenty-first century, in the early years of the twentieth century it represented a household revolution. While most of the spaces within American houses in the seventeenth, eighteenth and nineteenth centuries were made for the work and leisure needs of adults, architects increasingly planned the twentieth century's dwellings around the needs of children. Reformers urged parents to give up their parlors, rarely used and fairly useless spaces, for playrooms, which would get heavy traffic from children.[127] The proliferation of perceived dangers outside meant that it would be safer, and easier, to move the children inside. As sociologist Viviana Zelizer has commented, "If children lost the contest for public space, they staked in this period a new claim to indoor space; a separate domain for sleeping, playing or studying."[128] The space inside the middle-class home was increasingly the child's domain.

Another, perhaps more successful, attempt at environmental manipulation was the development of swimming pools. Children and water were a natural, if dangerous, combination. Urban children, and boys in particular, made active use of the rivers, streams and ditches to which they had access. Partially, their goal was to bathe, since so few late nineteenth- and early twentieth-century homes had bathing facilities. This led to serious adult objections. The problem was not so much the filth in which youngsters found themselves. The problem was the display that they made of themselves. Bathing often turned to swimming and other forms of recreation and horseplay. Swimming, in the late nineteenth century, generally meant nudity. This, in turn, meant that naked boys and youths disturbed the view of adults of both sexes. Many respectable folk found this objectionable. Little boys might get away with this; big boys could be arrested for public indecency. As Harold Gates, who grew up in Greenwich Village, remembered, "We didn't wear any clothes at all. We just went balls naked, and the boats that would pass, the kids would all be runnin' up and down wavin' at the passengers, not a stitch on. What we called the big guys, the kids around seventeen or eighteen, they would wear something, or they'd get locked up."[129]

Fairly early in American history, city councils began regulating the conduct of boys and young men in their waters. In 1786, Boston banned swimming on Sundays. In 1808, New York City forbade swimming in the East River during daylight hours, because it was "extremely offensive to spectators." And in 1856, Milwaukee banned individuals from swimming in Lake Michigan or the Milwaukee River within view of any home, walk, pier or business.[130] The boys responded vociferously: "if not allowed to swim, they may as well 'put on frocks and give up being boys.' For them, swimming was an essential part of male adolescence."[131] Legislating boys out of rivers and lakes was about as successful as banning them from the streets.

Again, reformers stepped in with solutions meant to control the public behavior of boys and young men, this time in the form of public baths and swimming pools. From the 1860s onward, municipalities began building pools, in order to provide the poor and working classes with bathing facilities. Their intended purpose was not to provide public recreation, but to provide those without appropriate amenities at home the opportunity to clean themselves. Reformers saw this as a means of preventing the unwashed from spreading disease. From the beginning, however, boys defeated their purposes. As historian Jeff Wiltse found, boys were far more likely to use the pools for their horseplay than adult working men were to use them for bathing. Women and girls hardly used them at all.[132] "Pools may have domesticated swimming, but working-class boys maintained cultural authority over the activity. Even in the supervised and regulated setting of a municipal pool, swimming continued to serve as an expression of adolescent independence and rebelliousness."[133] Frustrated supervisors decided to control boyish behavior by banning them, largely by charging entrance fees that poor and working-class youths could not afford.[134]

In the end, however, most progressive city planners came to see free or low-cost public swimming pools as a way to control boys' rebellion and to contain it within a relatively benign setting.[135] In Boston in 1904, the city reinstated free days as a way of keeping boys out of mischief. "The committee decided that it would rather have local youths roughhousing in the pool than betting craps, hanging around saloons and gambling dens, playing stickball in the street, fighting, and vandalizing property."[136] Although some cities, like Chicago, allowed children to do as they pleased (within reasonable limits) in municipal swimming pools, in most places, the desire was to contain children's behavior as much as possible, and to direct them toward constructive activities, just as reformers planned to do in city playgrounds.[137]

Slowly but surely, American cities embraced the swimming pool. By 1929, there were 700 outdoor pools in 308 American cities, and 310 indoor pools in 122 cities. Under the auspices of New Deal work programs, the nation's cities and towns built more than 700 new pools, improved approximately 350 existing facilities, and built 1,681 wading pools.[138] Although some municipalities, like Madison, Wisconsin, were extremely slow to build pools, instead preferring to maintain the use of natural waters, cities increasingly relegated youthful swimming to the more manageable and presumably cleaner confines of chlorinated, poured concrete swimming pools.[139] Recreation reformers and city planners were sanitizing the world in which children lived, worked and played.

This era also saw a number of attempts to bend nature to the cure of the ills of city life. Progressive baby-saving campaigns took a number of different forms, but just as urban reformers promoted playgrounds for older children, they also promoted fresh air for babies. Acting on the spike in infant mortality that typically occurred during the summer months, proponents organized "fresh air camps" in many large cities. In the summer of 1913, for example, various women's groups in the city of Des Moines launched a "save the babies" campaign, led by Cora Bussey Hillis, organizer of the Iowa Congress of Mothers. In addition to providing appropriate clothing and fresh milk for babies, the campaign included an outdoor camp to provide fresh air for tired mothers and their infants. An outdoor nursery in Good Park, supervised by nurses, allowed sickly babies to recuperate in the open air. The city promised to maintain the facilities. Over the course of the summer, more than 100 mothers and their children made use of the camp. In the summer of 1914, Methodist Hospital opened a "fresh air ward" on its roof and offered the same services as had been available at the park the previous summer.[140] Although it is impossible to quantify the degree to which the camps did or did not alleviate the problem of infant mortality in American cities, they provided mothers of small children the opportunity to get them out into the air, and out of stifling apartments and homes in the long, hot summers. Other improvements, such as sanitary sewers, purified water and clean milk would undoubtedly contribute more to the preservation of health in the very young.

A concern for health also fostered the adaptation of schools to the needs of sick children. Tuberculosis, one of the great scourges of the nineteenth and early twentieth centuries, killed numerous city children. This was a case where environment clearly played a role in mortality. Packed into urban slums, the disease spread easily from person to person. Living in dirty, cramped quarters, children had little chance of recovering from the disease in an era before antibiotics. Germans first developed the open-air school concept, bringing together doctors and educational reformers to provide infected students with fresh air, sunshine, and the opportunity to spend the majority of their day exposed to the healing powers of nature. Most children's health improved markedly under these conditions. The concept then spread to other points in Europe, and on to the United States.[141] One of the first open-air experiments in the United States was the Parker Hill School in Boston. The teachers planned all activities for the out-of-doors but moved children into tents in the case of storms. Nature study was at the center of their experience, with a garden plot the children tended. They also spent an hour each day in the "quiet study of the plants, flowers, and other living forms about the children, and to the application of the observations as lessons in natural history."[142] The children spent little or no time on academic subjects; instead it was "simply a day camp for tuberculous children."[143] In roughly the same time frame, actual schools following the open-air concept opened in Providence, Pittsburgh, Chicago, Hartford, Rochester and New York City. All of them emphasized fresh air, sunshine and healthy eating. Bundled children sat on roofs, and in tents, studying and exercising even in the coldest weather.[144] By 1916, the idea was so popular that over 1,000 of the fresh-air schools existed.[145] As with adult patients, doctors sought to control and cure tuberculosis in children by controlling the very air that they breathed.

While children adapted quite readily to their new place in urban America, adults had a harder time reconciling themselves to the wisdom of this move. Reformers, educators and many Americans who lived outside of the nation's cities deplored the very idea of urbanization and its potential impact on the nation's vulnerable youth. Cities did not hold a place of pride in the nation's consciousness. In spite of the economic growth occurring in cities, late nineteenth- and early twentieth-century Americans were more likely to associate cities with squalor than opportunity. What was visible to the naked eye (and nose) was belching smoke, rotting garbage and grimy buildings. Observers readily contrasted this picture with that of the countryside's green grass, leafy trees and bluer skies, leaving aside less positive images, such as mud and manure piles. The response was to try to find for children a way out—a way to live in the city without being consumed by it. Playgrounds and swimming pools were part of a concerted effort to humanize the urban environment for its youngest inhabitants. These developments were also the opening salvo in the "islanding" of America's youth—moving them into spaces out of the mainstream of the places in which they lived. Whether adults did this to protect children or to limit the inconvenience of youthful activities depended on the individual or group moving children out of the streets and into pools and playgrounds. Pools and playgrounds, how-ever, were not enough. Having access to these new play spaces did not nec-essarily mean that children had greater access to nature, either in a touched or untouched form. In fact, these venues were highly artificial, the product of human planning, planting and paving. Such places were no guarantee that children would grow to adulthood with a greater understanding of the world around them. More would have to be done to keep wild spaces alive for America's urban youth.

When reformers considered this problem, however, they did not advo-cate the wholesale adoption of a rural, agricultural model, turning children loose to play independently in the nation's farms and fields. Reformers who thought urban youngsters needed more fresh air and sunshine sought to humanize the urban landscape with playgrounds and supervised activity. Vigorous, unsupervised play, as most farm children experienced it, was not a part of the late nineteenth- and early twentieth-century vision of appro-priate immersion in nature and its wonders. Although children lived this way every day, from the point of view of many urban adults, it was simply too dangerous.[146] It also lacked purpose, from their perspective. The push for a full-fledged, adult-supervised children's experience of the outdoors truly began to take shape in the early years of the twentieth century, but the thought had been in adults' minds for decades. As early as 1880, Daniel Carter Beard, children's writer and one of the founders of the Boy Scouts of America, developed rules for "Snow Ball Warfare" after observing the fe-rocity and danger of children's snow play. Children's games and unfettered interactions with their environment and its elements (in this case, ice and snow) cried out to be regulated and tamed, not encouraged to run amok.[147]

Recognizing and lamenting this transformation, reformers tried to pro-vide urban youngsters an idealized and sanitized version of farm children's experiences with the creation of new outdoor activities that would bring children into closer proximity with grass, trees and fresh air. In doing so, they were providing urban children a drastically different experience of the natural world than the rural experience, the best of which they hoped to em-ulate. Instead, urban children would receive measured doses of the natural world at the appropriate times, largely stripped of the dangers with which rural children lived.

CHAPTER THREE

TEACHING NATURE APPRECIATION

Through the end of the nineteenth century and the beginning of the twentieth, Americans faced a serious question: where did the nation's youth belong? Clearly, the nation's population was moving to the cities, but many had grave doubts that urban locations actually were the best place for the nation's young. According to the values of the day, a relationship with the land was what had made Americans strong and independent. It was what had given the nation its character and democracy. What then, would happen to a nation that had moved to the cities? Little good could come of a childhood spent only in the human-made world, whether it was the grimy city street, or the hardly less grimy urban playground. While many were concerned by the separation of adults, and particularly adult male voters, from association with the virtues of the countryside, even more disturbing was the separation of children from the natural world. Experiences in the out-of-doors, far beyond the urban fringe, clearly provided a superior route to strength and maturity for American's children.

Americans knew against what they were reacting. Stark nineteenth-century photography juxtaposed impoverished city youth with their less-than-congenial environment. The lens captured sweet-faced children made filthy by their surroundings, playing in gutters and alleys and sitting on stoops. To the middle-class American, a picture of a group of children cavorting around a horse's decaying carcass was nothing less than horrifying. Danish photographer and social commentator Jacob Riis, who took many such pictures, lamented the absence of nature from the lives of New York's street urchins. He mourned the impoverishment of youngsters growing up without adequate sunlight, without flowers and without a patch of green in which to play. He wrote "The street, with its ash-barrels and dirt, the river that runs foul with mud, are their domain. What training they receive is picked up there. And they are apt pupils. If the mud and the dirt are easily reflected in their lives, what wonder?"[1] His experiences with inner-city children would lead him to advocate for programs to provide country outings for urban youth.

While Riis's concerns were largely for the impoverished children of the inner city, other observers worried about middle- and upper-class urban youth.

In the early years of the twentieth century, President Theodore Roosevelt, with his deep and abiding love for open skies and all things western, feared for the future of the nation. He believed that the United States had drifted too far from its rural roots. Too few children, and particularly young men, were growing up on farms. Farms gave boys both strong characters and muscles. He argued vigorously for exercise and competitive athletics for boys, in the absence of regular physical labor done in the fresh air. Still, he longed for a day when boys had partaken in what he called "natural outdoor play." Roosevelt wrote, "In the Civil War the soldiers who came from the prairie and the backwoods and the rugged farms where stumps still dotted the clearings, and who had learned to ride in their infancy, to shoot as soon as they could handle a rifle, and to camp out whenever they got the chance, were better fitted for military work than any set of mere school or college athletes could possibly be."[2] For Theodore Roosevelt, there was no equivocating. The right environment prepared boys to be real men. Those without the benefit of a farm background would have to be trained to take on vigorous physical tasks. A nation without such training for the young would surely falter.

G. Stanley Hall, an influential psychologist and educator, theorized along the same lines as Roosevelt. He believed that a too-civilized childhood made boys unfit for the rigors of adulthood. In fact, he believed that it made them both mentally and physically ill.[3] It gave youngsters an inadequate and stunted understanding of the world in which they lived. Hall opined "City life favors knowledge of mankind, physics, and perhaps chemistry, but so removes the child from the heavens and animate nature that it is pathetic to see how unknown and merely bookish knowledge of them becomes to the town-bred child."[4] His research and observations led him to develop a theory of "recapitulation." According to Hall, as children moved through developmental stages, they were experiencing the stages of development through which humankind had passed on its way to civilization. As a result, play and recreation were not a luxury, but a necessity. Running wild was an important developmental task, as children made their way toward maturity.[5] Hall encouraged parents and educators to allow the young to revel in the out-of-doors. Particularly necessary were children's (and particularly boys') experiences in nature. Nature gave the young the opportunity to experience the world in a way that most promoted their development toward healthy, normal, vigorous adulthood. Hall exhorted,

> Worship on a hill or mountain, at the shore, out at sea, under towering trees, or in solemn forests or flowery gardens, amidst harvest scenes,

in moonlight, at midnight, at dawn, in view of the full moon, with the noises of the wind or streams, the hum of insects, the songs of birds, or in pastoral scenes, is purer and more exalting for these pagan influences than it can ever be in stuffy churches on noisy city streets upon the dull or familiar words of litany, sermon, or Scripture.[6]

Although highly questionable from a scientific perspective, Hall's ideas had far-reaching appeal among reformers.[7] The development of organizations such as the Boy Scouts stemmed from fears that youngsters, and particularly boys, would fail to develop into competent, healthy and vigorous men in the absence of fresh air and strenuous muscle- and character-building work.[8]

William Byron Forbush, an incredibly prolific writer of child-guidance literature, echoed Hall's commitment to get boys out into the open air, declaring that "the country is a boy's own homeland."[9] Whether they hailed from the suburb or the slum, city boys lacked the character and wholesomeness of country boys. Forbush wrote, "No one who has dealt with boys successively in rural regions, large towns and the city could have failed to notice how much less potent in grasp, attention and efficiency are city boys, living between walls and pavements and among a thousand distractions and allurements, than country boys, with their freedom, contact with nature and wild life and opportunity for origination in work and play in woodland, pasture and carpenter shop in the barn."[10] Given that the population was rapidly moving toward the cities, another alternative had to be found for the over-citified boy. One option was camp. "If more workers with boys knew how simple an affair a camp is, they would try it, for a week with boys under a tent is worth more than a whole winter in Sunday-school or a club room."[11] Of course, the answer was more complex than a simple dose of the outdoors. Forbush prescribed many different kinds of character-building activities—but without sustained contact with the natural world, a boy was likely to lose his way.

These concerns continued on into the second and third decades of the twentieth century. Reports emanating from the 1930 White House Conference on Child Health and Protection acknowledged the drastic changes in children's lives wrought by urbanization and industrialization. Boys and girls were born to play, but the new world in which they lived challenged that birthright. James Edward Rogers, Director of the National Physical Education Service of the National Recreation Association, commented upon the impact of cities on child-life. "The environment in which they must grow is changing at the most rapid rate in the world's history. On all sides modern life seems to be conspiring to thwart the normal expression of a child's inborn urge toward play activity. It offers him a flood of impressions and stimulations, but little chance to explore and to create, and to develop his own personality as a child must do it, from within himself."[12] The contours of the physical space children inhabited had changed drastically as communities became more and more congested, and the larger portion of the nation's youth moved from countryside to city.

Some reformers, as noted in Chapter Two, saw the playground and the swimming pool as antidotes to the environmental challenges facing the urbanized child. Many, however, did not believe that access to better homes, parks and playgrounds was enough. These were simply panaceas. They did not get children out of the city and into fields and forests. They did not expand the child's knowledge of the natural world. Educational and recreational reformers sought to create the means for youngsters from all walks of life to develop a more intimate knowledge of the natural world outside of the city. One of these means was to infuse the curriculum of America's schools with study of wild flora and fauna. At the most basic level, this could be as simple as the creation of "outing clubs," meant to divert high school–aged students into the woods for a morning or afternoon each week, in order to study nature. As a turn of the century teachers' publication noted, "An ideal outing club is one which studies the trees and native shrubs, their bark, habits, etc., and observes the varieties of foliage, the geological formations about, and the many kinds of wild flowers to be found in the woods."[13] Many schools, however, took this several steps further and adopted "nature study" as part of their core curricula, in the hope of fostering in children a love and appreciation of nature. According to historian Kevin Armitage, educators hoped that "nonhuman nature would become a consistent part of the individual's practical and moral considerations. . . . sympathy for nature would harmonize the individual with his or her natural surroundings and in so doing would increase the quality of life, foster scientific inquiry and prompt an ethics of conservation."[14] An important component of nature study was fostering a love of the natural world.

For many educators who lacked an easy way to bring nature education to urban children, school gardens were the answer. Armitage noted that gardening provided "practical, results-oriented pedagogy that appealed to teachers and parents alike. . . . gardens broke down barriers between theoretical and applied work, beauty and science, preservation and use, household and school."[15] In short, they were the ideal place to teach lessons about love of

Students work in the Boston Branch school garden. Judging by the looks on their faces, this may not have been a favorite activity. Warren H. Manning Papers, by permission of Special Collections Department / Iowa State University Library.

nature in a way that provided youngsters with a practical reward for their work—a product that they could either eat or sell. This approach to nature study could be adopted in a number of different venues. Schools promoted gardening, as did boys' and girls' clubs and other community institutions, such as settlement houses. Neighborhood House, a settlement house serving the Italian American community in Madison, Wisconsin, sponsored a Better Homes and Gardens Club for adults, but also a Junior Better Homes and Gardens Club for children. The children were more active gardeners than the adults and threw themselves into planting fruit, flowers and trees. As the program's sponsors noted, "The children are gradually learning the appreciation of growing things." The gardens also had the great benefit of keeping the youngsters busy and off of other people's property.[16]

Another way in which to develop children's love of nature was to create special events to celebrate particular forms of nature. A prime example of this was Bird Day. Developed in 1894, its organizers intended Bird Day to run counter to the contemporary child culture, which encouraged harassment rather than the love of birds, particularly on the part of small boys.

Bird Day "was a teach-in for the conservation of birds," a day in which students wrote about birds, celebrated them in song and story, and improved wildlife habitat.[17] Properly educated children would (the naturalists and educators hoped) become young conservationists who would not unnecessarily disturb, injure or kill birds. Children would come to love undisturbed birds in the wild, rather than assaulting them with slingshots and BB guns. Whether this actually happened, of course, was another question altogether, but thousands of children participated in Bird Day activities, joined conservation clubs and entered contests to demonstrate their knowledge of birds.[18] Throughout the twentieth century, educators attempted to inculcate children with a love and understanding of the natural world, through nature study, environmental education, outdoor education and conservation and environmental events, from Arbor Day, to Bird Day, to Earth Day.

Studying nature in the classroom was one thing, but actually experiencing the out-of-doors was another altogether. Over the course of the late nineteenth and early twentieth centuries, adults organized many new activities meant to bring youngsters in contact with the world outside of their homes. In the United States, scouting, both for boys and for girls, had its origins in a desire to improve urban youth by bringing them closer to idealized forms of nature. Robert Baden-Powell, the British founder of the Boy Scouts, placed knowledge of the natural world at the center of his philosophy and at the center of the requirements for scouting. First and foremost, a scout was to know woodcraft. As Baden-Powell wrote, "WOODCRAFT means knowing all about animals, which is gained by following up their foot-tracks and creeping up to them so that you can watch them in their natural state, and learn the different kinds of animals and their various habits."[19] Woodcraft included the knowledge of animals, their tracks and other signs, as well as the knowledge of wild plants and their uses. Scouts were also to master "campaigning," or "living in the open; they have to know how to put up tents or huts for themselves, how to lay and light a fire; how to kill, cut up, and cook their food, how to tie logs together to make bridges and rafts; how to find their way by night, as well as by day, in a strange country, and so on."[20] Chivalry, life saving, endurance and patriotism rounded out the lessons of scouting. But lessons about the natural world and living in it came first, and Baden-Powell presumed that most boys would have to learn those lessons by way of structured scouting activities, rather than by exposure to nature on a daily basis by way of their residence on farms and in villages.

By 1910, Boy Scouting was spreading into the United States and soon had its own oath, handbook and magazine.[21] The Boy Scouts and similar

Boy Scouting took youngsters outside to introduce them to the wonders of nature. WHS Image ID 79841. By permission of the Wisconsin Historical Society, Madison, Wisconsin.

organizations such as the YMCA intended to provide an antidote to the cities and their disorder for urban youth. While the YMCA initially focused on activities in the gym, the Boy Scouts sought to get youngsters outside. Supervised recreation in the out-of-doors would help boys grow into fine, responsible men. Interestingly enough, the Boy Scouts placed their initial emphasis on middle-class boys, who reformers believed were being softened and weakened by life in the nation's urban centers. The nation's future leaders needed exposure to the great out-of-doors in order to grow up strong and capable.[22]

The 1916 Boy Scout Handbook placed familiarity with and love of nature at the forefront of the organization. Beginning with the question, "What is a Boy Scout?" the handbook first and foremost defined him in relation to the natural environment:

A Scout! He enjoys a hike through the woods more than he does a walk over the city streets. He can tell north or south or east or west by the "signs." He can tie a knot that will hold, he can climb a tree which seems impossible to others, he can swim a river, he can pitch a tent, he can mend a tear in his trousers, he can tell you which fruits and seeds are poisonous and which are not, he can sight nut-bearing trees from a distance; if living near an ocean or lake he can reef a sail or take his trick at the wheel, and if near any body of water at all he can pull an oar or use paddles and sculls; in the woods he knows the names of birds and animals; in the water he tells you the different varieties of fish.[23]

This young master of nature would be versed in "scoutcraft," a combination of many skills, including tracking, nature study, campcraft and woodcraft. As the handbook commented, "All that is needed is the out of doors, a group of boys, and a competent leader."[24] The organization acknowledged the limits that modern life presented to boys wanting to experience nature. "Some boys cannot go to camp for a summer, while others cannot even go to camp for one week or two weeks, but almost any boy, no matter in what city he lives or how big it may be, can go out into God's out of doors for a week-end hiking party or camp."[25] Getting away from the city, even for just a weekend, would give boys the opportunity to develop the skills that could only be acquired in the open country.

Properly trained youngsters could then apply the lessons learned from nature to life in the city. The handbook made clear that "a scout can apply his knowledge of prevention in the home, in the school, on the street." The observational skills that boys honed in the woods would make them valuable citizens in the cities in which they lived: "Through knowledge acquired on his hikes and in his daily intercourse, he becomes a master of preventive principles as applied to his community, its traffic regulations, its building laws, its sanitary regulations, and its industries."[26] There was evidently no venue in which the skills acquired from scouting would not be useful.

In all seasons, in all months, the scouting program enjoined boys and their leaders to immerse themselves in the out-of-doors. Some of that immersion was merely study of nature subjects, care of birds and reading of fiction and nonfiction devoted to outdoor subjects. The boys, however, would have to carry their studies into the field throughout the year. January might be the first and the coldest month of the year, but even then boys were to venture forth. The *Scoutmaster's Troop Program Note Book* for 1936 provided concrete suggestions. "Practice Troop requirements under winter conditions, snow or no snow—first aid as related to ice freezing and frost bite; safety; ice rescue; tracking—no greater sport in either mud or snow."

January was the appropriate month for "the Fourteen Mile Hike to find a suitable spot for a camp site."[27] As winter turned to spring it was time for overnights, in preparation for the summer camping season ahead. The big push began in May. No boy should miss out on camping. "Scouts are real backwoodsmen. Now is the time to talk summer camp. Get some of the Senior Scouts to tell about camping trips they have taken and show the Troop expert campcraft. . . . Have the Troop Committee pay a personal call, if possible, on the parents of the Scouts and tell them about camp . . . Don't let any boy miss camp because you fail to educate his parents."[28] As summer turned to fall, the organization exhorted its adult leaders to "Keep the 'Out' in Scouting. This is a grand month to do it."[29] The Boy Scout program offered youngsters a structured, vigorous encounter with the world outside their homes.

The Girl Scouts arrived in the United States just behind the Boy Scouts. While most reformers and educators were primarily concerned with boys and the problems posed for them by living in a modern urban world, there were those concerned about the girl problem, too. While reformers often worried about the corruption of boys, since they were to be the nation's next generation of leaders, they also worried about girls as the next generation of mothers. If girls lost their innocence and finer qualities, then the nation would suffer. Reformers saw too many temptations leading girls astray. The modern world offered plenty of opportunities to corrupt girls as well as their brothers, from romance novels and moving pictures to dance halls. Girls, like boys, needed an opportunity to get out into nature and away from the damaging effects of popular culture.[30] Juliette Gordon Low helped to organize Girl Guides in Britain and then brought the concept to the United States in 1912. The organization soon had much in common with the Boy Scouts, including its emphasis on camping and outdoor activities.[31]

In 1913, W. J. Hoxie published the first Girl Scout manual, *How Girls Can Help Their Country*. As evidenced in the manual, the organization exhibited many of the same preoccupations as the Boy Scouts. The Girl Scouts, first and foremost, focused on getting girls out of the house and the town and into the countryside. The organization instructed girls to engage in camping in order to discover nature. "Walks and picnics are all very well as far as they go, but to get the full benefit of actual contact with Nature it is absolutely necessary to camp out. . . . A camp can be nicely planned within daily reach of many of our large cities but should be far enough to escape city sounds and smells." Any location in which there were too many other visitors, too, was inappropriate for a true camping experience. Relative solitude

Girl Scouts gathered around the campfire in the evening. WHS Image ID 13786. By permission of the Wisconsin Historical Society, Madison, Wisconsin.

was important to the girls' relationship with the outdoors.[32] Once in camp, the manual offered any number of activities for the scouts. Stalking, tracking, shooting, archery, astronomy and botany were all worthwhile projects while in the woods.[33] The manual reassured girls that the wilds were no more dangerous than their everyday surroundings: "The 'deadly auto' will not get out of your way but all snakes will."[34] Girl Scouting also emphasized that the skills learned in the out-of-doors would translate into sensibilities useful in an urban context. "People who live in cities are often exposed to dangers, too, that make it necessary to *be prepared*."[35]

The Girl Scouts were not the only organization competing with popular culture for the attentions of America's girls. Camp Fire Girls also developed during the same years. In spite of its name, the initial purpose of the Camp Fire Girls was not, first and foremost, to encourage girls' knowledge of and familiarity with the out-of-doors. Founded in 1911 by Luther Gulick, an education and recreation reformer with the Russell Sage Foundation, the central thrust of the organization was to encourage womanly, domestic activities. Camp Fire Girls ventured forth for activities in the out-of-doors, but not for the sake of experiencing nature. When girls went out to cook around the campfire, the lesson to be learned was not necessarily to love the woods. As historian Leslie Paris wrote, the organization "explicitly tied participation in outdoor life to older ideologies of maternal devotion and domestic inclination."[36] Their primitive surroundings would help them to get in touch with their inner, domestic natures.[37] At the center of Camp Fire was an "emphasis on a strictly home-based domesticity."[38]

A shorter-lived organization that was far more concerned with a girl's experience with nature was the Girl Pioneers of America, founded by Lina and Adelia Beard. The sisters hoped to help girls to find "the can-do spirit of early settlers" and to reclaim their "pioneer heritage."[39] Although their organization came into existence at roughly the same time as the Girl Scouts and the Camp Fire Girls, the Beard sisters had a long history of encouraging girls in outdoor pursuits. The best evidence for this was their 1887 publication, *The American Girl's Handy Book*. As they explained in their preface, "We desire also to awaken the inventive faculty, usually uncultivated in girls, and, by giving detailed methods of new work and amusements, to put them on the road which they can travel and explore alone."[40] They hoped to provoke a spirit of inquiry and independence in American girls.

Their book, organized by the seasons, encouraged girls to venture—and adventure—outdoors in all weathers. In the spring, the Beards exhorted girls to sally forth in search of wildflowers. They were not to wait until the snow had melted, but were to find plants that were emerging even as the last snows lingered. Summer offered girls many opportunities for outdoor experiences, including making their own hammocks in which to lie, "idly listening to the hum of the busy bumble-bees at work among the red clover, or gazing up through the leafy canopy to the blue heavens where now and then fleecy white clouds float softly past, or watching a flight of birds skim o'er the distant horizon, who would not be lulled by the harmony of the summer day!"[41] In fall, the Beards suggested that girls harvest "nature's fall decorations" or venture out to gather nuts. Even winter offered opportunities for outdoor play, as vigorous as any available in the other three seasons. "It is well to follow the example of our Canadian sisters, and, clad in garments warm and appropriate, indulge in coasting, tobogganing, skating, sleighing and walking."[42] The Beards claimed that even in the coldest weather, outdoor amusements promoted physical well-being. "The cold winds will only bring the roses to your cheeks, and the keen, invigorating air, health and suppleness to your body."[43] There was a world of adventure outside their doors, and the Beard sisters encouraged girls to go out and find their place in it.

The same spirit infused their organization, the Girl Pioneers of America. Created in 1910, the Girl Pioneers of America called upon the nation's girls to find within themselves the spirit of their pioneer foremothers and to "heartily join in all work where they can be of service to their country."[44]

Girl Pioneers were involved in a complex program of civics education, home economics and outdoor pursuits. The Molly Pitcher (or Patriotism) Badge, for example, required girls to be able to recite from memory the Declaration of Independence, the Constitution, and the presidents of the United States. They were also to know the laws governing women and children in their state, including property laws. The Nancy Lincoln (or Handicraft) Badge required knowledge of such diverse (and often antiquated) home crafts as candle making, flax or wool spinning and caning a rush chair. To earn the Mary Moore (or Camping) Badge, a girl would have to choose a campsite, erect a tent properly and "cook an appetizing meal in the open without manufactured cooking utensils," among other skills.[45] The Girl Pioneers' program was academic as well as practical and infused with a significant dose of feminism.

The foundation of these activities was an abiding faith in the relevance of American pioneering to modern girls and a belief that girls could find much of the knowledge they needed in the out-of-doors. In reference to America's pioneer foremothers the Beards commented, "They learned without books the many things that nature could teach them. Woodcraft in all its phases, weathercraft and telling time by shadows. They knew the wild things of the woods, the animals, the birds, the trees, the plants. Though filled with danger, the early pioneering brought a happiness all its own."[46] A modern girl, the Beards argued, could also achieve this knowledge and happiness. "You must get out-of-doors when you can and stay out as long as you can. . . . You must run and walk, and when possible swim and row. You must learn to put up a shelter for yourself in the open and learn to live in the open."[47] Girls could then take the lessons learned outdoors and apply them to their responsibilities indoors. A Girl Pioneer would be at home in any environment.

The Beards followed in the 1920s with the publication of *On the Trail: An Outdoor Book for Girls*. *On the Trail* reinforced the message that being in the out-of-doors was the only way for girls to truly understand the wild. As they wrote, "There is a something in you, as in every one, every man, woman, girl, and boy, that requires the tonic life of the wild. You may not know it, many do not, but there is a part of your nature that only the wild can reach, satisfy, and develop."[48] It was not enough to simply be an observer of the wild, visiting a wilderness lodge or picnicking in a glade. Even the wilderness knew it was not enough. The Beards wrote, "At their careless and noisy approach the forest suddenly withdraws itself into its deep reserve and reveals no secrets."[49] Only by going into the wild and staying could any girl really know the land and its wonders. The Beards exhorted their readers to "plant your feet upon the earth in its natural state, however rugged or boggy it may be."[50] Following their directions, a girl could learn to do anything necessary to make a camp: how to use an ax, follow a compass and find her way by the North Star. She would also know how to erect a tent, make a bough bed and fry breakfast flapjacks in the morning, or cornmeal mush if she preferred. The Beards also provided handy directions for constructing a camp latrine, although they demurely called it a "sanitary facility."

Once the girls had properly prepared their camp, they were free to "make friends with the folk of the wild," also known as wild animals. "Make them understand that you will not interfere with or harm them, and they will go about their own affairs unafraid of your presence. Then you may silently watch their manner of living, their often amusing habits, and their frank portrayal of character."[51] They provided detailed instructions to their young readers on what to do should their observations lead to troubles, such as snakebite, including the wisdom *do not be afraid. Fear is contagious and exceedingly harmful to the patient.*"[52] There was a whole wide world to see, and no reason why the well-prepared girl could not spend many hours happily and safely camping. Interestingly, in neither text nor illustrations were there any adults present, supervising the girls' activities. Perhaps the Beards believed that a thorough education in camp craft was supervision enough.

As the Beards' preoccupations would suggest, at the center of all of these organizations was the activity of camping. As historian Michael Smith has argued, camping achieved two goals: removing youngsters from the city and providing them a structured experience in the wilderness. In essence, it married the goals of child-savers, such as the Children's Aid Society, with the methods of playground reformers.[53] The first American camps originated in the late nineteenth century, largely for the benefit of relatively well-to-do boys. Perhaps not surprisingly, their development proceeded from east to west. The camps first developed in eastern states with large urban populations, and spread only gradually to less urbanized western locations.[54] By the 1930s, organizations ran between three and four thousand camps, serving a wide variety of children and interests. Boy and Girl Scout camps focused upon training young outdoorsmen and women and good citizens. Charity camps brought the children of the urban poor to the countryside to improve their health. Other camps mirrored the religious and political interests of parents. As historian Leslie Paris aptly put it, "In an increasingly postagrarian economy, camp advocates aimed to return children to rural environments, not in the context of productive labor but productive leisure."[55]

All of the summer camps offered children the opportunity to spend a week or several weeks enjoying the benefits of fresh air and sunshine. Although different camps stressed nature study to different degrees, a central feature of many children's camping experiences was to "cultivate friendships" with the various elements of the natural world.[56] These connections could come in any number of forms: taking nature walks, observing plants and animals, collecting specimens and sleeping under the stars. Camping experiences provided children a structured, supervised experience with the natural environment, a chance to have a "touristic" and protected interaction with the wilds beyond. It was a gentled and safe experience, "worth a trip, but within boundaries, as a necessary additive to civilized life."[57] It was, according to Smith, "the *contrast* between the everyday world of a child's life and the camp world that had the potential to help children develop." They were experiencing "something more 'natural' and more 'real,'" as an antidote to the artificiality of their everyday surroundings.[58] It was a far cry from the unsupervised and often dangerous experiences that rural children had in their own daily interactions with the land. That, of course, was what camp organizers hoped to avoid.

The first summer camps were expressly for boys. Their founders wanted upper- and middle-class boys to escape from the too-civilized city into the wilderness where they would learn self-reliance.[59] Typical of camps for boys was Camp Mishawaka, founded in 1910, and located five miles from the Mississippi River in Itaska County, Minnesota. Although boys attended from all over the United States, the vast majority came from the Chicago area, escaping the city summers in the cool, green wilds of the north country. The camp served youngsters from age nine through the teenaged years, and the founder intended boys to return on a regular basis so that they could progress through a number of levels of outdoor and athletic skill building. Young boys lived in cabins, while older boys graduated to tents. Canoeing was one of the major activities in camp, and as they improved their skills, boys could take part in progressively more strenuous trips out of camp and onto more challenging waters. The camp director required boys who wished to take the more adventurous trips to prove their camping and canoeing skills before being allowed to participate. The most difficult trips ventured into Canadian waters, and included extensive, difficult portages.[60]

While the adventuresome canoe trips were the highlight of the Camp Mishawaka experience, other activities rounded out the boys' days. They participated in track, swimming, baseball and "Woodcraft or Tree Study," with athletics forming the core of the daily schedule. Parents expected their boys to return home in improved physical condition, with camp staff taking before and after pictures of each boy, illustrating his physical development over the course of the summer.[61] Athletic achievement, however, took place in a beautiful natural environment, replete with birds, deer, wolves, bear, moose and porcupines. Camp organizers even counted the local Native American population among the wildlife to be observed.[62] This association with the wild, camp organizers hoped, would encourage a love of nature in city boys. Camp records stated "Many and many an evening these boys, whom we think are so devoid of sentiment and of appreciation of the beautiful, stand on the high shore in front of camp and attempt to assimilate the beauties revealed in the skies."[63] For some boys, camp did seem to encourage a new appreciation of the world beyond their ordinary, urban experience. One Camp Mishiwaka poet, Ray Wallace, composed this piece in honor of his summers in Minnesota's back woods.

> As I sit and smoke in my room at night,
> And below me glares the city light,
> My mind goes drifting far away,
> Away to where the tall pines sway.
>
> It's back to the mountains and valleys and streams,
> Back to the wilds with man at his best,
> To the howl of the wolf and the wild cat's scream,—
> That is the land where life is no jest.
>
> There is no wining, nor dining, nor dancing,
> No gay white lights nor corners to stray,
> There Death lives, bleak, frozen, enhancing,
> The future for those who can stay.
>
> It's the chance, and the fight from beginning to end,
> That draws me away from the city's safe lights,
> To fill my lungs with nature's real air,
> And to win, if I'm lucky, or die fighting fair.[64]

The city was safe—a place to sit, smoke a cigarette and observe. Camp was an opportunity for boys and young men to experience the world and test their mettle.

Camping for girls developed more slowly than camping for boys, but by the 1920s, new camps for girls were being established at a higher rate than those for boys. The camps ranged from expensive girls' vacation camps to more rugged sites operated by girls' organizations, settlement houses, and other charitable organizations.[65] Although the original purpose of the Camp Fire Girls may have been to reawaken domesticity in the American girl, the camps run by the organization were much like others in their emphasis on love of the outdoors. The literature describing Camp Kiwadinipi, in north eastern Minnesota, emphasized that its location in the Superior National Forest provided girls with an exceptional experience of the out-of-doors. The girls took advantage of "five thousand miles of canoe trails" radiating out from the camp.[66] The camp offered girls the opportunity to "**Live** out-of-doors in the heart of the forest—**Canoe** on trips lasting a day or five weeks—**Hike** or ride horseback along trails made many years ago for the early lumber camps." They would also swim, paddle and fish, and live close to nature, sleeping "on fragrant balsam boughs—**And awake** to see the early sun drive the morning mists away."[67] Promotional materials for the camp emphasized the joys of living in the wilderness, but reassured parents that their children would not be too far from civilization: "girls enjoy intimate contact with the wilderness, learn the mysteries and secrets of the great woods, yet are in constant contact with civilization and Camp, as there is daily telephone connection, and the mail and provisions are transported by airplane."[68] Camp Kiwadinipi offered girls the best of both worlds.

In the pre–World War II period, the Camp Fire organization also encouraged girls to experience greater adventures and go "gypsying," or simply rambling through and exploring unknown territory, not necessarily with a goal or destination in mind. Camp Fire literature described the outing:

> You walk part of the time, ride part of the time, cook your meals over a camp-fire beside the road or in the end of a shady brook, sleep under the open sky or in the hay-loft of a friendly barn; you watch beside the fire in the quiet of night hours; you take a dip from the sandbar of an inviting river, or halt your caravan at the foot of a mountain, and climb up to view the sunset. You just vagabond, and do all the countless things that you want to do along any beckoning road you follow—you will be amazed at the variety of your days when you give your fancy rein.[69]

A gypsy trip was to be as simple and carefree as possible. The girls were only to pack staples, and to fish, gather berries or approach local farmers for additional fresh food. The girls were to make their beds on the ground, and to divide into groups and take turns keeping watch over each other. Gypsy

These Ames, Iowa, Camp Fire Girls were practicing their outdoor cooking skills. By permission of the Ames Historical Society.

trips included a healthy dose of nature appreciation, as well as the careful avoidance of "woods-vandalism. Gather sparingly of rare wild flowers; use a knife rather than stripping twigs or branches from shrubs and trees; don't make totem poles with your initials of every forest tree; and last but greatest, be sure that your campfire does no damage—know that every spark of it is dead before you pass on."[70] The gypsy trip provided the girls an opportunity to practice campcraft outside of the strictures of a camp schedule.

In 1933, teenager Alice Gortner of St. Paul, Minnesota, went to Camp Fire camp at Camp Ojiketa, at Green Lake, Minnesota. The older girls and counselors, who had all passed essential skills tests, had the opportunity to embark on their own 850-mile gypsy trip across a goodly portion of northern Minnesota, bound for other Camp Fire camps in the area. The highly anticipated trip, recorded in Gortner's diary, was one trial after another—one of the hazards of making a gypsy trip. Mere miles from camp, one of the girls became "terribly sick" and had to be returned to camp. "Too bad," Gortner remarked, "after Roberta had worked so hard for her gypsy."[71] Also on the first day, just outside of Duluth, one trailer broke down and one of the cars developed a flat tire. The next day, one car ended up in a ditch, "with two flat tires, a bent axel, the brakes locked, wheels out of line, fender bent but otherwise O.K."[72] The girls all had headaches from bouncing off of the car roof. Fortunately, the accident happened near a Civilian Conservation Corps camp, and the men put the car back on the road and repaired it as well as they could. The girls proceeded in somewhat haphazard form, minus one car, and half the girls were sick the next morning. A canoe trip on Thursday came to naught, because of rocks and other water hazards. On Friday night, the weather turned cold, and the girls had an uncomfortable time sleeping in thirty-nine-degree weather. On Saturday, on the way back in to camp, more car trouble plagued the gypsies. Travelling on Minnesota's back roads in the 1930s was anything but easy.

Despite the hardships, Gortner reveled in her experience. She had smelled the pines, enjoyed the air, listened to the wind in the trees, and had seen beaver and blue herons in the wild. Predictably, the hardships became a subject of fun. "Driving into camp was so exciting! We honked the horns all the way up to the lodge and we were yelling at the top of our lungs . . . At supper we laughed so hard my stomach ached and all of us talked at once. Later around the evening fire we told some of our adventures and then we went to bed for a much needed rest—and so ends our trip of 850 miles!"[73] From the perspective of the twenty-first century, the gypsy trip seems like a remnant of another world. Given the burdens of liability, it is highly unlikely that such a disorganized and haphazard trip would take place under the auspices of a youth organization today and that a strenuous day (including a car accident) that left half the girls sick in bed the next morning would be taken so lightly. Today, there would be a trip to the emergency room for all. Gortner and her friends, however, did not consider such issues serious ones. The Camp Fire Girls' gypsy trip had been an exercise in self-sufficiency and endurance, which probably added to its allure.

A considerably less rustic camp, constructed for the benefit of well-to-do girls, and contemporary with Camps Kiwadinipi and Ojiketa, was the American Girl Camp at Lake Wabana, Grand Rapids, Minnesota. Camp founder Mildred Sebo became dissatisfied with teaching, and opened her camp for "junior girls," or adolescents. By taking girls out of the city and into the "Great Out-of-Doors," Sebo sought to help girls develop "their characters into the highest type of American girlhood."[74] Sebo definitely thought of camping as an essential, character-building activity. As with Camp Kiwadinipi, the camp director attempted to balance the joys of the out-of-doors with amenities that would appeal to girls and their parents. The camp session lasted from late June to late August, encompassing most of the summer season. Although Sebo's emphasis was on girls experiencing the outdoors, rugged self-sufficiency and gypsy trips were not on the menu. The girls lived in comfort in bungalows, rather than "box-like buildings, tepee or tent." These bungalows featured sleeping porches, "so protected that one feels naught but the pleasant thrill of sleeping out under the stars, yet neither rain, wind nor chill can reach one."[75] Upon waking, girls would enjoy a full program of activities, including (among others) woodcraft, nature study, astronomy and canoeing. Girls would also have the opportunity to go hiking, horseback riding and motor boating.[76] Nature study included such activities as bird watching. In 1934, the girls engaged in a detailed yellow warbler observation, lasting two weeks. This entailed careful recording and summarizing of the activities of a pair of warblers and their young, including photographs.[77] This meticulous and systematic pursuit of nature study reflected Sebo's background as an educator, prior to her foray into camping for girls.

Despite Sebo's best intentions, the American Girl Camp was exceedingly short lived, succumbing to the economic stringencies of the Great Depression. By 1932, 80 percent of former campers were no longer able to afford to attend for a full session.[78] Despite reduced costs, reduced sessions and elimination of required uniforms, the camp was gone by mid-decade. Undoubtedly the Depression would force many middle- and upper-middle-class parents to rethink how their children would spend their summer vacations, and how they would experience the out-of-doors.

While the earliest camps tended to restrict their activities to relatively well-to-do youngsters who could afford the high cost of attendance, other organizations sought to bring the benefits of fresh air and sunshine to children from less advantaged families. A trip to summer camp was not limited entirely to relatively well-to-do youngsters, whose parents could afford six-week sojourns in the north woods of Minnesota or Wisconsin, costing several hundred dollars. A number of camps proliferated to serve the needs of a wide variety of children. In fact, the relatively less expensive organizational and charity camps served more campers than the private ones, like the American Girl Camp.[79] One of the best examples of this low-budget, low-income camping was that sponsored through Neighborhood House, a settlement house in Madison, Wisconsin, which served the needs of the city's working-class, largely Italian immigrant neighborhood. In 1941, Neighborhood House sponsored camping for a group of boys, for the first time in its twenty-five year history. The settlement house was able to undertake the project because of help from the Recreation Department of the Works Progress Administration. Children applied through welfare agencies and schools.[80]

The boys went to camp from July 6 to July 20, 1941, funded by both their own efforts and monies from the Community Union Camping Fund. The

This Neighborhood House boy was participating in a "pajama race" in the lake at camp. WHS Image ID 96664. By permission of the Wisconsin Historical Society, Madison, Wisconsin.

cost per child was eight dollars for a two-week session. The Neighborhood House boys worked hard for the privilege of camping. As their scrapbook proudly attested, "The boys did what they could to pay a portion of their expenses. They pulled weeds in the scorching sun for 35¢ a day. They visited the neighborhood business men for jobs at which they could earn a nickel or dime. Every boy that went to camp earned his share of the expense money." Thirteen boys headed off to Pigeon Lake Camp near Drummond, Wisconsin, in the far northern reaches of the state.[81]

While somewhat more spartan facilities set Pigeon Lake Camp apart from a place like the American Girl Camp, the activities available at the two venues were remarkably similar. Neighborhood House boys enjoyed a list of activities that were common to many different types of summer camps. As their scrapbook noted, "Generally the boys had a choice of Sports, Crafts or Nature Study. However, on the first day of camp this was put aside because each boy had to pass a swim test in order to be able to enjoy the 'Free Swim

A camper had to climb to the top of this fire tower to join the Squirrel Club. WHS Image ID 96560. By permission of the Wisconsin Historical Society, Madison, Wisconsin.

Period' or to be able to go into a boat with a leader."[82] The recreational options included many nature-based activities that were unique to summer camp, in addition to old favorites such as baseball. "Wholesome recreation" in the out-of-doors included stalking a deer by following its tracks through the woods, hiking, boating and fishing. The boys, in turn, ate the fish that they caught.[83] One of the biggest events of the week was a five-mile hike to a fire tower, which the boys then climbed. Any boy who made it to the top of the tower became a member of the "Squirrel Club." The Neighborhood House boys helped to take smaller boys up to the top of the tower, so they could see the view and join the Squirrel Club, too.[84]

The 1941 experience was evidently a success, because in 1942, Neighborhood House sent twenty-five boys to camp, divided into four different sessions. Several of the boys were repeat campers. This time, the boys travelled to America Williams Camp, a facility run by the Volunteers of America, forty miles from Madison.[85] This was an even more economical option than the

Pigeon Lake Camp, since two weeks would cost only $6.50.[86] The program was not much different from that of the previous summer: handicrafts, swimming, boating, hiking and fishing, in addition to sports such as ping pong, badminton, archery and baseball. As usual, it wasn't the activities that garnered the most discussion, but the food. "Some boys liked it, others did not. Many made vociferous complaints."[87] The sponsors, however, judged the experience a success.

In this era, Neighborhood House sponsored sleep-away camping for boys, but not for girls, even though both Pigeon Lake Camp and America Williams Camp offered separate sessions for girls. The reason for this could be deduced from the comments of Miss Gay W. Braxton, the head resident of the settlement house. According to Miss Braxton, Italian American parents gave their sons considerably more freedom than their daughters. As Braxton commented, "These girls lead very shut-in lives." It was difficult for her to persuade parents to allow their daughters to come to Neighborhood House for one four-hour activity each week, let alone allow them to leave town entirely for two weeks at camp. Activities outside the home defied social convention in the Italian American community and interfered with the household work that parents expected of their daughters.[88] This was not just true in Madison. Studies done in New York in the 1930s showed that among white children, Italian American girls were the least likely to attend camp of any, with just over 4 percent attending. In addition, only about 9 percent of their brothers went to camp.[89] Nonetheless, the settlement house was able to develop outdoor activities for those whose parents allowed some freedom and some time away from home. As an alternative to camping, or a supplement in some cases, Neighborhood House offered hostelling for both boys and girls, in a wide variety of ages, in largely sex-segregated groups (although one boy occasionally joined the girls on their hostelling trips).

Hostelling, as sponsored by Neighborhood House, involved substantial overnight biking trips throughout southern Wisconsin. The first of these trips occurred in 1940 and they continued throughout the decade, although they were somewhat sparse at the height of World War II. Neighborhood House helped to find bicycles and made the youngsters responsible for mapping out their own trails. The primary purpose of the trips was to get them out of the city and into the countryside for new experiences in the out-of-doors. As their American Youth Hostel scrapbook indicated:

> Hostelers got varied experiences. They knew how city folk lived, but to go to a farm and be allowed to milk the cows, to feed the chickens, and

even to ride a horse and drive the cows from the pastures was a real thrill. Unlike camping, where the immediate objective is the destination, the objectives in hostelling are the roadside scenery, adventure, meals out of doors, and the geography of our own country, with a good hostel to rest in at night.[90]

In 1940, Neighborhood House conducted ten hostelling trips with twenty-two girls and twenty-five boys, and leaders judged the activity to be a success. "This attraction promises to open new vistas for many boys and girls who otherwise would live in the confines of the Madison neighborhood. One hosteler remarked, 'I have never had such a thrill out of anything as from bicycling.'"[91]

The hostellers kept detailed records of their adventures. The first girls' hostel trip was typical. They left from Neighborhood House at 5:30 a.m. on June 19, 1940. Seven girls pedaled from there to Picnic Point, on Lake Mendota, on to Pine Bluff, then to Cross Plains and to the Gronethal Hostel. The girls came home by way of Cross Plains, and the Post farm hostel. Among the highlights of the trip were finding wild strawberries and "when we coasted down the loooooooooong hill and into Pine Bluff after walking up and up and up." Altogether, they pedaled fifty-five miles, on bicycles without anything more than a single speed. It was an inexpensive trip, with total costs for the group of only $2.80.[92] The girls came home tired, but happy.

A boys' trip to Mount Horeb and Blue Mounds in June of 1947 was rather more adventurous. Seven boys went on this trip, leaving Neighborhood House at approximately nine in the morning. The weather was challenging, cold and rainy, and by the time they got to Blue Mounds, they were "soaked to the skin but all were happy." While their clothes were drying, they went swimming. Afterward, they hunted for wood and cooked their soup, corn, beans, pork chops and hot dogs. Somehow they had miscalculated, and "since the hostel at Mount Horeb was not open it was decided to sleep in the lookout tower." It was an uncomfortable night, since it was "very cold . . . and the wind was blowing very strong. The boys made their beds on top of the tower where it was possible to watch the stars and clouds." The weather became wilder, however, and the boys moved into the tower and shared blankets in order to stay warm. The odd noises of the wind in the trees caused some consternation, and "four of the boys started to sing to pass away the time because by now the wind was so strong that it was almost impossible to sleep." After breakfast, they finally headed home. The report ended upon a somewhat chastised note: "The next trip will be to

A Neighborhood House girl repairing her bicycle. WHS Image ID 95522. By permission of the Wisconsin Historical Society, Madison, Wisconsin.

Devil's Lake and it is hoped the weather will be much better. Reservations will be made at the hostel." Clearly, the boys had experienced a bit more of the out-of-doors than they had planned.[93] But if the point of youth hostelling was inexpensive fun in the out-of-doors, the trips sponsored by Neighborhood House surely fulfilled the children's expectations.

For little boys, Neighborhood House sponsored one further type of nature-oriented activity, under the umbrella of hostelling. Small boys, in groups of roughly a dozen, headed off on day and overnight camping trips within the city of Madison. In 1947, boys made three trips to two locations in Madison: Hoyt Park and the Arboretum. The boys bundled up their supplies and hiked across town to their destinations, posing difficulties for those who had "not learned yet to make a secure bundle."[94] In both locations, they found and cleaned their campsites and gathered wood for cooking. They also cooked their own meals. During their trips to the Arboretum, the boys took part in nature education. They learned to respect the wildlife, since the Arboretum protected all wild animals within its bounds. The boys also learned to build a dam and a water wheel. Two of these trips involved overnight stays away from home. Sleeping in the out-of-doors was apparently a bit of a trial for the adult chaperones. The boys had a very hard time getting to sleep, and a tendency to wake at 4:30 in the morning, apparently before their chaperones were ready to face the day. The boys rounded out their trips with swimming and intense games of cowboys and Indians.[95] The outings were a great success. The report of one outdoor adventure concluded, "It was quite funny to see thirteen little fellows strung out the length of Vilas Avenue. They were all tired and wanted to get home but they could not all walk at the same rate and some were having trouble with thire [sic] equipment and had to stop many times. Finally all reached the neighborhood and went to their homes. They were very tired but happy."[96]

Activities at Neighborhood House were but one example of community organizations attempting to improve the lot of children by transporting them into new and presumably more natural environments. Reformers planned and executed these programs, intent on bringing an appreciation of nature to Madison's Italian American community. As historian Leslie Paris has argued, this impetus was not necessarily coming from within the community itself: "Poor children generally attended camps less on their own families' terms than on those of the charitable organizations that sponsored them." Nevertheless, children attended because the camping experiences more than likely served parents' needs and wants as well. Paris wrote, "Charitable and low-cost camps succeeded because they provided parents relief from the burden of caring for children at home during the school vacation, catered to their aspirations for their children's health and well-being, and offered children exciting opportunities for adventure." These camping experiences, even when designed by reformers outside of the community, were meeting a need.[97]

The Neighborhood House experiment was small, confined to the child residents of a single neighborhood. On a grander scale, one of the most enduring experiments in altering children by altering their environment is New York City's Fresh Air Fund. Founded in 1877, the Fresh Air Fund is one of the United States' oldest continuously operating children's charities. Reverend Willard Parsons of Sherman, Pennsylvania, was concerned with the conditions children faced in the nation's cities. The suffering of city children on hot summer days deeply disturbed him. They sweltered, while many country people did not value or even recognize the beauty of the landscape surrounding them. For a number of years various organizations in and around New York City sponsored day excursions for "children of poverty."[98] Parson's plan, however, was more ambitious; he wanted to provide children country vacations, not just day trips. He asked his congregation to open its hearts and homes to the children of New York City. His congregants were sympathetic, and within weeks, a group of nine slum children had arrived in rural Pennsylvania for two weeks of country living. Jacob Riis, a supporter of efforts to improve the lot of impoverished children wrote, "at the end of the two weeks, nine brown-faced laughing boys and girls went back to tell of the wondrous things they had heard and seen." Another group of children came to replace them, and so was born the Fresh Air Fund, which has operated every summer since, sending children from inner-city New York to rural and semi-rural locations throughout the eastern United States and Canada. Initially, the program sent children entirely to farming communities.[99]

In selling the program to potential donors and sponsoring families, newspaper editorialists focused the readers' attention on the terrible discomforts of a city summer. In July 1892, an article in the *New York Times* encouraged support of the Fresh Air Fund, saying, "Of course, everybody who had to be out in the sun was aware that it was hot, but whoever was rationally dressed and ate and drank rationally, did not feel nearly so uncomfortable, and was very much further from collapse. A heated term so dry would present no very great terrors, except to young children. The mortality among these may be expected to be very great."[100] Improving children's chances and exposing them to the wonders of nature provided the impetus for the program. Nearly 100 years later, environmental concerns still underlay the reasoning for the project. Although time had diminished considerably concerns about summer child mortality, the child's surroundings still weighed heavily in the continuation of the program. Children came to the Fresh Air Fund from communities where "it is the sidewalks that are green—with shattered pop bottles—and not the naked ground. The streets that run through the projects are as pocked and rough as dried-up riverbeds. Instead of trees they are lined with unoccupied teenaged boys, shirtless and muscular, staring at passersby with idle-eyed hostility."[101] By contrast, children could hope to spend a summer in a more favored location, with grass, streams and trees available for their enjoyment.

Although the program has changed in many ways since its inception, the principle today remains the same: to allow urban children from disadvantaged backgrounds the opportunity to experience the countryside during the long, hot summer. Initially, the program placed children with farm families who hosted them for two-week periods. Today, children go to live with a variety of families, not all on farms, and also to camps owned by the charity.[102] The program has had a number of benefactors. At first, the *New York Tribune* published the appeals for sponsoring families and donors, followed by the *New York Herald Tribune*. In 1967, the *New York Times* assumed responsibility for the annual drive. In the first 125 years of the program, 1.7 million children took part.[103] The goal always remained the same: to allow children to experience the world in a way that they otherwise might not. A 2002 profile of the program described inner-city children having the opportunity to swim, go to the beach, fish and ride horses.[104]

These two-week encounters with the land beyond the city often challenged children's perceptions of the world. A newspaper writer in 1890 attributed the following comment to a fresh air child: "The daisies out here are as thick as flies in New York."[105] Late twentieth-century comments were not much different. One boy noted that "before I came here . . . I thought swimming was me and my friends taking turns running through the open fire hydrant." He had never used a swimming pool or gone swimming in an open body of water. Ronald Rosario, who was a Fresh Air Fund child in the late 1960s, remembered, "I had never heard such silence. It hurt my ears it was so quiet." He also encountered his first cow during his Fresh Air experience.[106] For another boy from Queens, it was simply the open space that intrigued him. He looked forward to visiting a family in Postdam, New York, whose backyard was so big he could "run around forever, just free."[107] Another child from Queens marveled at the Vermont sky: "I've never seen so many stars."[108]

In its attempt to provide fresh air and sunshine to poor, urban children, the fund cast its net broadly, offering to meet the needs of children from any faith and without regard for racial or ethnic background. Sponsoring families were not always as welcoming as the program's organizers; in 1902 Riis lamented that no one asked for Italian children and that "prejudice dies slowly." They often had to explain to rural families why children did not arrive neat, clean and well-scrubbed, although volunteers de-loused children before they trundled off to their temporary homes. Program organizers were careful not to send ailing children to rural homes.[109] Initially, most of the children taking part in the program came from white immigrant families. The demographic composition of the participating children has changed over time. Today, most of the children who participate are African American or Latino. Most sponsoring families are still white.[110]

Scholars have done little research to evaluate the way in which the Fresh Air Fund experience affected children's perceptions of the inner-city environments in which they lived. What little information there is would seem to indicate that after their time in the country, children's feelings were profoundly ambivalent about the homes from which they came. Lawrence Wright's 1979 book, *City Children, Country Summer*, chronicled the Fresh Air experience of a handful of children sent to Pennsylvania's Amish and Mennonite communities. One Fresh Air boy told his rural Pennsylvanian counterpart that he would be unhappy changing places and going to New York City. Among other reasons, "you can't be walkin' barefoot . . . 'cause your feet'll get cut on the glass." Another child lamented the two cats and puppy she was leaving behind on the farm. In a conversation on the bus going back to the city, one girl exclaimed "I don't wanna go back to stinky New York." Another chimed in "Big Valley is nicer than New York." A conversation between two boys captured the environmental critique fostered by two weeks in the country. "When you're in the country with all that fresh air and then you come back, all that stuff gets in your lungs. Like the gasoline stuff and the trailer-truck smell." "And the ocean is so dirty. . . . Violence, pollution, and gossip . . . that's what's wrong with New York."[111] For many of these children, the ambivalence was reinforced year after year. More than 60 percent of the children received invitations to come back to their host families for a second visit.[112]

How the Fresh Air experience affected children's perceptions of their homes of origin was a rather different concern 100 years ago. When Jacob Riis reflected on the benefits of the Fresh Air Fund, he pointed largely to its health-giving properties. Slum children, abstracted from that environment, had the opportunity to regain their health and vigor. The two weeks in the countryside, reformers argued, had remarkable curative properties, making children tanned and strong. Sociologist Walter S. Ufford, who studied various fresh-air charities in the 1890s, believed that leaving the city for an extended period did much to improve the lot of the child, implying that the program gave the child an opportunity to reflect on the type of life he or she wanted to live. "The quiet influence of family life and the personal rela-

Jacob Riis, an early child advocate, used pictures like this to illustrate the benefits of a vacation in the country for inner-city children. Photograph by Jacob Riis. By permission of the Museum of the City of New York.

tion of the child to its caretaker have time to make themselves felt. Either directly or incidentally, a certain amount of instruction in the art of living is practicable."[113] Program founder Reverend Parsons also saw a great benefit in "'making the tenement house child thoroughly discontented with his lot. There is some hope then of his getting out of it and rising to a higher plane." The tenement child would then have the opportunity to teach "the shiftless parents the better way."[114]

By the second half of the twentieth century, although the overall evaluation of New York's Fresh Air Fund remained positive, criticism of the discontent created by the program had emerged. That discontent was no longer seen as an unambiguous force for good in inner-city children's lives. As Lawrence Wright wrote in the closing pages of *City Children, Country Summer*:

> For most of the children, their stay in Big Valley would prove little more than a momentary calm in lives so abused by randomness. The Fresh Air Fund is sometimes criticized for giving some children who are caught in the ghetto impossible expectations for the future, and others a depressing understanding of how deprived they really are. As a matter of fact, this criticism is often expressed in the black community. And yet intelligent and sensitive children already know the truth of their situation. The difference that the Fresh Air Fund can make is not so much that they expect better, but that they realize they deserve better. For some of them, coming home is the beginning of a lifelong outrage.[115]

All children had the potential to become angry with the disparities between their lives at home and their surroundings during their brief two weeks living as Fresh Air children. And what of the 40 percent of children *not* asked back for a second summer? As geographer Robert M. Vanderbeck has noted, "There is virtually no discussion."[116] There has been virtually no discussion either of the way in which the Fresh Air program affected children's ability to live within and respond to the environments surrounding them the other fifty weeks of the year.

One measure of the overwhelming appeal of this program has been its imitation elsewhere. Fresh-air experiments proliferated throughout the United States. The Fresh Air Fund's model has been interpreted and reinterpreted by dozens of organizations in different parts of the United States. In the 1880s, the Sunday school children of Philadelphia collected money to send less fortunate and ailing youngsters in their city to sanitariums and fresh-air camps.[117] As early as 1897, fresh-air charities flourished in seventeen of the nation's largest cities. The vast majority of these programs existed east of the Mississippi River, with St. Louis and Minneapolis being the only westerly cities with fresh-air charity programs.[118] Chicago was one of the first midwestern cities to establish its own program. Chicago-area reformers, searching for a suitable location for fresh-air camps for their impoverished children, looked north to Wisconsin, founding in 1887 the Fresh Air Association of Lake Geneva, and creating the Holiday Home Camp at

Williams Bay. Chicago children with disabilities camped at Brown's Lake, Wisconsin.[119] The railroads even made special half-fare tickets available for children travelling by rail to fresh-air charity events and camps outside of Chicago.[120]

Various churches have also adopted the idea of fresh-air charity, most notably the Mennonites. Although Mennonite and Amish families participated in the New York–based Fresh Air Fund program, Anabaptists organized their own efforts, too. In 1896, Mennonite mission workers in Chicago first began to send children to the countryside. In the middle years of the twentieth century, other congregations began to operate fresh air programs. One run by the Lancaster Conference took children from inner cities to Mennonite farms in Lancaster County, Pennsylvania. Because of its proximity to a Mennonite alternative service camp, another program took children from Gulfport, Mississippi, to Mennonite communities on the Great Plains, such as those in Kansas and South Dakota. In many ways, however, concern about children's experiences of nature was not the Mennonites' focus. Instead, they saw this as a missionary effort extending in both directions, bringing African American children closer to God and improving their own understanding of race relations. For the children, too, nature may not have been so much the point of the exercise as learning to drive a tractor, that ultimate symbol of mechanized, modern American agriculture.[121]

As large as these fresh-air efforts were, they did not make up the sum total of such efforts. Even at the very small, local scale, members of organizations such as 4-H attempted to bring the benefits of rural life to urban children. In June of 1968, the Mahaska County (Iowa) North Madison Happy Pals 4-H Club, an organization enrolling twenty-six girls, planned a July outing for urban children in their county. The club invited twenty-six children from Oskaloosa to join them for a day outing on members' family farms. "Two or three children will be placed with each of our 12 farm families and our town 4-H members will join us at the farms. There will be so many things to do— animals to pet, ponies to ride, games to play, good food and maybe you'll even want to bring your swimming suit in case there is time for a visit to Prairie Knolls swimming pool."[122] Although the visit would only be daylong, the intention was to provide children with the opportunity to experience an environment that they normally would not have known.

By the middle years of the twentieth century, dozens of organizations were actively plotting the course for youth in the out-of-doors. The rapid urbanization of these years challenged adult preconceptions of the proper place of children and their proper relationship to the natural world. Left to their own devices, children made use of their surroundings in (from the adult point of view) the most unfortunate of ways. They were more likely to be outdoors "just fooling around" as they were to be engaged in more constructive activities, such as organized games. The only choice of the caring and educated adult was to provide youngsters with the right way to know, enjoy and understand the world in which they lived. Boy Scouts, Girls Scouts, the Girl Pioneers of America and other youth organizations offered youngsters a controlled, educational experience of wild places. Nature education provided them the tools to see the world in a scientific way and to have sympathy with creatures different from themselves. Fresh-air charities extended the understanding of a different way of life to thousands upon thousands of inner-city children. Even rural children received instruction in appreciating the natural world and spreading that appreciation to the less fortunate. This proliferation of organizations and activities brought a wide variety of children into the out-of-doors—not just the middle class and privileged, but the poor and underprivileged as well. Leaders in these efforts and organizations believed there was a right and a wrong way for children to interact with the world; the right way involved supervised visits beyond the concrete jungle to commune with the animate and inanimate world, to understand that world's connections to people, and to appreciate its power to teach timeless lessons about the human condition. A 1922 poem, published by the Camp Fire Girls, captured the spirit and intent of outdoor experiences for urban children:

> Good-bye to Summer
> Good-bye to Camp
> We've packed our memories and bloomers and ties!
> We must get an education
> If we are to help the nation
> But it's hard—it's hard to be civilized![123]

CHAPTER FOUR

THE ENVIRONMENTALLY AWARE CHILD AT MIDCENTURY

In the middle years of the twentieth century, the United States was at a transition point. While many American children continued to experience a wide range of interactions with the world outside their homes, it was clear that the situation was changing. Radio, the movies and the newly commercial television increased the allure of the indoors, and larger numbers of children were involved with activities that programmed their after-school and weekend hours, such as ballet lessons and baseball. It is perhaps not surprising that these years saw a burst of nature education for children, from a variety of sources. Parents loaded their children into station wagons and hit the highways, hoping to expose their children to the wonders of the American outdoors. Both the Boy and Girl Scouts continued to bring youngsters into the wild and to emphasize the importance of these experiences for the development of young minds. Purveyors of commercial entertainment also focused on nature themes, bringing wholesome (though dubiously scientific) entertainment to the nation's young, such as Disney-made and commercially sponsored wildlife films and television specials for a young audience. This was the era of Disney's *Charlie the Lonesome Cougar* and *Mutual of Omaha's Wild Kingdom*, programming that captured prime-time family viewing hours on Sunday nights. Organizations increasingly used animal spokes-creatures to bring environmental messages to young people. Smokey Bear, Woodsy Owl and Ranger Rick had their genesis at midcentury. Although an indoor-oriented childhood had yet to become established, its outlines were revealing themselves, and organized adults were already poised to combat children's proclivities toward indoor, sedentary lifestyles.

The lure of the indoors, however, captured different children, in different locations, at different times. For many children, a rather free-wheeling, independent experience of the surrounding world persisted into the middle years of the twentieth century. On April 26, 1949, researchers spent many long and tedious hours observing every single minute of a seven-year-old boy's day as he made his way through his usual round of home and family activities in a small midwestern county seat town. What Raymond's observers found was a boy who was very much at home with his environment. Even at age seven, Raymond had a great deal of independence in his daily activities. His family home was only two blocks from the local school, and he walked himself there on a daily basis. On this "average" morning, he played on the playground essentially without supervision for approximately twenty minutes before being called in by the bell. During recess, he spent most of his time grubbing in a sand pit with another student, Susan Hebb. The two devoted themselves to an intensive period of road building. "Raymond vigorously pushed his shingle along the roadbeds as if it were a tractor or grader of some kind. The sound accompaniment was a 'Bzzzzzzzzzz,' in imitation of a heavily laboring motor."[1] Nobody seemed to care if he came back from recess with his clothing a little worse for the digging and building.

At lunchtime, Raymond walked home alone to eat with his parents, playing along the way. He borrowed a stray baseball bat and used it to launch rocks into the air. He also paused long enough to clamber around the bandstand located near the courthouse.[2] After eating lunch with his parents and before returning to school, he climbed a tree and climbed up the side of the garage, onto its roof. Even though he "swung back and forth on a tree limb in a daredevil manner," neither parent seemed to be concerned about his safety.[3] After jumping to the ground, he headed back to school for his afternoon's lessons, this time riding his bicycle. No one worried about that, either, since Raymond was apparently an experienced and careful rider. "He went so slowly that at times he had to maneuver the front wheel to keep his balance. His slow speed did not indicate lethargy or a lack of energy, for he was very alert in balancing the bike and used good judgment in knowing just how long he could coast without turning the wheel."[4] His afternoon recess included more efforts at road building.

After school, this seven-year-old continued his independent activities, riding his bicycle to the courthouse, where his mother worked, and playing on the grounds. He met up with a group of roving boys, also entertaining themselves in the interval between school and supper. From there, he and the other boys went to play in a vacant lot. He and a group of boys played in a pit, the sloping dirt walls of which boasted "miniature bridges, runways, and roads which show that the pit has been visited before by juvenile engineers." Raymond focused most of his efforts on digging a wooden crate out of the bottom of the pit.[5] After a brief trip inside to eat, Raymond headed

The midcentury child enjoyed outings in all sorts of weather, even snowstorms. WHS Image ID 11447. By permission of the Wisconsin Historical Society, Madison, Wisconsin.

back outside again, climbing on trees, the garage roof, and whatever structures presented themselves. He also dragged the crate from the vacant lot home, so that he could build a playhouse in the yard. His mother contributed an old comforter to the effort. At 7:49 p.m., his mother called him in for the evening.[6]

The degree of freedom and independence allowed Raymond seemed unremarkable, given the other equally unsupervised children populating this small town. Children took themselves to school, both on foot and by bicycle. They engaged in numerous games on the playground, many involving digging in the dirt. After school and into the evening, they played on vacant lots and in the town's public spaces, sometimes involved in activities—such as climbing on roofs or jumping off handrails—that were potentially dangerous. Adults appeared at the periphery of this activity, observing and not observing from a distance, rarely interfering. If the children's activities had become destructive, an adult surely would have noticed. As it was, the youngsters were free to make use of the environment as they pleased, largely without attracting attention or comment.[7]

At midcentury, freedom was also the watchword for older youngsters in somewhat larger places. In many communities across the United States, youngsters continued to take advantage of the open places in their communities for recreation. Teenagers showed a good deal of familiarity with the outdoors—even in inclement weather. In the winters of 1944 through 1946, fifteen-year-old Nancy Norg of Madison, Wisconsin, wrote to Molly Fisher, a pen-pal in Scotland, about her regular outdoor adventures, explaining the importance of such adventures in teenagers' social lives. She wrote, "Here, in Madison, almost everyone has ice skates, as Madison is between two lakes Lake Mendota and Lake Monona. I go on the lagoons though. Its zero outside today and snow is on the ground. Lots of kids are going skiing."[8] Norg herself skated, skied and tobogganed, and teachers incorporated vigorous outdoor activities into her school's physical education curriculum. "Our gym class went tobogganing last week," Norg wrote. "We had loads of fun, but only got three rides as we had a double class and only about 25 min. to do it in. The slide is a mile from school and we had to walk out and back in one period which is about 45 or 50 min. long."[9] Norg was completely unfazed by her vigorous midday exercise in frigid weather, which might have had something to do with her status as an active Girl Scout.

Another of Fisher's Girl Scout pen-pals was Alberna Herrick, also a Madison teenager. Herrick was every bit as outdoorsy as Norg, as evidenced by her own participation in tobogganing and other outdoor sports. In the winter of 1946, she wrote to Fisher, "You are probably wondering why I haven't written for so long but three weeks ago I broke my colar [sic] bone and haven't been able to right (I mean write) because it was on the right side and I am right handed. It happened when I was tobogganing." Herrick admitted to the fun of the sport, but also its danger, saying "It is a real lot of fun but you can get hurt awfully bad sometimes. At this one place where a lot of people go to tobogganing there have been 8 broken backs."[10] It would be interesting to know if there really had been that many serious injuries, or if Herrick was exaggerating for effect. The lakes that made skating possible

Tobogganing was a favorite winter sport for youngsters in Madison, Wisconsin. WHS Image ID 45571. By permission of the Wisconsin Historical Society, Madison, Wisconsin.

in the winter also lured youngsters outside in the summer. Herrick spent an early June day at a lake, a somewhat questionable activity in Madison, where Junes could be chilly. "Last Friday ten of us kids at school went on a picnic. We took our lunch and went swimming. The water was horribly cold and I just felt numb. Would you rather swim in a pool or in a lake? I would rather swim in a lake . . . it gets so crowded in a pool."[11] If frigid Januaries and chilly Junes were prime time for outdoor fun, imagine how much time these same youngsters would have spent enjoying Madison's open spaces in July or October.

Raymond, Nancy and Alberna spent untold hours out-of-doors, finding their entertainment in their environment. Forces of change, however, were beginning to work on American youngsters. Although Americans tend to think of the television as the most important force bringing children indoors, that transition was well under way before television became commercially available to the masses. Even before World War II, popular culture was beginning to loosen children's day-to-day contact with the world outside their homes. When sociologists Robert and Helen Lynd studied "Middle-town" in the 1920s, they found the radio beginning to make inroads into the leisure time of teenagers.[12] By the 1930s, the ascendancy of indoor, passive entertainment for children was evident.

A 1936 study followed the activities of 1,100 junior high–aged youngsters on New York's Lower West Side. These children lived in a largely immigrant and second-generation Italian American community. The boys and girls in this community spent a significant amount of their leisure time in inactive pursuits. The radio was the most important indoor activity. On a Thursday, for example, 47 percent of all boys listened to the radio and spent 35 percent of their time listening. Among girls who listened, 45 percent of their time was spent with the radio. On the weekends, children might spend 25 percent of their time with radio listening.[13] The movies also absorbed children's attentions. While few went to the movies on school days, 25 percent went on Saturdays and 50 percent on Sundays, taking up quite a bit of their free time.[14] Girls, because of the very large amount of housework required by their parents, spent a great deal of their time indoors, reading, visiting, and listening to the radio. Girls spent much more time than boys reading.[15] Compared to the amount of time spent indoors, the time spent outdoors was minimal. For girls it might be no time during the week and as little as an hour and a half on Saturday. Boys generally got out for about an hour and a half on weekdays and up to four hours on Saturday. Predictably, youngsters spent their hours out-of-doors "'hanging around.'" As the researcher noted, "Children do not want to play organized games all the time."[16]

By the 1950s, television was surpassing radio and the movies in absorbing the leisure hours of American youth. In 1940, television was an infant technology, and only 3,785 sets had made their way into homes in the United States. By 1953, half of all American homes had a television. By 1960, 90 percent of American families had at least one.[17] When television first made its appearance, some believed that it would be a short term fad—children would flock to it because of its novelty and then eventually lose interest. That, as we now know, was not to be the case.[18] By the early 1960s, the average preadolescent was spending more than twenty hours a week in front of the television. When summers were taken into account, television viewing had become children's most time-consuming daily activity, sleep aside.[19] Social scientists examining children's activities found that the new communication medium had become firmly entrenched in children's repertoire of weekly activities, without regard to gender, economic status or race. In November of 1954, a researcher in San Francisco followed 391 fifth-graders in three different communities of varying socioeconomic status. She found that boys and girls, across the spectrum, preferred television viewing to all other activities. She wrote, "The fact that 348 children mentioned watching television 2,035 times in the five days of log-keeping suggests a genuine addiction. Boys and girls seemed about equally involved."[20] The researcher also found that boys' second favorite pastime was active sports, but similar outdoor activities fell far down the list for girls. Most girls spent considerably more time with cooking, cleaning, and washing dishes than any type of outdoor play.[21]

In 1961, another California researcher tracked middle- and working-class children who were white, African American and Chinese American. He, too, found that children, regardless of race or family income, had become avid viewers. Noting that children would go outside or read a book if the television was out of order, he commented, "It would seem that television reduces considerably the amount of children's outdoor play and reading."[22] Like other social scientists, he suggested that given children's overwhelming preference for television viewing, their experience could be improved by diverting their interest into programs "featur[ing] good music, science, or the arts."[23] Even in the 1950s and 1960s, the educators and reformers seemed resigned to losing the fight against television. Parents seemed ready to concede their ground as well. Even though one study found that 68 percent of mothers interviewed believed that television viewing led to less outdoor activity among their children, they were remarkably ambivalent about controlling their children's viewing.[24]

Americans today may think of the 1950s and 1960s as a mecca of outdoor activity and vigorous play, but criticisms of flabby suburban children, too sheltered to walk to school or to play outside, emanate even from those halcyon years. In 1962, journalist Peter Wyden published his critique of the new suburban child's life in *Suburbia's Coddled Kids*. An experience with his own sons sparked his interest in the subject. "It all began to register with me one sunny Sunday afternoon near the North Shore Railroad tracks in Highland Park, Illinois. I had my two boys aged ten and eight with me, and we were doing something quite extraordinary. We were walking. Even more notable for week-ending suburbanites, we were walking without a plan, without a particular destination, without a deadline when we would have to be someplace else."[25]

Astonished and dismayed at his own sons' lack of perspective on the world around them, he set out to study the children of Highland Park, a suburb of Chicago, and Bellefontaine, a suburb of St. Louis. In both communities, he found children so isolated that they had lived their entire lives in the sub-urbs, without ever having been to the neighboring city.[26] Aside from certain usages in language that give away their era, the complaints Wyden made could have been made in 2002 as easily as 1962: "More and more kids come to know only their neatly manicured, fumeless, comfortable monotonous bedroom communities where there are almost no old people, no poor, no childless, no Negroes, either no Jewish families or many, no sidewalks, no places to explore except by mother-chauffeured car, no houses or incomes too different from those of their parents."[27] Wyden's parental concerns about the over-manicured, featureless suburbs have a familiar ring. He noted, "A mother said: 'There's no place here to make a mess. Everybody here keeps the yard just so. There's no place where kids can go dig a hole, no sidewalks to ride on, no fences to climb.'"[28] In the course of his investigation, Wyden found overweight children, children whose parents were terrified of germs and parents who never allowed their children to walk anywhere, especially in inclement weather.[29] From the perspective of the twenty-first century, Wyden's observations have a contemporary quality and are not the type of observations most readers would expect from the early 1960s.

Teachers, too, noticed the changes in children's lives. John D. Woolever, a high school teacher in Detroit, bemoaned the ignorance of urban children when it came to animal life. Woolever wrote, "Due to their environment, millions are not in contact with plants and animals as much as they should be, even with our expanding camp programs and outdoor field trips. As a result they acquire many little fears and undesirable attitudes toward living things long before they have a chance to find out for themselves."[30] While he expected children to fear the obvious, such as the lions and tigers in zoos, he did not expect fear of such a wide range of animals, or some of the reasoning children had for their fears. Worms, children mentioned, be-cause they wiggled and were slimy; caterpillars also wiggled and were hairy; rats, they said, were poisonous; and deer might bite. Three-quarters of the children Woolever questioned could not tell the difference between snakes that were poisonous and those that were not.[31] Woolever traced the origins of the problem to adults and particularly to the influence of mothers. "Since children spend more time with their mothers," he wrote, "it would not be surprising that it was from them that children learned many of the irratio-nal fears we are trying to correct."[32] The moms of America had, according to Woolever, imparted their squeamishness to their children, and to their daughters in particular.

Woolever might just as easily have come to a different conclusion. He noted in his study a discrepancy between the fears of higher-income versus lower-income students. While children from high-income families identified rats and insects as dirty, children from low-income families "rarely associated rats, roaches or bedbugs with filth."[33] The poorest children may very well have had some familiarity with these creatures and had come to the conclusion that there was little to fear. Perhaps, rather than blaming mothers, Woolever would have been more correct to blame a lack of familiarity for children's fears. Urban and suburban children at midcentury had limited opportunities to become familiar with the many creatures mentioned in the study. They may not have had any opportunity to make the acquaintance of snakes, bats, lizards, fish, turtles and deer. Although children claimed to have encountered all of these animals, and sometimes went as far as to say they had been chased by them, it's unlikely that they had spent any significant time with them. Perhaps the urban and suburban drift, as well as the increasing orientation of children toward the indoors, was fueling their fears of a wide variety of living things.

Another factor contributing to this problem was the increasing regimentation of children's lives. While the amount of regimentation in children's lives was certainly less than it would become in the late twentieth and early twenty-first centuries, the number of hours children spent in organized activities was growing. Families in the United States had gone through lean times in the thirties and had deprived themselves of many things they wanted during World War II. In the postwar era, parents sought to give their children many experiences and opportunities that had been unattainable during the thirties and early forties. Parents enrolled their daughters in ballet lessons and their sons in baseball and football. Both boys and girls found themselves taking music lessons and learning to swim. Because of the dispersed residential patterns promoted by suburbanization, fewer children were able to take themselves to their after-school activities by bus or bicycle or on foot. Mothers spent increasing amounts of time behind the wheel, ferrying their children to after-school and weekend activities.[34] One of the most popular activities in this era was scouting. While there had been 766,635 Cub Scouts in 1949, by 1959 there were 2.5 million. The number of girls involved in Brownies and Girl Scouts rose from 1.8 million to 4 million.[35] Here was a type of organized activity that actually counteracted the influence of radio, television and the movies and encouraged children to get outside.

One of the adult impulses behind the growth of the Boy Scouts, Girl Scouts and the Camp Fire Girls was to help children continue to forge strong relationships with the outdoors. The Boy Scouts, as ever, continued their emphasis on outdoor activities. A quick look at *Boy's Life*, the Boy Scouts' official magazine, confirmed the organization's ongoing emphasis on nurturing healthy boys by sending them outside. While the magazine at midcentury tapped into new interests, such as the development of jet engines, and promoted indoor pastimes such as basketball and radio building, it contained a healthy dose of outdoor adventure. The January 1950 edition encouraged boys to plan for the upcoming Second National Jamboree at Valley Forge, to make a tent for the occasion and to hold their meetings "out-of-doors around a campfire" like a troop of Explorers in Scotch Plains, New Jersey. As the author announced, these were "The Toughest Guys We Know!" New members "on their first overnighter, construct an emergency shelter and sleep in it. And this was really to be a night. The temperature got down to ten below zero."[36] The same issue included a piece of adventure fiction about the "Avalanche Patrol" and a nature story about a coyote entitled "Dangerous Journey." Other articles encouraged hiking, explained the use of snow shoes and demonstrated techniques for upland game feeding in the winter.[37] A decade later, the emphasis remained the same. In January 1960, *Boys' Life* lauded 400 Wisconsin Explorers for taking part in "Operation Snowbound," which tested lifesaving skills under seriously adverse conditions. As one organizer explained, "On paper, Operation Snowbound looks like a snap. Just a three-mile hike from a base camp to a crash site, but it could be the longest and coldest hike you ever took. This is more than just a survival trek. It's a rescue operation. You will have to use all your skill, knowledge, and training, not only for self-preservation, but to save the life of a crash victim."[38] In addition to this discussion of winter survival skills, the magazine also told the daring story of twenty scouts hiking to the top of Mount Fuji and prepared boys for that year's Jamboree, which would celebrate fifty years of scouting in the United States. An article, complete with patterns, explained to the scouts how to make a sail to use with their skates, so instead of "cruis[ing] along at a snail's pace," they could "speed across the ice at breathtaking speed."[39] Even in the depths of winter, the Boy Scouts kept their focus on the outdoors. They were either engaging in strenuous outdoor activities or making plans for what could be done when warm weather, and jamboree season, returned.

While the Camp Fire Girls did not place outdoor skills at the top of their list of objectives, it was the ninth of ten items girls were to acquire during their experiences with the organization. As the *Book of the Camp Fire Girls* noted, "The favorite sport of Camp Fire Girls is camping, hiking, cooking out of doors and exploring. This they do all year round, with a special splurge in the summer, when they go to the Camp Fire Girls camps."[40] Camping did seem to be the big attraction for most girls. In 1960, the organization claimed that 97 percent of their members liked outdoor activities best of all that Camp Fire had to offer.[41] Suggested activities included a whole host of earthy pursuits: making meals using some or all wild foods, making a bed from materials found out of doors, building a latrine and hunting for birds and nests without disturbing them.[42] The organization built its pastimes around a conservation ethic. While Camp Fire Girls were to build various sorts of nature collections, "All collections should be made with due regard for conservation." The Camp Fire Girls also emphasized "helping and protecting nature," encouraging girls to build their knowledge about plants and animals, to understand problems such as erosion and to seek out information about the workings of federal agencies charged with conservation.[43]

The Girls Scouts, too, put a strong emphasis on outdoor activities for all girls. At midcentury, girls of all ages were going to camp. In 1950, nearly 20,000 Brownies, age seven to nine, were attending camps of one sort or another, but mostly day camps. Nearly 88,000 Intermediate Scouts went to camp, and nearly a quarter of all Girl Scouts who went to camp were eleven-year-old girls. Another 8,109 Senior Girl Scouts, or the oldest girls, also went to organized camps.[44] Not all girls, however, were able to get away for a "proper" camping experience. One troop of girls described their activities developing a backyard camp, "about 200 feet from our house—No. 25 Main Street." One of the girl's fathers built a platform, upon which the girls set up a tent. They set up an ice box and put their kitchen in a lean-to. As the girls commented, "The kitchen was our pride and joy. At first we had trouble with ants, but we learned to keep all opened food in tightly covered jars or cans." They built a fire pit and "built a fire in it for supper every night." They overcame the problems of living out of doors. "At first we had trouble with mosquitos, but after a while we learned to fix our mosquito netting properly. All in all we had a fine time. My cat and all his friends slept on my bed every night."[45] While the organization preferred that girls get out and explore the world beyond their neighborhoods, it endorsed the many lessons that girls could learn, even from backyard camping.

In the early 1960s, the Girl Scouts' outdoor program was quite comprehensive. Under the rubric of "let's explore the out-of-doors," the organization encouraged Cadette Scouts (adolescent girls) to "walk out," "meet out," "hike out," "cook out," "sleep out" and "camp out." In particular, the Girl Scouts encouraged members to camp out. "Camp out for more fun than you can imagine, for days filled with activities you can't do in town. Do you love sports? You can learn to swim really well, to paddle a canoe down a winding stream, or perhaps to sail a boat. Do you love nature? It is all around you, offering miracles of beauty and science."[46] Being out and about required girls to learn a whole new set of skills: fire building, tent pitching, knot tying and wood chopping. Girls could earn a whole range of outdoor badges, including the conservation, family camper, campcraft, explorer, hiker and pioneer badges.[47] The Pioneer Badge was the most ambitious, requiring the girl to demonstrate all of the skills required for the campcraft badge and put them to use in planning and carrying out a four-day camping trip in primitive conditions. The girls took on every step of the process, from planning the trip, to purchasing, packing and preparing meals, to taking "outdoor good turns." When the trip was over, the conditions of the badge required the participating girl to "strike camp and restore site . . . return equipment, evaluate the success of the trip, and make a record of your recommendations for your next trip."[48] This was a fairly ambitious project for an adolescent.

Slightly older Senior Scouts also participated in a wide variety of events outside. As their handbook promised, "outdoor activity will be part of your year's calendar all through Senior Scouting."[49] The girls engaged in any number of projects, all of which required them to demonstrate a wide variety of skills. The project entitled "outdoor skills" required scouts to demonstrate toolcraft, knotcraft, fire building, construction, cooking and orientation skills and to be able to make, pack and carry a wide variety of equipment. For example, the girls had to be able to build from the materials on site a "Cooking fireplace, Baking fireplace, Incinerator, Grease pit, Drain." They also had to construct a "Lashed table, Outdoor shower, Outdoor latrine," several kinds of caches, and a kitchen.[50] The girl who could do all of this was well-prepared to take on even more ambitious tasks, such as teaching these same skills to younger girls as a camp counselor. She would know the out-of-doors, and even more importantly, be able to adapt to its requirements.

The Girl Scouts also sold the organization's camping program as an antidote for the ills of a Cold War world. As the Girl Scouts' *Annual Report* for 1950 explained:

> A complete picture of Girl Scout camping in 1950 must include reference to the part it played in plans for civil defense. Girl Scout councils in every State offered the State government their services and facilities, and, in particular, Girl Scout camps that could be used if evacuation of populated areas became necessary. The foremost contribution, however,

of Girl Scout camping is that it helps girls grow naturally and securely, even though the world around them is upset and tense. Camp life teaches them to stand on their own feet and to meet emergencies without panic—probably the best preparation youth can be given in the world today.[51]

Much like founders of American scouting who, in the early years of the century, thought of their organizations as antidotes for the problems of industrialization and urbanization, the Girl Scout organization continued to see itself as providing girls defenses against a potentially hostile world. No matter what the world threw at her, the well-prepared Girl Scout would have a whole host of skills and abilities that would allow her to adapt to just about any circumstance short of nuclear war.

Parents did not entirely leave their children's outdoor experiences to organizations such as the Boy and Girl Scouts and the Camp Fire Girls. Summer vacations became another venue for outdoor education. Family camping boomed in the postwar era. As historian Susan Sessions Rugh noted, "It was seen as inexpensive, fun, and wholesome to be outdoors."[52] As more and more families moved to the cities and suburbs, parents perceived camping as an activity that would bring children closer to nature, while at the same time teaching them responsibility and essential outdoor skills. A number of forces converged in the postwar era to make outdoor camping for families easier and more accessible. The growth of the interstate highway system connected more of the country. The dam building of the 1930s created new play spaces. The National Park Service added to the number of camping spots at popular destinations such as Yellowstone National Park. Camping was also inexpensive, compared to other sorts of vacations, as long as parents resisted the urge to purchase a shiny, all-the-comforts-of-home Airstream camper.[53] Perhaps unsurprisingly, it was in the midst of the 1960s camping boom that the KOA (Kampgrounds of America) campground was born, with its restrooms, showers, laundry facilities and convenience stores.[54] For the squeamish, camping no longer had to entail all of the hardships involved in sleeping in tents, on the ground and without access to electricity and modern plumbing. It could be, if parents wanted, an indoor/outdoor activity.

Parents planning vacations were not the only adults trying to bridge the gap between changes in child life and the need to connect children with the natural world. Children's drift indoors coincided with a burst of entertainment opportunities that sought to bring the outdoors in for this generation of youngsters. The growing divide between children and the out-of-doors certainly represented a commercial opportunity. The movies offered an ideal medium through which to provide children with additional insights into the natural world. One of the earliest and most engaging examples of this was the 1942 Disney studio release, *Bambi*, based on the novel by the Austrian writer Felix Salten. Viewed by millions of children worldwide, one critic has dubbed the film "the single most successful and enduring statement in American popular culture against hunting."[55] In spite of Walt Disney's desire to make the visual depiction of the movie's animal heroes as accurate as possible, the film's interpretation of nature was anything but realistic. The forest in which the fawn Bambi was born was a paradise, filled with sweet, sleepy animals, living in harmony. They even spoke the same language, heralding his birth with the cry: "It's happened, it's happened! The new prince is born!"[56] The animals not only spoke the same language, but also lived entirely harmoniously with each other, loving, respecting and teaching each other the skills necessary to life and survival. In this celluloid world, there were no animal predators, even those that existed in the natural world. As environmental studies scholar Ralph H. Lutts wrote, "Friend Owl, who appears to be a great horned own, is Thumper's [a rabbit] and Flower's [a skunk] friend. Apparently great horned owls do not consume their normal quota of rabbits and skunks in Disney's forest because Disney's world is a world without predation."[57] Other natural forces that might normally kill animals, such as conflicts over mating, winter's cold or a forest fire, also did not. The filmmakers left that distinction to "Man."

Humans were forces of evil in the film, either through their carelessness with fire, their hunting or their vicious dogs. Bambi's mother summed up the situation when Bambi asked, "What happened, Mother? Why did we all run?" by answering, "Man was in the forest." "Man" shot and killed Bambi's mother (although entirely off-screen), shot and wounded Bambi and burned the forest to ashes with a carelessly tended campfire. Seen by millions of youngsters, "Bambi" imparted a powerful pro-animal, anti-hunting message to generations of American children. Disney-critic Ralph H. Lutts commented in reference to the film:

> Bambi has become one of our most widespread and emotionally powerful national symbols of nature, one that motivates deep concern, and dedicated action to protect wildlife. However, Disney's Bambi is an empty symbol, because the concept of nature that his fawn represents is impoverished. The film motivates, but it does not educate. It may stimulate action, but not understanding. Instead of affirming nature, it represents a

flight from the natural world into a comfortable nature fantasy. Ironically, it offers no hope for us poor humans to be anything other than destroyers of the natural world.[58]

Ironically enough, while humans were the enemy, the Disney studios endowed the animals in "Bambi," and numerous other Disney nature films, with remarkably human motivations and behavior. For the next three decades, Disney used a parade of anthropomorphized animals to introduce American children to the natural world.

Although there was little market for live-action nature films in the years before World War II, opportunities expanded in the years immediately after.[59] World War II had taught the Disney studios a great deal about documentary and educational filmmaking, and the studios sought to apply that knowledge to a peacetime market. Disney released an impressive number of live-action nature movies from the late 1940s into the 1960s. In the first half of the 1950s, Disney released *The Living Desert* and *The Vanishing Prairie*, two feature-length nature productions, which the studio called *True-Life Adventures*. Both won "Best Documentary Feature" academy awards.[60] Miles of film, careful selection and engaging soundtracks helped to create "a harmonious vision of nature through editing, music and commentary."[61] With anthropomorphized animals and "the more gruesome aspects of nature" sanitized, Disney produced perfect nature films for a family audience.[62]

The Living Desert purported to be a *True-Life Adventure*, where "Nature sets the stage and provides the actors."[63] The most important character in the movie was the desert itself, "incredibly ugly but fantastically beautiful." In the opening minutes of the film, the director set the tone with mud pots in the Salton Sea moving in time to symphonic accompaniment, made both animate and comedic. "Where we find only a dead and desolate wasteland," the narrator intoned, "nature finds life." In just over sixty minutes of film, the movie led the viewer through the hours of the day and the season of the year in this desert environment. The narrator told a series of domestic stories, with an underlying message: "In the living desert, nature's theme is always the preservation of the species." Tarantulas found their mates, as did owls. Kangaroo rats built homes and protected their young. The filmmaker portrayed the animals as human cousins, with very familiar behaviors. Take the kangaroo rats, for example, celebrating in the moonlight, having defeated a malevolent sidewinder. The rats frenetically played to the tune of "Hail, Hail, the Gang's All Here." "Then in typical human fashion, the affair degenerates into a brawl." Other animals, seeing this, took advantage of the situation. A ring-tailed cat arrived, as did an owl. "The squabbling rats are about to learn one of nature's oldest laws: a single moment off guard can be your last. It's a lucky rat who gets away to live perhaps another day."

The film was full of near misses and deaths. Interestingly enough, it was only the ugly and the villainous that died in "The Living Desert." Lumbering tortoises, cute pocket mice and saucy bobcats lived to struggle another day. Rattlesnakes and tarantulas, however, met gruesome endings. The violence of a flash flood, too, threatened all. But lest the film end on a grim note, the desert bloomed with the storm's passing. Gorgeous time-lapse photography showed the desert's flowers in full bloom. The narrator asserted, "There are no endings, only beginnings. . . . and so it will be through all of time." A number of narrative threads made their way throughout the movie: life was precarious, the desert was full of surprises, and animals were people, too. *The Living Desert* took young viewers to a place they most likely had never been and purported to teach them lessons about geography, biology and natural history.

The Vanishing Prairie, released a year later, had a stronger environmental theme.[64] As the title suggested, the film placed its emphasis on the problem of extinction, and animals' struggle to survive in the presence of modern humans. Native Americans, mentioned in passing as "red men" in their "happy hunting ground," who lived lightly on the land, gave way to settlers in their prairie schooners. The film, the narrator opined, was an attempt to "re-create the wondrous pageant that was nature's prairie" before the arrival of human beings. Again, the story involved long and careful examinations of animals in various domestic scenes, choosing mates and rearing their young. Pied-billed grebes, watching their nest, could not have been more like humans, or the commentary more like 1950s discussions of appropriate gender roles:

> At the home of the pied-billed grebe, it's father who is presiding over the unhatched half of the family. Like most males he's rather careless about domestic chores, and wanders off with an egg still clamped in his chest feathers. Well that's typical, perhaps if he had to lay these eggs, he'd be more careful. Mother makes a hurried check. One, two, oh, here we are. I declare, these husbands, always leaving things for someone else to pick up.

Perhaps a bit more surprising for the era, the film showed the birth of a buffalo calf, more than likely leading to some interesting post-movie discussions between parents and children.

Throughout the film, every creature was a part of a vanishing species, and the film's makers focused on both the predation by humans and the predation by other animals. Mountain lions stalked deer. Black-footed ferrets chased prairie dogs. Coyotes found it "both a duty and a pleasure" to kill rattlesnakes. Inanimate nature, in the form of prairie fire and prairie flood, also threatened the animal inhabitants of the prairie. In the end, it was all a part of the web of life. The narrator proclaimed, "And so on nature's prairie everything has its place, even catastrophe and disaster. And the raging flood is as much a part of her mysterious plan as the wind and the grass and the howling of the coyotes at a prairie moon." At the film's end, the narrator became philosophical and made a pitch for environmental consciousness, since "nature's prairie, in part at least, still survives." The film ended with the observation, "Nature preserves her own, and teaches them how to cope with time and the unaccountable ways of man. Mankind, in turn, is beginning to understand nature's pattern, and is helping her to replenish and rebuild, so that the vanishing pageant of the past may become the enduring pageant of the future."

The director surely meant the overriding environmental message to disguise any problems and inconsistencies in the film. The film's writers were geographically confused, throwing in mountains on many occasions for good measure. Rather than examining animals on their own terms, the narration explained their actions within a human context, providing Disney's usual anthropomorphic explanation for animal behavior. Grebes were lazy husbands and buffaloes were proud mamas. Mountain lion cubs were just like domestic kittens. Male animals in mating season were good for a laugh in both *The Living Desert* and *The Vanishing Prairie*, their foolish antics highlighted with appropriate classical music accompaniment. As cinema scholar Nicholas Sammond wrote in his book, *Babes in Tomorrowland: Walt Disney and the Making of the American Child, 1930–1960*, "The True-Life Adventures revealed a strange landscape—a tundra, desert, or prairie—that reproduced the social world of the American suburb in its animal life. Thus, nature appeared exotic, independent, and distant, yet familiar and comforting."[65] And again, it was largely the unattractive, or just less cute, animals that died. A coyote killed a rattlesnake and an adult deer succumbed to a female mountain lion, hunting to feed her incredibly cute cubs. A fawn, still wearing its spots, survived by way of its natural camouflage and careful waiting. In the end, all was harmonious on the prairie.

Although *The Living Desert* and *The Vanishing Prairie* received the most critical acclaim, they were only a small part of the steady stream of nature movies Disney produced in the 1950s. In 1955, the Disney Studios released another "true-life adventure," this one devoted to the study of the African lion in its native environment. As in similar films, the producer followed the lions through a year in their lives and examined the many other animals sharing the lions' domain. The narrator, as he usually did, gently chided the male lions for their ungentlemanly ways. "If only friend husband would do his part here, things might be easier . . . but this is no time to worry about lazy males, there is a meal yet to be won, and a whole pride to be fed. And now the ladies join forces."[66] Baby animals provided comedy, the dry season tragedy, and in the end, the rains came again, making all things right. A 1956 "true-life adventure," titled *The Secrets of Life*, must have frustrated many a young viewer. While the title promised a voyage into the great mystery of "What life is and how it came to be," the film never got much closer than seed pods bursting, bees pollinating and grunion leaving their fertilized eggs on the beach. Anyone hoping, as an adolescent might, for enlightenment on the topic of human and animal reproduction, would have remained in the dark.[67] There were no bison giving birth in this film.

In 1957, the Disney studios found a point midway between the animated storytelling of *Bambi* and the more serious filmmaking of the *True-Life Adventures*. In that year, the studio released *Perri: The First True-Life Fantasy*. *Perri*, which like *Bambi* was based on the writings of Felix Salten, used live-action animal photography to follow the story of Perri, a precocious female squirrel. Like the other *True-Life Adventures*, *Perri* followed a year in the life of an animal. Unlike the other films, it followed a distinct story line, from infancy to adulthood, with many adventures in between. *Perri* was also a bit more bloodthirsty than Disney's previous offerings. While the narrator was careful to intone that mother animals in the forest, such as martens, foxes and wildcats, killed to support their young, the marten featured in the film was "the face of death," stalking, killing and eating Perri's father, mother and siblings and attempting to kill her.[68] Like *The Secrets of Life*, *Perri* was rather coy on the subject of reproduction. When spring came, the narrator intoned not that it was mating season, but "together time." Perri, having become acquainted with a young male squirrel, Porro, proceeded toward the inevitable. The voice off-camera announced, "Perri awakens with a new awareness in her breast," and "Her moment of fulfillment is at hand." After the predictable last-minute confusion provided by a forest fire and the final appearance of the evil mother marten, Perri and Porro headed off into the woods to have some "together time." With its live-action depictions of animals and educational tone, *Perri* could claim to be more fact than fiction, although the viewing children were more likely to remember the nightmarish quality of the marten than the natural history lesson about mother animals and feeding their young.

By the early 1960s, Disney had moved even farther toward entertainment disguised as education. *Flash, the Teen-Age Otter*, which Disney released in 1961, continued in an anti-hunting, pro-wildlife management vein, attempting to educate young viewers about wildlife refuges and the work of game wardens. Based on a story by nature writer Emil Liers and filmed in Wisconsin, *Flash, the Teen-Age Otter* followed the adventures of a young otter, beginning life in a backwoods mill pond. Flash's story began with the intonation, "Ever since the frontier wilderness was turned over by the pioneer's plow, the wild animals of America have been looking for another home, but they never found it." Animals like Flash had to make accommodations to fields and farms, unless they were lucky enough to find a wildlife refuge. Flash began his life in one of those refuges, but following instinct, had to make his way with his family in late summer to a wintering ground more than 100 miles away. This odyssey, as the narrator called it, was the source of adventure after adventure, from a harrowing encounter with a bobcat, to a near-fatal interlude with a fisherman/trapper. Mr. Slocum, the fisherman/trapper, caught Flash, and took him home to fatten him for slaughter for his pelt. As winter came, the narrator ominously stated, "A change of seasons, but no change of heart. For of course to the man there was no sentiment here. This was business. Flash was just a piece of merchandise to be disposed of at the most profitable time. That time was now." Only the appearance of a deer and the help of a dog at an opportune moment saved Flash's life. After further near-fatal adventures, including saving his beloved, Tina, from a fisherman and a gamekeeper, Flash faced almost certain doom. "In his short life, Flash had faced all the worst that man could throw against him. Surely now his ordeal would be over; nothing more could happen to him. But it did." Surprise! It was a game warden, come to save him and return him to his mill pond wildlife refuge, where he and Tina could forge a lifetime partnership. The story ended with Flash, Tina and the whole otter family frolicking on the mill wheel. The narrator bid farewell to "The joyous, fun-loving carefree otters, the happiest animals in nature."[69] *Flash* dealt with a number of topics in nature education: the problems agricultural development posed for wildlife, the development of wildlife protection and the commodification of animal products.

Further films carried on in the same vein, using supposed wildlife education to entertain. Further offerings, however, strayed even farther from the educational model. In 1963, the *Wonderful World of Disney* broadcasted *Yellowstone Cubs*, the live-action story of two black bear cubs, Tuffy and Tubby, temporarily separated from their mother, Nokomis. Although mother bear and cubs lived comfortably through the spring, summer brought intruders to the park. When summer came to Yellowstone Park, the tourists came, too. In spite of signage exclaiming "Danger: feeding bears is prohibited," tourists continually fed the bears, even to the point of causing "bear jams." Chaotic interaction with tourists caused Nokomis to become separated from her cubs. The rangers branded her as a "bad bear," and she nearly lost her life in her struggle to be reunited with Tuffy and Tubby. In the end, however, "old faithful" Nokomis found her cubs, and the rangers let them escape back into the wild. They were happy to let her be, since "She was an awful good mother bear." Sympathy for the bears aside, *Yellowstone Cubs* was full of mixed messages. While Disney's filmmakers may have conceived *Yellowstone Cubs* as a way of teaching people young and old the dangers of feeding wildlife, the entertainment value of the marauding cubs subverted the message. Even though it was probably not the director's intention, the film made feeding the bears look ever so much more interesting than watching from a distance.[70] Entertainment trumped education.

A final example showed the degree to which Disney had drifted away from the educational model of the *True-Life Adventures* and toward entertainment. One of the most successful and best loved of the Disney pictures featuring wild animals was *Charlie, the Lonesome Cougar*, released at Christmastime in 1967 and shown (at least in some markets) in a double feature with *The Jungle Book*.[71] Set in the Cascades of Oregon, termed "Timber Land, U.S.A.," the film followed the adventures of Charlie, an orphaned cougar. The film worked to counter the opinions of those who thought cougars were "about the biggest mistake Mother Nature ever made," consisting of "two hundred pounds of tooth, claw and trouble."[72] The orphaned cub had the good luck of happening upon Jess Bradley, a lumber company forester for the Carbon County Lumber Company. Jess did the "only thing for a nature-loving man to do" and brought Charlie home to live with him in the lumber camp. Predictable mayhem ensued, with Charlie making his way into the wild, the lumber camp and back and then finally heading off into the wilderness to find his way in life, side-by-side with a fetching "cougarette." The narrator intoned, "So that's how Charlie's lonesome days ended in the best of all possible ways. He was a king cat now. From this time on he'd reign over all this bountiful wilderness domain. He'd have a whole new life, with a brand new mate. Now it's time for us to state, so long Charlie."

Charlie, the Lonesome Cougar was very much a product of its time, featuring a highly unrealistic (but live-action), anthropomorphized animal hero, while at the same time attempting to impart a message of environmental sensitivity. One of the more dubious and potentially dangerous messages embedded in the film was that until he had tasted freedom as an adolescent cougar, Charlie was essentially tamable and not truly wild. Mountain lion Charlie, while content to be somewhat domesticated during his kittenhood, eventually succumbed to the seduction of the wild (the passing "cougarette"), becoming dangerous to humans. Once living free, he had to find his place in the world of wild things, including learning how to hunt and kill his prey, although the filmmakers always showed him devouring his dinner at a distance. Although Charlie started small with mice, rabbits and other diminutive game, the narrator assured his listeners that Charlie, like all cougars, was "born to play a bigger part in keeping nature's balance. A deer is the natural prey for a king cat." The narrator also reassured the audience that when Jess Bradley ultimately relocated a wayward and now-wild Charlie to a wildlife preserve, he would be able to roam free in 1,000 square miles of wilderness, "all out of bounds for dogs and guns and bounty hunters." The anti-hunting message within *Bambi* continued twenty-five years later in Charlie's story.

Unlike the commentary that would most likely develop in a nature film today, the Carbon County Lumber Company received uncritical mention, and instead, its operations and its action-packed spring log drive became the center of much of the film's story. As one critic of Disney nature films has commented, "The influence of human civilization on the natural environment was not yet an agenda item."[73] Or, to put it another way, animals were on their radar, while trees and natural landscapes were not, a somewhat curious development after *The Vanishing Prairie*. The type of filmmaking exemplified by *Charlie, the Lonesome Cougar* became less popular in the late 1960s, when more educational, made-for-television wildlife programming came to the fore and when such anthropomorphized depictions of animal life succumbed to environmental sensibilities.[74]

The most familiar example of this type of educational programming was *Mutual of Omaha's Wild Kingdom*, a weekly half-hour of television devoted to the examination of animals and their habitats and beloved by a whole generation of children. *Wild Kingdom* premiered in January 1963 and remained on prime-time, network television until 1971, when it went into syndication. During its long run, the show won four Emmys and received the P.T.A.'s endorsement as a show approved for family viewing. Marlin Perkins, whose career included directing both Chicago's Lincoln Park Zoo and the Saint Louis Zoo, hosted the program. Zoologist Jim Fowler often served as co-host and did most of the show's heavy lifting.[75] While Perkins sometimes joined in the action, Fowler more often tackled the wildlife and dealt with sticky situations. On Sunday nights, the show brought the outdoors, and exotic locations and animals, to the average American family's living room.

From the first episode, *Wild Kingdom*'s producers made the educational intent of the series clear. Marlin Perkins, in a suit and standing in a "laboratory," introduced the show. The episode emphasized his credentials as a zoo professional and conservationist. In the pilot, Perkins and Fowler examined the theme of survival, intoning, "In the wild kingdom, where death is swift, life depends on a design for survival." Perkins introduced his viewers to cute lion cubs, who relied upon their speed to keep them out of harm's way, as well as turtles of various sorts, who relied upon their armor, their odor and their strong jaws for survival. The episode also introduced young viewers to the protective features of armadillos, porcupines, ducks, fawns, rhinos, ant-eaters and snakes. The excitement came from a live-action segment showing Jim Fowler chasing and lassoing an anteater in South America, and the two men, back in the lab, pestering a cobra until it spit venom at them. At the end of the half-hour, Perkins and Fowler gave their attention to a pair of cute lion cubs, taking their dinner from bottles. Perkins turned to Fowler with a question: "Isn't it interesting Jim, that lions with their great ability to defend themselves are actually losing the battle for survival?" In his closing remarks, Perkins emphasized the importance of wildlife conservation to lions as a species. "They've had those same abilities to protect themselves for hundreds of thousands of years, and yet their range is much smaller today than it was just a few hundred years ago. But so it seems with many animals. Protective devices that have been effective for millions and millions of years now seem to be out of date. Many animals are losing their battle with man. They are being killed out, their ranges are being reduced in size, and every day we travel a little bit farther to find the wild kingdom."[76] *Wild Kingdom* began with education, conservation and just a touch of excitement.

Wild Kingdom continued as it had begun, with its legitimacy derived from Perkins's authority, its use of animals borrowed from both the Lincoln Park and St. Louis zoos, and snippets of live-action footage from various parts of the world, often featuring the young and outdoorsy Fowler. In his narration, Perkins generally did not anthropomorphize the animals, but attempted to explain their behavior in terms that young viewers would understand. Keeping small viewers' attention meant highlighting the weirdly fascinating chameleon, with its incredibly long tongue and independently moving eye-balls. Entertainment value also dictated the show devoting a large portion of an episode to otters, with their fun-loving, almost child-like antics. As Perkins chuckled, "I've never seen anyone who has more fun than an otter."[77] The show attempted to highlight animals and animal behaviors that would pique the average child's interest, without depending upon a fictionalized story line, as Disney did. But lest we start to feel too smug, *Wild Kingdom* was just as much a product of its own time as the Disney nature films. In episode four, featuring the "strange but true," the producers wandered into questionable territory in a misguided attempt at explaining cultural diversity. While delving into a number of rather disjointed stories about strange animal behavior, the writers inserted a discussion of South America's Ticuna tribe. Their puberty rituals for young women were their "strange-but-true" activities, and Perkins intoned, "We call the customs of the Ticuna Indians strange, but after all, that's only our point of view. I'm sure that a Ticuna visiting our land would find many of our customs strange. Strange, and to him, utterly incredible."[78] As with the animals, Perkins was trying to understand the Ticunas on their own terms—but they were being observed side-by-side with animals, not with others of their own species also engaging in strange-but-true behavior.

Wild Kingdom ranged far and wide over its years as a prime-time series, covering a multitude of conservation issues in many different places. Wherever the story took place, however, Perkins kept the focus on animals and habitat. He used the story of the polar bears of Churchill, Manitoba (Canada) to illustrate the serious problems caused by animals and humans crossing paths. Every fall, waiting for the ice to form on Hudson's Bay, polar bears inundated the Churchill town dump, looking for food. The same bears often strolled through town, looking for a meal there as well. As Perkins noted, "For the most part, they're not aggressive toward humans who keep a respectful distance and don't bother them." Hungry bears, however, could be short-tempered, and not everyone kept a respectful distance or avoided teasing the bears. Rather than destroy the bears, scientists working in conjunction with wildlife management experts relocated the wayward animals. As they released yet another bear hundreds of miles south, Perkins commented, "For the twenty-fourth time this season, concerned conservationists have preserved another magnificent polar bear of Churchill."[79]

Wild Kingdom's central emphasis on wildlife conservation, rather than ecology, led the show into some directions that similar programs might not go today. A two-part episode on wildfire focused on the destructive power of fire, rather than the role that fire has to play in woodland and grassland ecosystems. Perkins, this time with co-host Stan Brock, travelled to western Montana to study the behavior of animals in the face of wildfire. From the beginning, the program clearly defined fire as a problem, and the Forest Service's lookout towers and smoke jumpers as essential parts of the solution. As Perkins commented, "Speed is everything. The smoke jumpers must reach the fire before it has a chance to spread." Perkins and Brock joined the action, and Brock even plummeted out of the plane with the smoke jumpers. He landed in a tree, then slid down to the forest floor. He said, "Not quite what I had in mind, but no harm done, thanks to the padded jump suit." Perkins contented himself with observing the fire from a helicopter.[80]

While the two spent some of their time observing the wildlife, they devoted even more to trying to save animals that had gotten too close to the fire. Observing a porcupine up a tree, potentially in harm's way, the two sawed down the tree, bagged the reluctant porcupine, and released him near a stream. When a fawn floated by, swept up in the current while attempting to avoid the fire, Brock dove head-first into the water to save it. Perkins then took the scared animal by helicopter to safety. A few minutes later, a bison herd appeared to be wandering too near the fire, so Perkins and his pilot used the helicopter to direct them toward safety, commenting, "the huge animals were in real danger." The final message for the young audience was one worthy of Smokey Bear. "While lightning starts many fires every year, the majority of forest fires are man-made and preventable. . . . Man is the major cause of wildfire. By taking extra care with camp fires and matches, he can also be the main hope for reducing the annual destruction in our great forests, hoping to preserve a unique part of the wild kingdom."[81]

Promotion of fire safety in the nation's parks and forests was certainly a laudable goal; the message, however, was single-minded and delivered in an overly dramatic fashion. The program wasted no time on the discussion of naturally occurring forest fires and the role that fire plays in forest and grassland ecology. The program also avoided the obvious limitations of Perkins's and Brock's actions. They might be able to save a limited number of animals, but many more faced peril in the burning forest. Was saving one or two animals really worth the danger and the expense involved? Did bison that had survived in the wild for centuries really need human intervention when confronted with fire? This being children's programming, and programming aimed at children who loved animals, the producers naturally avoided exploring these questions. Even more obviously, should anyone ever dive into unknown waters, as Stan Brock had done, in pursuit of the fawn?

Mindful of the liability issues involved, producers today would probably avoid featuring such reckless activities in a live-action children's program. This is not meant to suggest that *Wild Kingdom* was without value and that children would have been better off without this and similar programming. Instead, my purpose is to suggest that the midcentury environmental messages purveyed to children, even from a show like *Wild Kingdom*, tended to be one-dimensional and uncomplicated and created the impression that wildlife biologists spent their time physically rescuing the wildlife from the dangers of life in the wild.

This proliferation of wildlife programming in the movies and on television coincided with another development: the creation of a host of cartoon animal characters meant to promote sensitivity to the wild. The first of these was Smokey Bear (not Smokey *the* Bear, as he is often called), who made his appearance in 1944, during World War II. The Wartime Advertising Council first borrowed Bambi from Disney to promote a fire safety message, but developed the idea of Smokey Bear as a long-term solution to the need for a wild fire safety spokes-creature. While fawns like Bambi could be victims of fire, only a large and powerful animal could be a part of the campaign to prevent fires. The advertisers settled on a bear as an animal that the public would find "appealing, yet strong."[82] That they were able to add a real, live bear cub, saved from a forest fire, as a supplement to the cartoon image, was a stroke of genius. In fact, there are very few people who remember that the cartoon came before the cub. While the cartoon bear was born in 1944, the cub went to the National Zoo as Smokey Bear in 1950.[83]

Smokey soon made a favorable and dramatic impression on the nation's youth. As a reporter for the *Science News* wrote in 1955: "What has he done? He has captured the children. The kids will lecture for an hour if you get careless with matches or cigarettes. Today's youngsters will tell you exactly what the ashtray is for, and what car windows are not for."[84]

The Forest Service plastered Smokey Bear's image over a plethora of products, in addition to mounting a very successful ad campaign in which the bear proclaimed, "Only YOU Can Prevent Forest Fires." As historian Hal Rothman commented, Smokey taught "environmental responsibility to children through the remarkably pleasant device of a friendly animal with human characteristics."[85] By the mid-1950s, around 500,000 children had become junior forest rangers.[86] Every child who became a junior forest ranger received a kit, including "A letter from Smokey, signed with paw print. Smokey's photograph, with his true story printed on the back. A pledge card. A membership card. Four Smokey prevention stamps. A bookmark.

A song sheet of 'Smokey the Bear.'"[87] Young enrollees took the "conservation pledge": "I give my pledge as an American to save and faithfully defend from waste the natural resources of my country—its air, soil, and minerals, its forests, waters and wildlife."[88] Fires not only injured and killed animals, but also were a waste of the nation's precious resources.

Interest in Smokey Bear also led children to action. Some, as the foregoing would suggest, educated their parents about the dangers of careless use of fire. Others wrote to Smokey with questions, concerns and contributions. In the mid-1950s, he was receiving about 1,000 letters every day. James, a boy from Pasadena, California, wrote, "Would you please send me another Smokey badge mine broke." A girl from North Dakota sent a nickel and a note: "I read that it cost billions of dollars to pay for the damage caused by

The Forest Service used posters like this to educate young conservationists about the dangers of fire. By permission of the U.S. Forest Service.

fires so I am contributing five cents to help pay for the damage." One little girl wrote, "I have tried to break daddy from throwing out cigarettes from the car."[89] Another girl asked for a Ranger kit, and then proceeded, "I want to be a forst [sic] ranger. But in the meantime I want to know how to take care of the horn-toad. if you have a booklet on them would you send me one? I found him in my front yard. . . . P.S. It's a Girl Horn-toad." When the original Smokey died at the National Zoo in 1976, there was an outpouring of grief. A fourth-grader wrote to the chief of the Forest Service, "I am very sorry that Smokey had to die. I liked him very much. I saw a lot of his commercials. They are very good. I hope the new Smokey is as good as the old one."[90] As these children's letters indicated, Smokey and his story struck a chord and provoked reactions.[91] As in the case of Disney's movies and *Wild Kingdom*, the message was a bit flat and one-dimensional: forest fires were bad, animals could be harmed, and "only YOU can prevent forest fires."[92] Nevertheless, a campaign that provoked children to pressure their parents into using their ashtrays instead of littering the highways and by-ways with their spent matches and cigarettes certainly constituted a public good. Smokey Bear had given America's children something constructive to do in the cause of conservation.

The National Wildlife Federation's contribution to the whole genre of animals as educators was the raccoon Ranger Rick and his many animal sidekicks, such as Wise Old Owl. *Ranger Rick's Nature Magazine* provided a whole range of environmental education to the younger set and also allowed children the opportunity to air their questions and concerns. Ranger Rick arrived on the scene in 1959, when the National Wildlife Federation published its book *The Adventures of Rick Raccoon*. The book was a statement against pollution, with Rick Raccoon and his forest pals joining forces to clean up a creek and pond. In 1960, the organization published a follow-up, *Ranger Rick and the Great Forest Fire*. This time, Ranger Rick and his friends saved the forest from a catastrophic fire.[93] The first issue of *Ranger Rick's Nature Magazine* went to press in 1967. In the first issue, the publishers explained their objectives: "To give boys and girls a year-round program of activities, adventure and knowledge which will help them appreciate and enjoy nature. To help them know and respect all things that grow and creatures that move, that all may desire to conserve and wisely use the vital natural resources of the world."[94] *Ranger Rick's Nature Magazine* has remained in print ever since and in 1980 was joined by *Your Big Backyard*, a publication for preschoolers.[95] As one scholar has put it, Ranger Rick has evolved into "a kind of raccoon steward, working to put out fires when needed, but more likely to engage with complicated environmental degradation."[96] In appealing to children, the National Wildlife Federation was hoping to build a constituency that would last for generations.[97]

Ranger Rick's Nature Magazine presented a wide variety of conservation issues to young readers, but also gave them a forum in which to express their own interests. Part of the magazine's appeal was its success at finding children at their own level. A 2000 issue featured the article "Animals Eat

Woodsy Owl, who once proclaimed, "Give a hoot, don't pollute," now says "Lend a hand, care for the land." By permission of the U.S. Forest Service.

the Weirdest Stuff," which included pictures of animals eating each other's feces, or "poop tarts."[98] Children's letters to the folks at *Ranger Rick's Nature Magazine* displayed a whole range of interests in (and confusion about) the workings of the natural world. One youngster wrote "Dear Wise Old Owl: Why do dogs have black lips?" Another wrote to tell Ranger Rick about a school project: "In school I made an incest [*sic*] collection." And yet another child in his or her enthusiasm for environmental education betrayed the limitations of their knowledge: "Dear Ranger Rick: I have decided to learn all about nature. Please send it to me at once." As Judy Braus, who for a time was the Wise Old Owl, commented, "How would you answer that? Now you can see why I moved on to new jobs."[99] Children were more than passive recipients of nature education. They responded with curiosity and concern. The magazine also encouraged them to value the nonhuman world and to feel responsibility for it—or stewardship.[100]

In 1971, the Forest Service invented Woodsy Owl, an apparently less successful spokes-animal than Smokey Bear or Ranger Rick. Woodsy was the face of the Forest Service's anti-pollution campaign, with his tagline, "Give a hoot, don't pollute."[101] Somehow, Woodsy never mustered the support of Smokey, lacking the cute factor, and a real, live, particularly adorable animal counterpart. He also lacked the sort of forum that Ranger Rick had in his monthly magazine. In 1997, the Forest Service rolled out a revamped Woodsy, featuring "a backpack, hiking shoes, and field pants—smart and safe for exploring the 'great outdoors.'" Instead of saying "Give a hoot; don't pollute," the new Woodsy said, "Lend a hand, care for the land!" which the Forest Service claimed was "positive, easily understood, and generates a new interest in the stewardship of natural resources. As Woodsy flies across the land, he invites children to see the world around them and explore their surroundings."[102] The new Woodsy seems to have had even less of an impact than the old.[103]

Sometimes, human beings were more powerful environmental messengers than cartoon (or real) bears, raccoons and owls. Adults of a certain age more than likely remember a little bit of the "Give a hoot, don't pollute" campaign, but they probably have even stronger memories of a very successful "Keep America Beautiful" anti-littering advertisement featuring actor Iron Eyes Cody. In this classic public service announcement, broadcast again and again in the 1970s and 1980s, an Indian in native garb paddled a canoe through polluted waters and past a smokestack spewing filth. In the last moments of the commercial, the Indian stood next to a busy highway. Garbage landed at his feet, thrown from a passing car. A single tear slid down his face, and the narrator intoned, "People start pollution, people can stop it."[104] Although his movie career spanned decades, this was, perhaps, Cody's most famous role, and the one most children of that era would remember.[105] Correctly or not, Indians were enormously important as symbolic exemplars of correct environmental relationships between human beings and the land. As historian David Rich Lewis wrote, "Modern whites embrace the image of Indians as the ultimate environmentalists, beings who lived at peace with each other, who utilized everything they took from the land and left no mark of their passing." As Lewis further commented, this stereotype "denied native peoples their humanity, culture, history, and modernity."[106] But by using a tear on an Indian face to promote this particular environmental message, the commercial's makers chose a potent symbol that was sure to stay with a generation of viewers, both children and adults.

The release of the commercial coincided with the first celebration of Earth Day, on April 22, 1970. In 1969, Senator Gaylord Nelson of Wisconsin started a national teach-in on environmental issues. In 1970, Harvard University law student Denis Hayes converted Nelson's idea into a nationwide educational event, meant for everyone. Hayes hoped that converting Earth Day from a protest-oriented teach-in to a more "centrist" event would capture the attention of individuals who might not otherwise be interested or participate. In this vein, elementary and secondary school students from places small and large joined in on activities aimed at building environmental awareness. [107] For example, in central Iowa, programming occurred at most, if not all, schools, in response to Republican Governor Robert Ray's proclamation of the week as "Environmental Week in Iowa." In Nesco and Collins, students picked up litter from the areas adjacent to their schools. Students in neighboring Nevada began their school day with an assembly where a panel of three Iowa State University students discussed the problem of pollution and answered questions. Students from the same school visited their town's sewage treatment plant and tested water below the plant for contamination. Teachers also incorporated the topic of pollution into the day's classes. Students from Roland-Story High School walked to school and then visited the sewage disposal plant in Story City.[108] At Ames High School, students engaged in a whole week of activities. On April 16, students from several classes cleaned parts of the school grounds. Later in the week, a biology class "cleaned the native prairie . . . during class time." The school also hosted an assembly on "environmental improvement," and a student "sang several anti-pollution songs." The students observed Earth Day itself by "encouraging students to walk or ride bicycles. Those who drive will be asked to donate money which will be sent to an organization for environmental improvement." The final event of the week was radio transmission to "interested teachers and students" of an address by Stanford University's Dr. Paul Ehrlich on "The Population Explosion: Facts and Fiction," which he presented at Iowa State University.[109] Between the local schools and the college campus, there was an explosion of educational activities on environmental themes.

These same Ames youngsters would have heard additional environmental messages in their churches on the Sunday after Earth Day. Ministers planned to present sermons on Earth Day themes at Ames's Memorial Lutheran Church, Northminster Presbyterian Church, Collegiate Methodist Church, University Lutheran Church, First Baptist Church, the Church of Christ, Ascension Lutheran Church, the Seventh-day Adventist Church and St. Thomas Aquinas Church. Stan Borden, pastor of the First Baptist Church, planned to speak on the "Theology of Ecology," and James Jerrell of the Church of Christ on "God's Property." Reverend Wilbur Wilcox, of Collegiate Methodist, made available copies of his March 1 sermon, "Care of the Spaceship Earth."[110] Earth Day, in Ames's churches, was a truly ecumenical event and a shared concern for nearly all denominations. At least for that week, environmental themes were front-and-center in the minds of boys and girls in central Iowa and throughout the nation.

It was an interesting moment. Everyone, it seemed, had their attention focused on the outdoors, young and old, urban and rural. Everyone was thinking about planet Earth, and taking a look at what was happening to the health of the environment in their communities. Even if the children were watching the television, perhaps they were tuned in to *Wild Kingdom*, and a half-hour's lesson on wildlife conservation. Perhaps they were convincing their parents not to throw cigarette butts out of their car windows, in the spirit of both Smokey Bear and Woodsy Owl. Or perhaps, as will be examined in Chapter Five, they were enjoying the last hurrah of a truly free-range childhood.

CHAPTER FIVE

ALONG THE HIGH LINE

In visiting various housing developments, I have been puzzled by a curious fact about children's play areas. The children seem to play somewhere else.[1]

—William H. Whyte

In 1968, William H. Whyte, editor and advocate for urban open space, commented on a phenomenon apparent since the turn of the century: children rarely played where adults thought they should and generally scorned play spaces specifically developed for their use. In the early years of the twentieth century, interested observers noted that children avoided purpose-built playgrounds like the plague, preferring to frequent vacant lots and other locations of their own choosing.[2] In post–World War II America, that situation continued, with children neglecting those spaces adults designed for them—but seemingly without their desires in mind. Whyte wrote, "In most housing projects, private as well as public, the play areas appear to be designed by administrators. Administrators who dislike children. Everything is geared for order and ease of maintenance, and signs and fences are meant to keep the little beggars at bay. Some of the play areas look like small prison compounds, and not wholly by inadvertence."[3] Not surprisingly, children were everywhere else, playing in streets, vacant lots and other "nonplanned" places, as opposed to the planned ones many adults preferred.[4]

Although reformers such as Whyte advocated for the creation of more imaginative, friendlier spaces for children and touted the adoption of European inventions, such as adventure playgrounds, America's children at midcentury continued to do what they had always done: they appropriated their favorite play places, taking over vacant lands or making use of places for which adults had other, more grown-up purposes.[5] These places were often aesthetically unappealing to grown-up eyes: busy streets, vacant lots and other waste lands, littered, untidy and chaotic. As naturalist Robert Michael Pyle wrote in his autobiographical account, *The Thunder Tree*, children had an affinity for these landscapes. "They are places of initiation, where the borders between ourselves and other creatures break down, where the earth gets under our nails and a sense of place gets under our skin. They are the secondhand lands, the hand-me-down habitats where you have to look hard to find something to love."[6] Children, who had the time to explore and examine such places in detail, were able to see and appreciate the anthills pushing up through the cracks in the concrete and the flowers growing out from between chunks of asphalt.

Often, children had no other choice than to claim wastelands for themselves. In America's post–World War II building frenzy, millions of previously open acres became a part of the nation's suburban sprawl. Many of these new communities had little in the way of parkland.[7] (Or, as Whyte argued, planners had developed parklands with something other than children's needs in mind.) Indeed, builders like Arthur Levitt, the father of the Levittowns, expected that each family's property would eventually become a park unto itself.[8] Children looking for more appealing places to play appropriated their neighborhoods' undeveloped tracts, only to lose them to the next round of bulldozers and building. In 1962, a seven-year-old California boy wrote to President John F. Kennedy, lamenting the loss of his neighborhood's open spaces: "Dear Mr President we Have no Place to go when we want to go out in the canyon Because there are going to Build houses So could you setaside some land where we could Play? thank you four listening love scott."[9] With sanctioned play spaces unavailable or unappealing, children pleaded for open space to call their own.

Children were not alone in their pleas for open space. William Whyte was not the only adult who was listening. In 1956, planners Alvin Lukashok and Kevin Lynch appealed to their peers to consider the children as they developed urban spaces. After interviewing a number of MIT students about their childhood preferences, they noted that youngsters did, indeed, have deeply held convictions about what kind of spaces they preferred. In their conclusions they commented, "The child wants variety with a chance for some adventure; he has a strong need to act upon the physical environment, to be stimulated by it, and to realize his imaginative fantasies through it." They had their doubts about the ability of the modern urban landscape to meet those needs.[10] Parents chimed in, too. In 1966, Margo Tupper, a mother angry at the loss of her children's play places to development, penned a book-length appeal for open spaces titled *No Place to Play*. On page one, she wrote, "If you are planning a trip to the scenes of your childhood to show your children the play places of your youth—DON'T! The chances are that they are not there any more. When you have been long away from your home place the changes that have taken place can be shocking, cataclysmic."[11] Although parents often moved to the suburbs "for the children's sake," the undeveloped, open and park-like environs they sought were in turn destroyed by the next wave of parents, seeking the same environmental amenities for their children.[12] Urban and suburban open space was disappearing at an alarming rate, as development gobbled up acre upon acre of land, leaving children with remarkably few places to play.

Nonetheless, in many locations, urban wild places persisted, offering children an alternative to the planned and scripted play places preferred by developers, city planners and others primarily concerned with issues of liability. The urban wild place at the center of this chapter is metropolitan Denver's High Line Canal. This is the second-hand land with which Robert Pyle fell in love; it was this author's own favorite haunt in childhood. From the 1950s through the 1980s, the canal was one of Denver's premier play places, in spite of its many limitations. Basically an unadorned irrigation ditch with its adjacent access road, its beauty was in the eye of the beholder. The water only ran during a few weeks per year, and people disposed of all manner of garbage along and within it. When the water ran, it was an opaque brown. Nevertheless, the canal had all of the features necessary to a great play place: water (at least some of the time), dirt, shade and seclusion. It provided one of the necessities of child life (at least from the point of view of midcentury youngsters): an opportunity to gather and play, relatively free from the observation and restrictions of adults. In the second half of the twentieth century, the High Line experienced a transition common to most remaining urban wild places: a transformation from preferred playground to adult-oriented recreational space, with little or no place for children.

The High Line Canal's origins had nothing to do with recreation. It began its life as an irrigation ditch, running from the South Platte River near the foothills of the Rocky Mountains to farmers on the eastern plains. Construction on the canal lasted from the spring of 1880 to the fall of 1883, and the Northern Colorado Irrigation Company received water rights to the South Platte River in December of 1884. The completed canal wandered along for seventy-one miles, across only twenty-five miles of the plains as the crow flies.[13] At the Platte, the High Line is seven feet deep and forty feet wide. As it nears its end, it is only four and a half feet deep, and twenty feet wide. Its optimistic designers envisioned it carrying more than 1,200 cubic feet of water per second out of the Platte.[14] First and foremost, the canal served an agricultural purpose. Its builders' intentions were purely practical. As a practical matter, though, the canal served its purpose rather poorly. Although at the time of its construction it was the longest irrigation canal in

Colorado, the High Line never fulfilled its promise of successfully watering the semi-arid plains.

Unlined earthen canals lose a great deal of water to seepage, and in a semi-arid environment, to evaporation as well. Cottonwood trees soon grew up along its banks, sucking up even more precious water. Unpredictable rainfall also led to nearly constant litigation over water rights.[15] The Northern Colorado Irrigation Company never acquired more than "junior rights" to the waters of the Platte, meaning that those with more senior rights always received first dibs, particularly in dry years.[16] Farmers learned quickly that the water was unreliable. John Bowen, who farmed along the canal first with his father and then with his wife, experienced the drought of 1952–1953. That season, the High Line delivered water for precisely one day, forcing the family to sell its cattle.[17] Such stories were not unusual.[18] Eventually, the canal came under the control of the Denver Water Board and served a dwindling number of customers. By 2000, only sixty-seven individuals still held water rights in the High Line, and the last twenty-two miles served only five customers.[19] Major holders of water rights included such nonfarm interests as the Wellshire Country Club, Fairmount Cemetery and the Rocky Mountain Arsenal.[20] The canal no longer really served an agricultural purpose.

Year by year, as the canal's agricultural purpose waned, its recreational potential grew. There was no general public access to the High Line before 1970, but by that time, many communities had grown up along its course. Additionally, the service road along the canal offered interesting possibilities. Even though the canal was not officially open for public recreational use, the canal drew children into its intriguing green environs. As mentioned in the second chapter, streams, rivers and lakes seem to have a magnetic pull on children, no matter how unappetizing and filthy they may appear to adult eyes. Children flocked to New York City's East River, in spite of its unappealing smell and look. They waded, swam and played amidst garbage, rats and sewage. The somewhat cleaner High Line Canal had a similar effect on children in its reach. After all, it was as close to a river as many metro Denver children had. As naturalist Robert Pyle wrote, "Denizens of the Great American Desert, we were drawn to water wherever it was to be found. We gravitated to plastic wading pools. We sought out lawn sprinklers, broken hydrants, and warm rainwater running ankle-deep in concrete gutters of the streets. But the slippery brown flow of the canal was best."[21] The High Line's water was anything but clean and clear, and it only ran during irrigating season. In the spring, fed by run-off from the mountains, the water was icy cold. Full of water in some seasons, but dry in most, its banks were covered with plants encouraged by the periodic wetness of the canal. Cottonwoods, that staple tree growing along watercourses in semi-arid environments, proliferated. There were also wild plums, chokecherries and any number of other western plants.

Brown water aside, the canal could be an appealing location, but the restrictions on its use were significant. First and foremost, the High Line existed as an irrigation ditch. In the 1930s, the Denver Board of Water Commissioners allowed only very limited recreational use of the High Line and its environs. By special agreement with the Department of Improvements and Parks of Cherry Hills Village, the Cherry Hills Saddle Club obtained permission to use portions of the maintenance road along the canal as a bridle path, provided that Cherry Hills Village maintained the bridle path and did not interfere with the operation of the canal as an irrigation ditch. Cherry Hills Village also assumed "all responsibility of any kind or nature incident to the use of said bridle paths by the public."[22] The right to use the maintenance road did not extend, however, to other users. The Denver Water Board employed ditch riders, one of whose jobs was to discourage trespassing, but the children came anyway.[23]

From 1933 to 1951, Mae Swan Woodruff grew up along the High Line. Her father was one of those ditch riders, working for the Denver Water Board, and her family lived in a home provided by the board. Although an important part of his job was to "'shoo' out any kids who attempted to walk or play along" the canal, Mae was free to enjoy the High Line from the age of seven onwards. As a ditch rider's child, what was forbidden to others was permitted to her. Her father found a small rowboat abandoned in the canal, and repaired and painted it so that she would have her own watercraft for exploration. "It was great fun. . . . The Highline was a very beautiful, peaceful place. The trees lined it/leaned over the water, there were plants, vines, wild flowers. In places it was nearly like rowing along a jungle river." She also borrowed her father's hip boots to go into a pond along the canal and look for crawdads and minnows. She sought out shady spots in which to read. In the winter, she enjoyed ice skating in the canal and sledding down its banks. It was her all-season playground, and a bit of a lifesaver, as she was an only child and permitted few friends. Her father taught her some basic safety rules, and the canal became her very own. She commented, "I never had supervision."[24]

Other youngsters found a playground in the canal as well. In the wake of World War II, Craig Barnes's parents brought him and his brothers from

Denver to a small farm along the canal in Arapahoe County, in what would eventually become Centennial. At the time, however, their place was well beyond Denver's limits, "a couple of acres next to a sumptuous brown irrigation canal lined by great shuddering green cottonwoods."[25] In the 1940s, the canal and its cottonwoods lured city people out for picnics along the water. They also lured teenagers out for somewhat more dubious activities, the canal always being a bit of a lovers' lane.[26] The children in Barnes's rural neighborhood also used the canal—or what they called the ditch—as their own private swimming hole, in spite of mothers who objected to the filthy water that ran through it. Barnes's friend, Arnie Coughlin, taunted him into the freezing water one early spring day. Arnie made his case in favor of swimming:

> On the first day . . . when the ditch has to be washed out, there is going to be dead sheep. Sure. But to say that a person don't have no right to swim in the Highline Canal just because once't there was a dead sheep is just dumb. . . . This first day when the ditch runs there are always logs and boards and pop cans and such, but they don't never hurt nobody. . . . Except maybe city kids.[27]

The jibe about city kids was pointed enough to get Barnes into the ditch, in spite of the brown water, blobbed with "fluffy yellow creamy foam."[28] The water was far too cold to be enjoyable, but Barnes had to dive in to prove his credentials as a country kid.

At other times, visiting the canal was a far more pleasurable experience. When the water level fell, Barnes and his brothers scooped bewildered trout out of the fast-drying puddles. When the canal was more or less completely dry, they rode horses in its cool depths.[29] Another, perhaps less common activity was learning to rappel from the heights of the cottonwood trees that grew along the canal's banks.[30] In defiance of their mothers, who often feared polio, the local boys went swinging over the canal on a gunnysack filled with straw, dropping into the canal's dirty depths.[31] Young Craig Barnes defined himself in relation to the canal that wound its way around his family's little farm. He thought of himself as the "Highline King." Identities, however, could be destroyed, if a young person's relationship to a treasured place was disturbed, and that is what happened to Barnes's attachment to the canal. A stranger named Carlos Rhea chose to commit suicide not far from the Barnes house, and two of the Barnes boys found his body. It was a sobering, deeply disturbing event. Craig Barnes's reign as the High Line King was over. As Barnes remembered, "Carlos Rhea took away the ditch and the hawks and the pheasants and the golden grain in the world around me."[32]

Barnes would never feel the same warmth for the canal again; not long after, his family left Colorado for a long sojourn abroad.

Craig Barnes was not the only youngster to feel the pull of the canal. In the 1950s and 1960s, entomologist and naturalist Robert Michael Pyle grew up near the High Line Canal in Hoffman Heights, beyond Aurora but within commuting distance of Denver. Like Barnes, he fell in love with "the ditch" despite its obvious shortcomings, such as its weediness and dirtiness. Given that he was growing up "on the wrong side of Denver to reach the mountains easily or often," the canal was his "sanctuary, playground, and sulking walk. It was also my imaginary wilderness, escape hatch, and birthplace as a naturalist."[33] His experiences were much like those of Craig Barnes. After discovering the canal with his brother at age seven, he had more or less free rein to visit, although his mother wanted them to stay on the banks, out of the water. Parents associated the canal with death by drowning, injuries from broken glass and debris, and infection with polio. The first two were serious if intermittent hazards, the third was not.[34] Part of the temptation of the place was that it was forbidden: "No Trespassing signs, posted by landowners and the Denver Water Department, drew us on."[35] The canal would be the location for many adventures throughout Pyle's growing-up years.

Pyle wrote "I sought out the winding, cottonwood-shaded watercourse for purposes of exploration and play alone and with friends; discovery of crawdads, birds and butterflies; sulking and kicking the dust through a troubled home life; hiding, camping, fort building, stealing corn, cooking out, and pretending every kind of life in the out-of-doors; and ultimately, walking and parking and petting with girlfriends."[36] Pyle credited his career as a biologist to his early years on the canal, and the curiosity and familiarity with nature that his experiences inculcated. "It was the place that made me," he asserted. Pyle wrote, "Had it not been for the High Line Canal, the vacant lots I knew, the scruffy park, I'm not at all certain I would have been a biologist. . . . The total immersion in nature baptized me in a faith that never wavered."[37] While Craig Barnes came away from his experience of the canal largely with loving memories, Robert Pyle found his life's work as he examined the many creatures making their home along the High Line.

Like any other really good play place, the canal could be anything. It could be a place to challenge one's fears, a place to exercise the imagination or the body, or perhaps a place to study for one's vocation. There was far more to these places than usually met the adult eye. As Robert Pyle wrote, "Nothing is less empty to a curious, exploring child than a vacant lot, nothing less wasted than waste ground, nothing more richly simmered in promise than raw ground."[38] What was important was it was there, and it was available. What was true for the urban playground was equally true for urban wild lands, "kids need habitat right there, underfoot."[39] Then (and perhaps even more so now) they could not be expected to find play places miles from home. The closer the resource was to a child's backyard, the more likely he or she would be to make use of it. And find the High Line they did.

As development along the High Line continued, child after child discovered its uses. David Von Drehle, whose family lived over a chain-link fence from the canal in Aurora, composed an encyclopedic list of the many uses to which the High Line Canal and its accompanying trail could be put. As Von Drehle demonstrated, children could take that space as far as their imaginations could send them. He enumerated:

> Fort building, fighting dirt-clod wars, sledding and 'skiing,' embarking on epic hikes, playing with knives and bb guns, playing with matches, building various failed rafts, running away from home, tree-climbing, rope-swinging, chasing birds/butterflies/snakes/frogs, exploring for hidden treasures, archeology, reenacting the Civil War and World War II, sneaking looks at scandalous materials like *Mad* magazine and *Playboy*, attempting to convert a tree stump into an Apollo spacecraft, attempting to forecast the weather, attempting to smoke cattails (by lighting the fluff and sucking on the reed), bridge-building, dam-building, wading and mud-fighting, the collecting of leaves/rocks/sticks/items of garbage, digging holes to China, fruitless but exhilarating jack rabbit hunts, lost golf-ball collecting, picnicking, kite-flying, strafing and bombing flotsam with rocks and dirt-clods, jogging, biking, skateboarding, horseback riding, treehouse constructing, ice hockey, speed-skating, hide-and-seek, approximately one million hours of crawdad fishing, trying and failing to get girls to kiss us.[40]

Some of these activities, such as perusing forbidden reading, could have happened at home, but were made easier by the privacy the canal afforded. Other of these activities, such as raft building, could only have happened on the canal, the only available water in this corner of dusty suburban Denver. Von Drehle's list ran the gamut from purely physical recreation to journeys of the mind. Canal experiences could also be either entirely solitary or intensely social. While some youngsters saw it as a place for quiet contemplation and deep thought, even more used the space with friends and siblings, building the tight bonds that could be forged in the sharing of imaginative outdoor fun.[41]

Many remembered the canal as the site of epic building efforts. The cottonwoods provided a particularly inviting venue for forts and tree houses of all shapes and sizes. Dan Hoglund, whose family lived near Bible Park, remembered the structures as "a kind of communal property." As children matured and left behind their tree-climbing ways, their younger brothers, sisters and neighbors were waiting to take over and make them their own.

> One generation or group of kids would take ownership for awhile, building better ways to access the upper branches, and using it for their enjoyment. There would be steps nailed in ladderlike fashion to get you up to a platform or resting place. Forts and treehouses were built with leftover plywood and found objects. There were rope swings fashioned. 'Keep Out,' and 'No Girls Allowed' signs posted. Then, when our group/generation of kids stopped using them, they were taken over and improved by the next.[42]

No one, of course, paid attention to the water board's stern admonitions against the building of forts and tree houses.

For other youngsters, recreation along the canal was all about getting wet. Then and now, the water department strictly forbade floating on the canal. No one was to go into the water. Nevertheless, it was a favorite activity among children, and especially teens. They built rafts and "makeshift platforms" for the purpose, in addition to using inner tubes. As a group of friends remembered, "The Canal was about waist deep, had a constant gentle current, and made for a great way to spend a summer afternoon. On one memorable occasion, about 10 of us had decided to do a 'midnight float.' We headed down to the Holly Bridge, put in, and in all of our excitement, ended up making too much noise, and got kicked out by the police." Interestingly enough, the youngsters had embarked on their adventure with their parents' permission.[43] Although ultimately a truncated trip, they remembered it fondly.

Children exercised their imaginations as they made their way along the canal. For lovers of the *Little House* books, the canal could be the location for many a pioneering adventure, heading west into unknown territory.[44] Other literary adventures beckoned as well. As one woman remembered, "Friends and I pretended we were Alice in Wonderland and some of my fondest memories were getting lost down rabbit holes, the smell of the Russian olive trees and the soft sand between our toes when there was no water in the canal."[45] The idea of what *could* happen also figured prominently in her adventures, in almost biblical fashion. "We created drama for ourselves by

Many a creature, in this case a salamander, could be found on the High Line Canal. Photograph by permission of Mary Thompson Riney.

imagining that the water was going to come rushing down the canal at any moment and we be swept out to sea. It was my idea of heaven as a young child."[46] The Labak sisters took their imagination in a different direction: "We'd pretend to have spa mud treatments by smearing canal mud all over our arms and legs."[47] For others, as enchanting as the mud was the "snow" that the cottonwoods shed in early summer, which "was always a delight."[48] Dustan Osborn floated down the canal, imagining a wilder world. "Magpies watched and my fantasies saw more wild animals than were there."[49] The canal could become anything a child wanted it to be.

The detritus of the High Line inevitably ended up at home. Mothers found some of it quite welcome, such as the wild asparagus, plums, choke-cherries and other bounty that could be gathered along the banks. The remains of abandoned gardens also took root there, such as rhubarb.[50] Other "treasures" were perhaps not so welcome. As Dan Hoglund remembered, "We would catch crawdads along the muddy sides and bottom when it was shallow and bring them home. I don't really remember what we would do with them. Probably scare the little kids and put them into the sink or bathtub to scare mom and then, since I love all animals and would never hurt anything, probably take them back to their home in the canal."[51] Other chil-

This salamander, named Hobart, was a beauty. Photograph by permission of Mary Thompson Riney.

dren, with and without their mothers' permission, cooked and ate the craw-dads they captured.[52] The canal was also home to salamanders, frogs from modest to awesome size and numerous other creatures that often came home with the children.[53] Joan Chiang's children brought home bees, bull snakes and muddy clothes.[54] High Line mothers ignored or tolerated a good deal of dirt and disorder.

The parents of the 50s, 60s, 70s, and 80s had a remarkably relaxed attitude toward their children's use of the High Line Canal. Most parents laid out some basic rules of behavior, such as demanding that children use the buddy system or stay out of the water when it was running high. Young children had more rules than older children, and girls more than boys. Some parents, who otherwise gave their children free run of the canal when empty, were careful to reinforce the message that the canal, when running full, was a dangerous place. Scott Riney, who grew up directly across the street from the canal, remembered his parents' admonitions. "They did impress upon me that I should not go into the water when the canal was full, because of the strength of the current. Dad pointed out to me that our golden retriever, Beau, couldn't make headway swimming against the current. If he couldn't, I couldn't." They emphasized the same lesson when one of the neighborhood children released the parking brake on his parents' Volkswagen bus, causing it to roll across the street and into the canal. "The current turned it 90 degrees, and it started to float downstream. . . . The car had to be pulled out by a tow truck. We all thought it was pretty funny, but the moral of the story was that the current was surprisingly strong."[55] The message was simple and direct; running water was dangerous.

Once they had delivered their messages about safety, parents went about their business and allowed their children to go about theirs. As one woman remembered, "They did not require adult supervision, but they did want some accountability."[56] Fern Marston, whose children played along the canal from roughly 1969 to 1979, noted, "I let my children play unsupervised and I did not worry about them although I have learned since that I probably should have worried a little bit. . . . If I lived there with a young family now I would worry about them and would probably move."[57] But these, for the most part, were not the concerns of the 1960s and 1970s, and children did a good job of hiding the canal's dangers from their parents. Interestingly, the parents who seemed to have had the most qualms were those whose children did not roam the canal on a regular basis. Doug Miller and his siblings visited his grandfather's house on the High Line often, and his grandfather even led Boy Scouts on regular boat trips down the canal. Doug's mother, however, tried to keep her children away from the water. As he remembered, "We actually didn't use the canal all that much that I can recall. I think my mother was nervous about our getting dirty and/or hurt."[58] While the grandfather wanted his grandsons to play in the canal, their mother did not, and she largely prevailed.

Most of the time, children played along the canal in relative safety. Predictably, however, there were accidents both small and large. One man remembered "There were some broken bones. A LOT of cuts and scrapes and bruises. Some concussions." The youngsters tried to deal with as many injuries as they could by themselves but occasionally experienced problems that "required the intervention of adults, which we tried to avoid at all costs."[59] A persistent theme of protecting parents from knowledge of the dangers of the canal runs through people's reflections on those years. Darryl Harris avoided telling his parents when he and his bicycle tumbled into the canal. "I crashed into the canal when it was full of water once when riding my bicycle too fast from the steep hill on E. Dickenson Pl. . . . It was like a right of passage to do this hill. . . . I also lost my bike in the deep water and remember lying about it."[60]

Dunstan Osborn, too, knew that his activities were dangerous. Among his friends, the canal was the location for epic fireworks battles. "One fourth of July we got a bunch of Roman candles and had a war. Trees and the Canal bank were good hiding places and we reconnoitered where the enemy was then shot off fireworks at each other. No one died, but surely we tempted fate. Had my parents known of this, I might have been kept closer to home."[61] Kim Miller Bierman and her friends literally played with fire.

> There was an old silo building that we darned near killed ourselves in one day when we thought it would be brilliant to build a fire in there. When we realized what a bad idea it was, we covered our little fire with a piece of flagstone to put it out. The smoke filled the silo so fast we were all trying to climb up the little ladder at the same time to get out. I remember the bigger boys hauling us up and out without us even using the ladder.[62]

Because these activities did not end in disaster, they could be kept hidden from parents, who otherwise might have forbidden their children from playing along the canal.

Other youngsters were not so lucky. Because of the severity of their accidents, parents could not help but know about their misadventures. Benjamin Fitzpatrick's feats of daring landed him in the hospital. About his experiences, he wrote, "The only time I got hurt, the ditch was empty. We had a cable that ran across the ditch on which was a pulley device called the 'space trolley' that you could hang on. You pushed off one tree it was anchored to and crossed the ditch, then pushed back off the tree on the other side. One afternoon the cable snapped when I was doing this and fell on my back onto the sandy bottom of the ditch. I spent the night in Children's Hospital, but suffered no more than a sore back."[63] Deborah Spencer grew up along the canal in the 1950s, and knew of two deaths among neighborhood children, one of whom was swinging and fell and broke his neck. Another child fell into the water, was washed away and drowned. Both events dampened her enthusiasm for playing in and along the High Line.[64] A generation later, children were still involved in the same sorts of accidents. In 1978, a Littleton youth mistook a diversion bridge, used for water flow control, for a footbridge, and fell a considerable distance, resulting in facial cuts and bruises, as well as oral and dental injuries.[65] In 1980, a Denver girl fell from her horse into the canal, and drowned.[66] Like any play space, dangers and potential dangers abounded.

Children's experiences with the canal evolved as they grew, and with greater age came greater pushing of boundaries. The innocence of crawdad hunting often gave way to more "mature" activities, often to the chagrin of those living nearby. In the late 1940s, Bill and Eleanor Foley purchased approximately eleven acres of land adjacent to the High Line in undeveloped Arapahoe County. Although their home was at that time in the country, teenagers found their section of the canal and used it as the location for many an unauthorized party. In her memoirs, Eleanor Foley noted the "aggravations caused by humankind. Initially the High Line Canal road, unpoliced and secluded, provided refuge for all manner of transgressors. Lovers parked behind the house to avoid detection by patrol cars on South Quebec." The lovers' lane, however, was the least of the homeowners' worries: "We had all sorts of problems with young people clamoring behind the house and among the trees. The spot became a hideaway where they could indulge in smoking marijuana, drinking liquor, and using other drugs. Freed inhibitions meant they'd whoop it up, swinging across the canal on ropes they slung over the branches of giant cottonwood trees. Occasionally they'd lose their grip and plop in the water, which only heightened their glee."[67] The Foleys' protests resulted in the Water Board posting "no trespassing" signs and banning motor vehicles from the trail. With enforcement by the Arapahoe County Sheriff's department, automobile traffic on the canal eventually ceased, at least in the Foleys' location. [68]

Many youngsters lost interest or found the focus of their interest shifting as they grew. Although as a teenager Deborah Spencer continued to float in the canal occasionally, her love affair with the canal was more or less over. "We outgrew the imaginative games we played as children," she commented.[69] Don Drake, whose family lived in Littleton, recalled that his children seemed to lose interest with the canal at about age sixteen, "when cars and the opposite sex became important in their lives."[70] Little did he know that the canal could be incorporated into teenaged experiences with the opposite sex. Donna Judish, his daughter, succinctly commented that unbeknownst to her father, "it was a great place to make out."[71] For Andrea Labak, it was a place to steal away to smoke.[72] When Stacy Norton Wareham was a teen, the canal offered her a degree of privacy unavailable elsewhere. "As I grew older, and without my parents knowledge, I would often sneak out in the middle of the night especially during a full moon just to walk on the canal. I loved nature and felt called to it."[73] David Von Drehle, who grew up in Aurora and spent many hours along the canal in the 1960s and 1970s, noted, "The canal was for friends and for being alone. This was because what happened on the canal stayed on the canal. It was best if family didn't know too many details."[74] Parents, who, of course, had once been young themselves, probably had a pretty good idea of the kinds of activities that could be taking place along the canal's secluded banks. Most of the time, though, they chose not to ask too many questions.[75]

It was not a sense of danger and misbehavior that predominated in people's memories of their young adventures along the High Line, however. Instead, it was a sense that this was a special place, and for many, their favorite place in their neighborhood. For Benjamin Fitzpatrick, it was a place that meant warm weather and freedom.

> The very best memory relates to some undated spring morning. . . . I was still sound asleep when one of my brothers shouted up from downstairs: 'The ditch is in!' I can not describe the youthful excitement this engendered. It meant a whole season of fun on the ditch had begun. . . . Tubing, jumping off our tire swing into the water, throwing sticks for our dogs to fetch from the water. We had a blast. Of course, the sunny warm weather added to the mix. And it was all pent up in that waking moment.[76]

Kim Miller Bierman's description of a kiss experienced on a branch over the canal carried the same sense of wonder and excitement about the canal as a place. "It wasn't my first kiss, but it was by far the best because it was unexpected, and it happened in my favorite place on earth."[77] Years later, the canal inspired a deep feeling of attachment.

For many others, the canal had a strong feature of "otherness." While the city and suburbs might predominate in their lives, the canal provided them an alternative. A group of friends remembered, "During the 60s and even into the 70s, living near the canal gave us a feeling of 'country' even though we were living in the big city."[78] Rachel Myron, who grew up in Littleton but chose to live her adult life in remote locations in Alaska, had much the same sense. "Everything else in our world was manicured, mapped and known. Sidewalks and paved suburban streets, mowed lawns, two car garages, and neatly painted houses—one next to another. The canal was our unknown, our wild . . . our wilderness."[79] For some, the childhood associations were so strong that they precluded a continuing adult relationship with the place. "For a kid it was paradise within the city—a place to run free for hours. . . . I've never been back across the canal since I moved because civilization got to it."[80] While the canal remains, many of the open fields that once surrounded it are gone, sacrificed to the dramatic growth the Denver area experienced following World War II. Craig Barnes's family's acres are now in the midst of town. In many locations, the landscape surrounding the High Line Canal in the 1980s and 1990s bore only the slightest resemblance to what had been there twenty, thirty or forty years before.

Given its allure, the High Line Canal and its accompanying trail were probably fated to become a public amenity. As all of these accounts would suggest, respect for the canal as private property tended to be a little thin. Those adults with a stake in the canal as an irrigation ditch worked hard to try to keep the kids out of the canal. Robert Pyle described their exertions in Aurora. "The water company men told us to scram, while the landowners slung barbed wire across the canal on wicked, branchy poles to snag our inner tubes. More than once we looked down their double barrels. The shotguns were just for show, but we didn't know that and skittered away like pink water striders."[81] David Von Drehle never faced a farmer with a shotgun but experienced the wrath of the water board's ditch riders:

> The Denver water board's official position was that the canal was off-limits, and men would patrol the road in scary green trucks. We'd scatter or hide at the sight of them—which was easy because you could see the plume of dust from a half-mile off. But even though the Green Truck Man would occasionally scold our parents over the back fence for letting us run loose, I think all the adults understood that this was just too wonderful a resource, too magnetic, for kids to keep away from it.[82]

Although before 1970 the water board prohibited most recreational use of the canal, parents knew their children played there and approved. John Prescott and his friends used the canal in the pre-1970 period, and two neighborhood fathers, including his own, regularly inspected tree houses and tree swings for safety, with veto power over any design that was "too radical."[83] Other youngsters simply learned how to evade the water board's rules, putting up and taking down their rope swings on a daily basis.[84]

Other adults undermined the farmers' and the water department's interests in different ways. They, like their children, appropriated the canal for their own recreational purposes. Robert Pyle's father sometimes joined his sons for cookouts along the canal.[85] A Boy Scout leader used the canal for impromptu floats and other water activities.[86] A mother took her young children for bicycle rides along the canal even though it was not, technically, open for that type of activity. In a letter to the Denver Water Board, she argued for greater public access to the watercourse, writing that the use of the "foot, bike or horse path should be a considerable benefit to those who wish to use the country but do not live in the country."[87] Another mother who also took her baby along the canal for bike rides particularly enjoyed her daughter's "delight upon seeing the horses, cows and other animals" grazing along the ditch.[88] As the canal snaked through Cherry Hills Village,

People used the water in the canal (in this case, to train a hunting dog) even though it was against the rules. Photograph by permission of Mary Thompson Riney.

women could be found floating along the canal in tubes and galvanized tubs, playing bridge or sipping sherry as they went.[89] A father who actually worked for the Denver Water Board trained his hunting dogs in the water.[90] It was clear that it was not just children who appreciated the canal as a community resource; adults had a stake in the canal's use as well. Negotiations with the Denver Water Board began.

The path toward recreational use agreements was not direct. As late as 1967, the Denver Water Board entirely rejected the idea. When Glen Stenson, director of recreation services for the South Suburban Metropolitan Recreation and Park District (hereafter South Suburban) wrote to the water board, suggesting opening the maintenance road for "recreational use of hiking, horseback riding and bicycle riding," the Engineering Division dismissed the idea out of hand, writing, "Until such time as the use of the High Line Canal for conveyance of irrigation water is no longer required, it is not possible to consider recreational use of this property."[91] The objections extended beyond the water board's engineers. As one local paper, the *Littleton Independent*, began agitating for the canal trail's opening to bikers and horseback riders, property owners began voicing their disapproval. They objected to the possibility that motor vehicles might make their way onto the path, thereby violating their privacy and property rights. They objected to the possibility of dust, dirt, noise, garbage and the use of the area as a "lover's lane."[92]

Local ranchers also submitted their objections. In spite of the fact that the area was supposed to be closed to trespassing, recreational users had wreaked havoc on private property. Picnickers had left gates open, allowing cattle to wander off. Vandals had opened irrigation headgates, flooding newly mown hay fields. Trash littered their fields, and "horse back riders [were] using our hay fields as rodeo grounds." Just as homeowners along the canal had protested, the "seclusion of the ditch" allowed youngsters to use the area for "immoral purposes." The idea of the High Line as a recreational amenity offended those whose livelihood depended upon its waters. One rancher wrote, "As a tax paying user, we feel that our money should be used for upkeep and expenses in maintaining this right-of-way as an irrigation system not as a public play ground."[93]

The weight of public opinion, however, was in favor of recreational use of the High Line. The larger canal-coveting public vastly outnumbered the concerned ranchers and homeowners adjacent to the ditch. Another local newspaper, the *Arapahoe Herald*, echoed the majority's sentiments: "Its potential for recreation and native beauty is great; it will be a loss to the entire area if it continues to be closed off from the public by gates and more gates."[94] Others who loved the canal launched their own efforts. Robert Pyle, who would eventually write about his own High Line experiences in *The Thunder Tree*, campaigned for the preservation of portions of the canal in Aurora. He proposed creation of a "canal conservancy" dedicated to the preservation of the High Line as urban wild space. He asked that the canal corridor be kept as a place apart,

> where a biology class can study a living community, an Audubon member can go to list birds, or a business-man or housewife can go for a peaceful, leisurely and convenient walk, while reflecting on the abundance of wonderful living things in this strange place between the mountains and the plains; where a roaming child can discover Nature nearby, as I did ten years and more ago; and most of all . . . to establish a living ethic of conservation in Aurora.[95]

Pyle's childhood experiences fueled his desire to see the canal converted into a public amenity, enjoyed by a wide variety of users.

In 1970, South Suburban was able to come to an agreement with the Denver Water Board, and the City of Aurora soon followed. The park districts began maintaining the service road through the communities they served. The City of Denver followed.[96] The negotiations, however, were for the use of the canal's access road, not for use of the water. The water board carefully spelled out the limits of recreational use: "'Public recreational use or purpose' means use for horseback riding, bicycling, picknicking [sic], hiking and similar activities. Swimming and the use of all motor vehicles, including motorized bicycles, scooters and go-karts shall be prohibited at all times, except as the use thereof may be required for law enforcement and maintenance purposes."[97] The preservation of the High Line's waters for irrigation remained paramount. In the semi-arid west, where every drop of water belonged (and still belongs) to someone, the canal's waters continued to be private property.

With this transition came rules, although their enforcement tended to be somewhat hit or miss. The Parks and Recreation Districts strictly forbade some activities, such as the building of tree houses and the hanging of swings. Nobody wanted the liability that would result from children falling out of structures or swings onto property for which they were responsible, and when maintenance workers found tree houses and swings, they removed them as quickly as possible. There were no exceptions, although some parents tried to bend the rules on their children's behalf. A Littleton father wrote to the water board, concerned about South Suburban's demand that he remove a tree swing adjacent to his property. He argued that "the swing is a great source of enjoyment to my children and their guests. The swing is locked when not in use and is generally supervised during use." He also offered "to hold harmless the Denver Water Board for any injuries and/or liability which would be incurred as a result of this tree swing." In response, the water board issued a strongly worded "Tree Swing Memo" reiterating its adamant refusal to allow such activities. "If we make an exception in this case, it weakens the whole agreement, and destroys our credibility with the management entities." Penciled in at the bottom of the memo was the parting comment, "No Tree Swings!!!" The father glumly complied.[98]

Although parks administrators generally enforced water board regulations and forbade tubing and swimming, favorite activities among children and teens, they sometimes forgot their own rules. In 1971, the manager of the water board wrote to Ray Printz, executive director of South Suburban. South Suburban had erected signs along the canal stating "Tubing, inflatable rafts, canoeing and other non-motorized boating permitted only with U.S. Coast Guard approved life jackets or life belts in use," implying that the parks district and water board allowed this kind of use. This clearly violated the agreement with the water board, which "prohibits all boating except in instances mutually agreed upon." Additionally, Denver's health department, Tri-County Health, discovered that physical contact with the water was inadvisable, because of its polluted condition.[99] Although individuals and groups (especially Boy and Girl Scouts) often just got into the water with their boats and went, the water board officially allowed these trips rarely.[100] Preventing liability problems and preserving private water rights meant forbidding unnecessary contact with dirty, fast-moving water. Turbidity, chemicals from run-off, and human and animal fecal contamination rendered the water suspect.[101] The official line was, "Considering the contamination of the waters in the canal it is inconceivable that anyone would consider using the waters for body contact recreation of any type."[102] What the water board wanted to encourage was the dry and orderly use of the canal: walking, biking and leisurely horseback riding along the canal trail.[103] Since there were no regular patrols of the High Line, however, enforcement of these regulations remained a hit-or-miss proposition.

Over time, however, that became a less and less relevant issue. The days of free-range children running riot along the canal, or in any other urban wild space, are largely over. By some time in the 1980s, 1990 at the latest, the children gradually stopped going to the canal by themselves to play. As the water board paved larger and larger portions of the trail, slower-paced children's activities gave way to fast-paced running and biking by adults.[104] This change coincided with cultural and environmental changes, such as the proliferation of malls, indoor playgrounds and other indoor spaces accessible to children. Houses became larger, and families increasingly installed central air-conditioning, making the prospect of playing at home more appealing. These developments also came at a time when the pleasures of the indoors proliferated, such as video games, VCRs and MTV. As a fourth-grader told a researcher, "'I like to play indoors better 'cause that's where all the electrical outlets are.'"[105] Children increasingly had enough privacy, and enough toys, in their own, indoor spaces that they no longer had to go outside to find a congenial place of their very own.[106]

This abandonment of free play in outdoor space also coincided with a sharp increase in parental anxiety about the dangers of unsupervised outdoor spaces. Unsupervised outdoor activity had always entailed a certain amount of risk, and play along the canal was no exception. Up to and through most of the 1970s, however, there was little parental panic about the dangers that menacing creatures, animal and human, might pose to their children as they played in the out-of-doors. By the end of the 1970s all of that would change. Media attention to the problem of missing children increased substantially in the late 1970s, with the first "milk carton" campaign intended to locate an abducted child launched in 1979.[107] Although the actual number of stranger abductions per year hovered between 500 and 600 nationwide, with approximately 50 of those children murdered, exaggerated reports of up to half a million abductions with 50,000 resulting in murders heightened parental fears. Although studies showed that children had far more to fear from their nearest and dearest than from strangers, parents responded by allowing their children less and less freedom outside of the family home.[108] Mothers no longer told their children to go outside and not come back until dark.

These attitudes affected the use of the canal. Throughout the 1980s, 1990s, and early 2000s, there was just enough bad publicity about the canal to convince parents that the High Line was a dangerous, or potentially dangerous, place for unaccompanied children. Increasingly, wildlife sightings raised concerns about the safety of using the canal trail. Coyotes, which had long been residents of the High Line Canal area, became bold, attacking small pets as they walked with their owners. As an animal control officer commented about the canal trail, "This is their highway. . . . They can move across the city along the canal."[109] Even more worrisome than the canal's coyotes were the larger predators that also appeared to be using the trail as their highway into and through the city. Mountain lion sightings began to appear in the news in 1992, causing state wildlife officials to warn users about keeping their pets and their children safe. In 1999, South Suburban posted temporary warning signs after a mountain lion sighting on the canal trail between Colorado Boulevard and Dahlia Street.[110] Periodically, bold and potentially dangerous animals made their presence known along the High Line.

Even more disturbing were the incidents of crime along the trail. For a seventy-one-mile-long, rather secluded trail, the criminal activity did not occur with any great frequency. Nonetheless, the incidents that did occur were reminders to parents that bad things could happen even in a bucolic setting. Disappearances, sexual assaults and other violent crimes appeared in the news. On July 16, 1984, seventeen-year-old Jennifer Anne Douglas left her Park Hill home to ride her new bicycle, never to be seen again. The search for the young woman focused on the High Line Canal trail.[111] Ten years later in 1994, a Denver County jury found Robert Glasgow, Jr., guilty of being the High Line Canal rapist. The moniker was somewhat misleading. Glasgow did not commit his crimes on the High Line, although he did use it to travel to the attacks, committed in 1993 and 1994.[112] An unknown assailant attacked a Heritage High School student, walking along the High Line in July of 1995, taking his money and knocking him unconscious.[113] Just four years later, a man walked through the High Line to gain access to an Arapahoe County home and raped and attempted to strangle a woman living there.[114] In 2001, another unknown assailant attacked and stabbed a Hinkley High School student who had gathered with others along the canal during lunch hour. It was an area where students often went at noon to visit and smoke.[115]

A 2003 crime particularly shocked the canal's users. A man armed with a stun gun and a gag abducted a female jogger from the High Line Canal trail and repeatedly raped her. Arrested, tried and convicted, Michael Jesso is now serving a sixty-five-years-to-life sentence.[116] While most of the previous sexual assaults had occurred in proximity to the canal, in this case, the rapist actually used the canal to stalk his victim. It was an opportune place to find women walking or running alone. This crime, like each of the others, was associated with a specific, short section of the canal, and after the 2004 attack, the Cherry Hills Village police reassured residents along that portion of the trail that "there were no violent crimes associated with either the trail, or any of the homes bordering it, in recent history." According to the police, walkers and joggers were more likely to encounter menacing wildlife (read coyotes) than hostile people. Even so, local residents took the attack as a warning. Angela Smith, who regularly used the trail with her thirteen-year-old daughter, said that in the future she would not allow her daughter to run ahead of her while they strolled.[117] A generation earlier, her daughter would have been playing alone or with other children in the same locations.

Parents who themselves played freely along the High Line as children did not give their own children the same freedom to explore their surroundings. David Von Drehle cherished his childhood experiences along the canal and would have liked to foster similar experiences in his own children. While living in the Washington, D.C., area, he and his children found Rock Creek.

> It reminded me so much of the canal. I took the kids down there from time to time and tried to let them roam free. But never REALLY free. I was always close enough to see and hear them, and they didn't get to decide when we went or when we came home. There was no chance to be devious and very limited chance (very limited) to take ill-advised risk and make educational mistakes.[118]

Von Drehle later moved his family to Kansas, to provide the children more freedom, but they still had far less opportunity to explore urban wild space than he had, growing up along the High Line.

John Prescott, who lived near and played in the canal from 1958 to 1970, still lives near the canal, but has allowed his own children little of the free play he experienced when he was young. He wrote: "We are still able to enjoy summer time walking and riding bikes along the canal. We have the beauty of fall and spring, with the lush big cottonwoods. We have winter time outings in the snow. However, it's not the same amount of use, and certainly not the same adventurous activities. No tree swings or forts allowed, and the monitoring of such is visible and frequent." His primary concern, like that of many parents, is that "strange adults" might pose a danger to his children.[119] Joseph Brookshire put it succinctly, "I can only wish my children had the freedom that I enjoyed. . . . It is a different Day and Age."[120]

At the turn of the twenty-first century, the Denver Water Board began to consider the future of the High Line. Its use as an irrigation ditch had dwindled into insignificance. In January 2001, 350 recreational users flocked to public meetings to express their concerns about the future of the canal. The flora and fauna along the High Line figured largely in the discussion, with people pleading for a large enough flow to meet the continuing needs of various forms of wildlife, especially the large cottonwoods growing along the trail. The preferences of adults riding bikes, walking for health, and walking their dogs also elicited serious concern and comment. Many expressed a desire to keep the canal as wild and unpaved as possible. Children's needs, however, had few advocates. A Littleton resident did argue for maintaining the canal as a location for youngsters learning to ride bicycles, "safe from traffic."[121] A small number of older users lobbied for their grandchildren's nature walks. As a Denver grandparent commented, "The canal is a sanctuary from the hullabaloo of urban life. I can take my grandson for peaceful walks and share nature as it exists in more rural parts of Colorado."[122] A handful of comments aside, children were curiously absent. In 2001, no one mentioned, or even seemed to imagine, the wants of High Line children past, who reveled in the canal as a place of vigorous, unstructured and independent play. No one mentioned children catching crawdads, building rafts, digging in sand or playing pioneers. That day had passed.

The imagined uses of urban wild space had changed dramatically. Margo Tupper grew up in Florida, and watched the conversion of the wild spaces of her youth into suburban tract housing. She wrote, "When I was a child it was not necessary for my parents to take us on long trips to seek out natural play places for us. They were right at our back door. Summertime meant complete freedom and play. We would race barefoot down to the lake where we would spend the day fishing, catching tadpoles, or finding turtle eggs buried in the sand." As a midcentury mother, she wanted her own children to enjoy those same experiences, but even in the 1960s, the opportunity was disappearing.[123] Over time, the High Line had changed, too. The open fields, small farms and vacant lots that had once surrounded the canal were gone. What remained, however, was the canal itself, winding through metropolitan Denver, largely dry, but still shaded by the cottonwoods that once were home to children's playhouses and swings. Unlike many places in the United States, the canal as an open space resource remained, but its use had changed several times and now served a completely different constituency than its builders had imagined.

By the late twentieth century, the High Line's open space had become an adult-oriented amenity, rather than a family- or child-oriented desire. When the opportunity came to discuss the canal's continued use, no one spoke out for the preservation of the canal as a site for free, unsupervised children's play. Even supervised play rated barely a mention. The outdoor children of the 1960s and 1970s became the indoor children of the 1980s, 1990s and 2000s. Threats that Tupper did not anticipate seem to have been the ones that killed the High Line as a children's play place. It's hard to say if the children responded more to push factors, such as the fears of parents, or pull factors, such as the lure of the television and the mall, but the open space used and cherished by adults has become empty space—as far as children are concerned. Children and teens choose other locations for their quiet contemplation, as well as their intensely social moments. Even purpose-built outdoor environments suffer from a dearth of children. Just like the playgrounds William Whyte observed, youngsters have largely abandoned the parks and playgrounds of today, unless herded there and supervised by parents and day-care providers.[124]

And if someone had spoken out for children's continued use of the canal, would anyone, adult or child have listened? The news does little to allay parents' fears, and cottonwood trees do less to entice children than the internet. Air conditioners supply most of the noise outside on summer evenings. While the environmental history of childhood in 1950 has everything to do with intense personal experiences with outdoor places, by 1980 those experiences were largely a thing of the past.

CHAPTER SIX

CHILDHOOD MOVES INDOORS

When writer Bill Bryson described his middle-class midcentury childhood in Des Moines, Iowa, an essential feature of that childhood was that so much of it happened in public spaces. As he commented in his memoir, *The Life and Times of the Thunderbolt Kid,*

> kids were always outdoors—I knew kids who were pushed out the door at eight in the morning and not allowed back until five unless they were on fire or actively bleeding—and they were always looking for something to do. If you stood on any corner with a bike—any corner anywhere—more than a hundred children, many of whom you had never seen before, would appear and ask you where you were going.[1]

Although exaggerated for effect, Bryson's observations ring true to most anyone raised in America at midcentury. He wrote, "Life in Kid World, wherever you went, was unsupervised, unregulated, and robustly—at times insanely—physical."[2] All of the city was his home—downtown, the river bottoms, the grounds of the state fair. He visited these places not necessarily to do anything, but to hang out alone, or with other young people like himself. America at midcentury was a place where grownups, to a large extent, tolerated children doing nothing, unsupervised, in public places.[3]

By the last decades of the twentieth century, however, the world in which Bryson had operated as a child had profoundly changed. In many ways, it no longer existed. As he explained, "A new, cheaper park was built down by the river bottoms . . . but the last time I went down there it was overgrown and appeared to be abandoned. There was no one to ask what happened because there are no people outdoors anymore—no kids on bikes, no neighbors talking over fences, no old men sitting on porches. Everyone is indoors."[4] The children (and their parents) had found indoor spaces to inhabit, abandoning the out-of-doors during most of the day. When youngsters were, in fact, outside, it was often in controlled spaces. They were no longer doing nothing. Instead, they were engaged in adult-scripted, planned and organized activities. Increasingly, children followed a blueprint provided by adults. Structured pastimes took the place of unstructured, with children spending long hours involved in activities such as sports, play dates and church. While the youngsters of the 1990s might spend nearly five hours per week involved in sports, they spent a mere half hour outdoors in unstructured activities. The small number of minutes spent in the out-of-doors was consistent across all age groups, from infants and toddlers to twelve-year-olds.[5]

Geographer Stuart Aitken has critiqued the relationship between children purposefully doing something and the imposition of adult direction. "When a child is doing something (swimming in the public pool) it is usually sanctioned by adult authority and structured to be unresponsive to individual whims and fancies (no running or jumping in the pool)," unlike the situation in the past remembered fondly by individuals such as Bill Bryson.[6] Over time, the adults increased the number of children's purposeful hours in the day, while reducing their access to the "individual whims and fancies" allowed and encouraged by unstructured hours. In fact, at least one study done in the early 2000s associated "hanging out" (another term for doing nothing) and spending time in outdoor play as a predictor for depression, poor grades and behavior problems in children aged ten to twelve. Children hanging out were "unstructured and unorganized," spending their time in places "unsupervised by adults." The relatively limited number of children parents allowed to hang out were involved in "alternative" activities, such as skateboarding, which was appealing to "non-conformist youth."[7] In other words, youngsters outside, doing what they wanted to do, were up to no good, taking part in activities that would stunt, rather than enhance, their development.

This perception may partially explain why parents were willing to give up some of their own freedom associated with sending children out to play. Because they were shielding their children from the dangers of the unstructured out-of-doors, parents were happy to have their children indoors and safe, even if they were, potentially, more often under foot. Whether or not they would even be under foot was questionable as well. By the 1950s, parents were consciously looking for homes with segregated indoor space for children. This included the development of the "family room" and the basement rumpus room. Part of the impetus was to provide space for relatively free play. Parents also hoped to segregate teens and their use of two modern technological developments, the television and the phonograph, from adults looking for peace and quiet.[8] Not only did houses have new rooms specifically designed for youngsters, they were growing in size as well, particularly in the 1980s, 1990s, and beyond. While in the early 1970s, 89 percent of all new homes had 1,999 square feet or less, by 2005, 20 percent of new homes had 1,600 to 1,999 square feet, and 37 percent had more than 2,000 square feet.[9] America's available domestic space had grown significantly, making room for myriad new indoor activities that could be separated into their own private or semi-private spaces. Children, for their part, were happy to find diversions involving these and other enclosed and monitored play places. This was a new world.

One way of addressing the world's dangers, perhaps not so new, was to construct home playgrounds and private outdoor play spaces as a substitute for public playgrounds and the streets. In the early years of the twentieth century, child development experts recommended that parents have substantial backyard play areas for their children. In part, this reflected a desire to provide children opportunities for constructive play. It also reflected new urban realities. With the advent of the automobile, play in the streets held heightened dangers. Fatal encounters between children and automobiles were startlingly frequent.[10] A backyard playground, available of course to only private homeowners, distanced children from careless drivers and allowed a large measure of parental control.

By the late twentieth and early twenty-first century, parents' concerns had undergone a metamorphosis. More than fear of speeding automobiles, fear of the activities of potentially malevolent adults drove their actions. Melodee Martin Helms, a Steilacoom, Washington, mother, lamented the way that adult perversity had limited her children's freedom. "We don't let our children play in the front yard, because a sex offender lives two doors down. Instead, like other families in this neighborhood, we've built private playgrounds in the back." Those private playgrounds were well equipped and provided youngsters a presumably safe place to play. "From my kitchen window," Helms commented, "I see two wooden play structures, three trampolines, and four basketball hoops including our own. The kids on our street don't play unsupervised on common ground. They have play dates now, arranged by protective parents."[11] In the face of a potentially dangerous world, other parents went even further, moving their children into gated communities. As one resident of such a community in San Antonio, Texas, commented, "That's what's been most important to my husband, to get the children out here where they can feel safe, and we feel safe if they go out in the streets and not worry that someone is going to grab them. . . . We feel so secure." In particular, she worried about a cruising motorist who might "grab a child."[12] Keeping children confined to controlled spaces helped to assuage parents' fears about the dangers outside the home.

It would be a mistake to assume, however, that all parents were so worried about their children's exposure to urban environments. While some parents reacted by building walls around their children, others allowed them to venture into the larger world. In 1986, a columnist for the *New York Times* briefly examined urban childhood, looking for children's relationships with the surrounding city. The author acknowledged the dangers of urban living: "The streets of the city can also be a treacherous place for children. Crack is sold alongside candy. Muggers wait in doorways for the unsuspecting. Arcades are the offices of pimps. Alleys can't be used for games of cops and robbers—real ones might be there."[13] Hazardous or not, children ventured out into the street in search of adventure. Fifteen-year-old Emil Chudnovsky, an immigrant from Moscow, played his violin in the streets of the Upper West Side. Nandalal Lutchmansingh, an immigrant from Trinidad, traipsed for blocks and blocks around the city, just to "see the world." Twelve-year-old Erin Manning liked to walk to the movies or to go ice skating. She commented "'If you live in New York you don't feel closed in. When I walk on the street, I feel like I can do anything.'"[14] These children reveled in the city and its many opportunities. "These are New York City's children, undaunted and unafraid, independent and interested. Strangers to shopping malls, car pools and afternoon soap operas, they have made the bastions of the civilized world—libraries, museums, concert halls and studios—their after-school playgrounds. They are testaments to the possibilities of city life and are proud of it."[15] These city kids saw more opportunities than hazards in the world around them. They were unafraid in their explorations, and their parents, too, seemed willing to let them go. That a large number of these children came from immigrant families may have affected their attitudes and activities. Perhaps New York City looked no more dangerous than the worlds from which they had migrated.

These children and their parents, however, were bucking the trend. Worry, rather than acceptance, seemed to be the order of the day, and parents looked for more protected environments for their progeny. Public indoor space became an alternative to the public outdoor spaces that caused parents such stress.[16] Increasingly, youngsters turned to the available space in shopping malls. While shopping malls were not completely a post–World War II creation, the enclosed indoor shopping mall was. Built in 1956, Southdale Shopping Center in Edina, Minnesota, was the first indoor, climate controlled mall. By the early 1970s, indoor malls were the standard.[17] Before long, malls had become central features of American suburban, and often urban, culture. In 1973, *U.S. News and World Report* noted that Americans were spending more time at shopping malls than virtually anyplace else, excluding work, school and their homes.[18] Historian Kenneth Jackson beautifully summed up the American affinity for the shopping mall. Many Americans, he wrote,

> regard the modern shopping mall—clean, safe, convenient, and cheerful—as superior to any downtown alternative, as in fact the re-creation of the city with a suburban setting. The mall has become the place where senior citizens walk in comfort and security, where parents lead their young to Santa Claus, where singles court, where teenagers socialize, and where everybody consumes. . . . legions of young people . . . spend their free time cruising indoor corridors. It is something to do when there is nothing else to do. And there is nothing else to do, according to many young people.[19]

Shopping malls gave young people a reasonably controlled and comfortable space in which to watch each other, socialize and perhaps even have a bite to eat. By the 1990s and the first decade of the 2000s, other large (to gigantic) malls, such as the Mall of America in Minneapolis, even boasted their own indoor amusement parks, ice skating rinks and water parks.

Malls catered to the whims of a broader range of youngsters than just those in the teenaged set. As one father commented, he liked to take his young son to the mall because of its "safety, comfort and predictability. 'It's like McDonald's,' he said. 'If you go in, you know you're going to get the same thing all over the country."[20] More recently, many malls have incorporated indoor playgrounds for parents toting babies and toddlers, giving them an alternative to outdoor venues, which might be too hot, too cold or too wet, given the vicissitudes of the season. The mall gave mothers a place to take their young, wailing progeny. As one woman commented, "All mothers know that there is something magical about the mall. It puts children to sleep. Theories run from white noise to sensory overload."[21] West County Mall in suburban St. Louis, Missouri, had its own "Kids' Club," which offered entertainment each week as an attraction for caregivers of small children. While the retailers thought of it as good business, the mothers and day-care providers came to think of the mall as a place for reliable entertainment, adult company and perhaps a little peace in an otherwise overloaded day.[22]

Developers transported amusements once found out-of-doors into large, climate-controlled indoor spaces. Their appeal was both the climate control and the illusion that this kind of space was safer and more child-friendly than less controlled outdoor parks and playgrounds.[23] The illusion of malls as safe spaces may have been further reinforced by activities such as those in the mid-1980s, when volunteers set up stands in 2,800 malls across North America and hosted mass fingerprinting events for children "to protect them against abduction."[24] Outside the mall was danger; inside, people were working to keep children safe. Malls across the United States also began to assume responsibility for another activity children had once enjoyed in their own neighborhoods, trick-or-treating. Knowing that parents were uncomfortable with allowing their children to gather treats, roaming freely, merchants began to offer malls as a safe venue for the annual event. One Minnesota mother explained her reasons for taking her children trick-or-treating at the mall, "It's fun, convenient and most importantly it is safe." The fact that it was also "a pedestrian-only, lights-on, smiling-sales-clerk kind of experience," in a climate-controlled environment, surely encouraged the practice as well.[25] Parents, however, have had to learn that the mall's safety is in part an illusion. Any place that attracts children and teens can become a magnet for people with less than honorable intentions. A spate of abductions from malls in the mid- to late 2000s must have given pause to parents looking for safe spaces for their offspring.

Malls were not the only controlled and confined play places. McDonald's, the fast-food giant, was an early purveyor of indoor play venues and outdoor, enclosed playgrounds. The first of the McDonald's PlayPlaces appeared in 1971 in Chula Vista, California.[26] In areas with limited playgrounds or with inclement weather, the PlayPlaces gave harried mothers an alternative to sitting at home with their children. These playgrounds, open only to paying customers, afforded mothers and other caregivers a place to take the children, feed them lunch, and drink a cup of coffee or a soft drink while they played. It also gave McDonald's greater opportunities to sell its food to families with young children.

Scholar Holly Blackford argued that the parent-child interactions in a McDonald's PlayPlace were significantly different than those in modern suburban playgrounds and were actually reminiscent of early twentieth-century urban street play. Children inside the play structure were almost invisible, swallowed up by slides, tubes and ball pits. Parents wanting to find or rescue a child within the structure were stymied by its architecture. She commented, "It is impossible to either find or reach a child when they are in the structure. Adults are specifically excluded from the small entryways to the equipment."[27] Except in emergencies, parents seemed to like this situation. They surrendered a good bit of their surveillance to the place. "Parents of today," Blackford commented, "feel that commercial spaces share their adult responsibility."[28] As she noted, the PlayPlaces were as much for the parents as for the children. The play structure took over the task of monitoring the children, leaving the parents free to interact with each other, rather than constantly maintaining their vigilance.[29] Within the PlayPlace, children explored and played on their own, while parents attended to their own conversations and meals, confident that their children were safe within that space, much as early twentieth-century parents trusted that the many eyes of neighbors and friends would keep their children safe during street play. The PlayPlace operated as a large, plastic playpen; while the children were inside, the structure protected them from harm and their parents from worry. The McDonald's PlayPlace, perhaps, stands as "the historical culmination of middle-class efforts to contain free play" and control children's interactions with a potentially dangerous world.[30]

The McDonald's experience also illustrated a major late twentieth-century reality: safe, bland play spaces were essential to avoiding litigation. In 1999, the corporation paid out four million dollars in fines to the Consumer Product Safety Commission for "failing to inform [the] CPSC of playground injuries at some of its restaurants." In particular, these accidents involved Big Mac Climber, "a metal platform resembling a hamburger" upon which several children had been injured. This was McDonald's second offense. The first time, McDonald's had failed to report injuries, including broken bones, involving a Tug-n-Turn merry-go-round installed in other restaurants. The company promised to report promptly other incidents of playground equipment injuries in the future, or face up to a five million dollar fine.[31] The fines and the bad publicity generated by incidents such as these help to explain why McDonald's adopted increasingly smooth, rounded plastic playground designs, with few opportunities for children to encounter sharp corners or steep drop-offs. In order to make the most of the marketing possibilities of PlayPlaces, the playgrounds had to offer parents a safe experience for their small children. Keep in mind, though, that parents had long demanded safe play spaces. In 1915, parents in Tacoma, Washington, had sued the school board on behalf of their son, injured falling off of a swing. The school board lost, and schools across the state modified their playground equipment offerings. The threat of lawsuits, however, had yet to become the guiding force that it would be in the later years of the century.[32]

Another twist on the indoor play space was the invention of "soft contained play equipment," also a playpen in a public place for children ranging from toddlers to teens. One mother called the structures "habitrails for kids," since the children inside were as contained as hamsters, moving through their exercise tubes.[33] As defined by the Consumer Product Safety Commission (CPSC) soft contained play equipment, or SCPE, was "a new type of playground characterized by plastic tubes for children to crawl through, ball pools, climbing nets, slides and padded floors." These play spaces became popular in the mid- to late 1990s and could "be found in fast food and family restaurants, theme parks and shopping malls."[34] Owners of "pay for play" indoor playgrounds also integrated the structures into their sites. Park and recreation districts, too, purchased these "play systems." The Elk Grove Park District in Elk Grove, Illinois, experienced such overwhelming demand for a small indoor SCPE that it soon opened a larger unit, charging a $2 entry fee for children, while admitting adults for free.[35] Children seemed to enjoy the structures, especially the ball pits, into which they could jump and bury themselves. The appeal of this type of play equipment to adults as well was obvious: padding, soft surfaces and containment. Falls onto hard surfaces were the single largest cause of playground deaths and injuries. The design of SCPE play structures minimized these dangers. To quote a research team from the CPSC:

> The staff observed that the design of SCPE addresses the fall hazard. Padded floor surfaces inside the SCPE play space would minimize injuries due to falls from ground level equipment. Upper level equipment contained the user inside an enclosed structure such as a tube, box, or netting that prevents falls from the equipment to the ground surface. Netting blocked off exterior access points to crawl tubes or tube slides, preventing the user from climbing on the outside of the surface of the tube and falling onto a hard surface.[36]

To keep children safe, all that remained was to control their behavior, keeping older children away from the younger and discouraging them from launching themselves from equipment and landing on each other. In 1995, a thirteen-year-old boy died in a ball pit in a restaurant play structure. He had buried himself in the balls, and another teen, not knowing he was there, jumped on him. These types of problems, however, were not inherent in the equipment, but in lax parental supervision. If properly supervised, the CPSC allowed that these soft play structures were "a safe alternative to traditional playgrounds."[37]

The development of indoor play spaces of many varieties coincided with the development of "dumbed down" outdoor spaces. Playgrounds took on a uniform, rounded plastic profile, without corners and with limited risk. If the "soft contained play equipment" model could have been easily trans-

This Ames, Iowa, playground in a city park is typical of modern American play spaces. Notice the woods behind the playground. It would be extremely rare to see a child in them or the ravine below them. Photograph by permission of Richard Kehrberg.

ported to the average suburban playground, no doubt it would have been. Instead, manufacturers relied on smoothing and rounding exterior play surfaces and exhorting installers to provide sufficient and approved cushioned surfaces underneath their climbers and slides. Playground equipment manufacturers integrated placards of safety checklists into their packages of plastic components, instructing children and their parents on the proper and safe way to use their slides, swings and climbing walls. (Interestingly enough, one study done in the early 2000s showed that such signs had no impact on the supervisory behavior of 69 percent of adults in playgrounds.[38] The messages most assuredly had even less impact on children.)

The CPSC took an active role in enforcing playground safety throughout the United States. During the 1980s and 1990s, the agency conducted investigations of various manufacturers, based on reported injuries and deaths involving playground equipment. Sometimes the agency called for the recall of old favorites, such as cast plastic and aluminum animal swings, installed in parks and playgrounds nationwide. Between 1951 and 1991, children had swung on approximately 10,000 horses, zebras, ducks and other animals. The problem with the swings was their weight: between

This photograph shows a Giant Stride on a very early twentieth-century playground. Warren H. Manning Papers, by permission of Special Collections Department / Iowa State University Library.

thirty and eighty pounds apiece. As a result of being hit by the swings, two youngsters had died, and forty-two others had suffered head injuries. In 1995, the CPSC worked with seven manufacturers to remove and replace the swings with new toys or lighter weight versions of the swings.[39] At other times, the CPSC required manufacturers to provide repair kits for potentially dangerous equipment, such as the Miracle Recreation Company's "Flying

This photograph, taken on an Ames, Iowa, school playground, illustrates why school officials, worried about liability, removed equipment like Giant Strides. From the collections of the Ames Historical Society, by permission of the *Ames Tribune*.

Gym," an apparatus that was a large, rotating swing. In 1984, a Flying Gym on a Seattle playground had lost a part that had fallen and killed a ten-year old boy.[40] The CPSC also provided educational materials intended to reduce children's exposure to other playground hazards, such as lead (found on older painted equipment) and arsenic (used to pressure treat wood found in some playground structures).[41] In an age of litigation and heightened concerns about product safety, the CPSC sought to provide children with less dangerous play spaces.

While CPSC activities, in part, included prosecution of manufacturers of dangerous and defective products, the agency also published materials meant to improve children's playground safety. One publication, *Little Big Kids*, encouraged safe playground behavior for the preschool set. Supposedly conceived and written by children, the book discussed safety in the simplest of terms. "Say Hey" the frog, in rhyming form, encouraged children to avoid dangers on climbing towers, swings, and other equipment. Also included in *Little Big Kids* was "The Story of 'Bluey,'" a little girl who always wore blue and always played safely, in order to avoid the bumped heads, sprained ankles and other injuries resulting from careless behavior. As the text noted, "So 'Bluey' did everything safe. She did not climb up the sliding board. 'Bluey' also did not jump off the swing, and held on to the chain in case anyone pushed her. When 'Bluey' returned home, she had not hurt herself, and her mother was proud of her."[42] While Bluey was unscathed by her playground experience, it was also not entirely clear if she had any fun.

The CPSC's publication was not just for children, but for their adult care-givers as well. The appended "Adult's Corner" encouraged parents to follow through on "Say Hey" and "Bluey's" lessons. Play, the author wrote, was essential to children, but even more essential was safe play. "If children are to grow and learn, they must do so safely."[43] Teaching safe play meant dis-couraging roughhousing and teaching children how to use play equipment properly. The instructions flew in the face of centuries of children's inter-actions with the world around them and decades of interaction with play-ground equipment. There was to be no jumping from swings, no twisting of chains, no climbing up slides or sliding down two and three at a time, no "speed contests" on jungle gyms and no standing on seesaws. The CPSC's instructions certainly fell within their motto of "play happy, and play safely," but they seemed to fail the time-tested children's motto of play creatively and play fun.[44] The instructions left children no room to learn from their mistakes. While it is quite easy to see how both the CPSC and playground equipment manufacturers, and even many parents, would endorse this, it was harder to understand the way in which this carefully controlled play would help children "learn about life by imagining, creating, and design-ing their own life situations," one of the CPSC's other observations about the value of play.[45] Officials at the CPSC were somewhat bewildered by the whole situation. "As the Consumer Product Safety Commission concluded with some despair, 'Walking up and down slides, climbing onto any aspect of playground apparatus that allowed a grip or foothold, and rough-housing were evident in the in-depth investigation.'"[46]

Observing the tug-of-war between children, parents and playground de-signers, scholars have questioned the degree to which modern suburban playgrounds were really meant for children at all. The "play value" of such playgrounds tended to be low, and the parental supervision of children quite high. They seemed to be more a place for mothers to show off their supe-rior parenting skills than for children to have a raucous good time.[47] Holly

Blackford's description is apt. "Mothers spread paraphernalia across the park bench. Snacks, toys, jackets, strollers, and even back supports, pepper the seats of the ring on any sunny day. They forge a kind of domestic apparatus on the playground, bringing their domestic authority to organize their children's bodies and space. The ring becomes an extension of domesticity, bringing the nuclear family's privatization of mothering into public view, where it is reviewed and approved."[48]

Parents, and mothers in particular, were organizers and active participants in the playground experience, leaving very little room for free play among children. Children had limited opportunity to explore and experience this environment on their own terms, and in their own way. Blackford termed the circle of women a panopticon, the term English reformer and philosopher Jeremy Bentham used for his prison design.

The American playgrounds of the late twentieth century were also very much at odds with a post–World War II European development, the adventure playground. While the CPSC might have preferred to have children playing on carefully planned structures with no obvious room for injury, other more daring models existed. A Danish invention, the "adventure playground," generally included "a number of hand-made shanties, some two-stories high, rickety forts, rope-walks across water, mud slides. There may be individual flower or vegetable plots being tended by youngsters and a crude grill for cooking hot dogs. Typically each youngster is assigned a small plot of land on which he can do whatever he pleases."[49] The goal of the adventure playground was to encourage child-directed creative play. Although these playgrounds usually came with paid adult supervision, the adults supervised at a distance, and in nonintrusive ways. Children were there to shape their own environment and design their own experience.[50] If their play became messy and a little dangerous and even included some cooking over open campfires, so be it. Researchers discovered that children liked adventured playgrounds considerably better than most other types of playgrounds. While the average stay at a traditional playground was only twenty-one minutes, children generally remained at adventure playgrounds for seventy-five minutes, more than three times as long. Researchers also found that children enjoyed the "ambiguity" of adventure playgrounds. "An important difference in the meaning of the environment to the users was that the built playgrounds were planned by others, they were permanent, and the potential for original combinations was minimal; at the adventure playground, the form was created by the users and was only as permanent as they chose it to be." The playgrounds "allowed children to create their own form and structure and level of complexity."[51] While this innovation flourished in Scandinavia, it never really caught on in the United States, perhaps because it so successfully mimicked the very elements of unstructured, vacant lot play that worried parents.

Other innovations have also failed to catch on. While researchers discovered that children loved to play on "properly stripped" automobiles and boats, adults balked at providing this type of playground equipment. As was noted by one expert, "unfortunately, some of the most meaningful play activities, from a development perspective, are not supported by adults."[52] Adults, in the form of school administrators, saw stripped cars and boats as "unsightly" or "junk yard" materials, rather than acceptable play structures, without consideration of what children might prefer.[53] Adventure playgrounds and stripped vehicles had a certain allure to children. Children, it seems, preferred playground activities with "the illusion of risk." As one researcher put it, "Mastering perceived threats results in growth spurts and affirmations of personal power."[54] As the twentieth century closed, risk, even as an illusion, retreated further and further into the past of children's play.

The CPSC's standards became the metric by which the legal system measured the safety of playgrounds. In 1999, the Fair Oaks Recreation and Park District in California ran afoul of the CPSC standards for playground maintenance. In 1988, the district had acquired an arch climber for one of its eight parks. An arch climber required a child to use both arms and legs to move up and over, as it curved and climbed. The district's climber, when installed, met the CPSC's 1981 standards for playground equipment and was not an entrapment hazard for children's heads. In 1991, the CPSC revised its standards for entrapment, including narrowed dimensions meant to protect additional body parts, such as arms and legs. Now, the district's arch climber was an entrapment hazard, and the district was in violation of the CPSC's entirely voluntary guidelines. When a 1998 inspection revealed problems in the playground equipment, the inspector recommended the arch climber's prompt removal. The park district superintendent, however, did not order that the arch climber immediately be removed but recommended that it be replaced in the next year when the park district planned a major renovation.[55] In the interim, a ten-year-old boy, playing on the arch climber, broke his leg due to an entrapment: "His left foot missed a rung and his leg fell into the space between two rungs. When he tried to extract it, his femur snapped."[56] In the ensuing lawsuit (*Clark v. Fair Oaks Recreation and Park District*), it was the district's knowledge of the dangers of the equipment in relation to the CPSC's guidelines that resulted in the plaintiff's eventual victory. The appeals court's decision focused in upon the district's failure to act on established safety guidelines. "Even the District's biomechanics expert . . . conceded that the arch climber's noncompliance with the 1991 guidelines made it more likely that if a child slipped and fell, he would suffer the sort of injury the plaintiff did. The District knew of this hazardous violation four months before plaintiff's accident, yet did nothing to correct it or warn against it."[57]

The case, and its presentation in *Parks and Recreation*, the official publication of the National Recreation and Parks Association, served as a warning to facility operators across the United States. The CPSC's guidelines, voluntary or not, served as a nationwide standard for safety, and maintaining parks and playgrounds that deviated from these standards opened a noncompliant district to lawsuits. This did not mean, however, that every parks and recreation district or municipality in the United States raced out to correct the safety hazards on its playgrounds. Even a quick tour of small town parks and playgrounds in the Midwest (let's say, in Iowa) will reveal a host of hazards, from dangerously heavy, long-since-recalled flying animal swings to funky, old outer space– or wild west–themed equipment, full of sharp corners and covered in peeling layers of old paint, that the locals love too much (or are too broke or lazy) to remove. Just as likely, their local budget situation precludes replacement of older equipment that the city or county might remove. Nevertheless, the precedent existed for the CPSC's standards to be interpreted as binding. Older, battered-but-creative playgrounds opened a municipality or county to litigation threats, and adventure playgrounds were entirely beyond the pale.

The modern, ultra-plastic water park mimics these developments. In the last decades of the twentieth century, these structures began to make an appearance in communities across the United States, some as public and others as private ventures. Water park designers took the molded plastic playground concept to new heights but substituted water for other soft landing places. Water parks made the most of curved plastic tube structures, and the addition of water allowed riders, both young and old, to rocket along at great speed. The water slides, the water parks' central feature, ranged from the slow and mild to the wickedly vertical and fast. Their very existence would seem to contradict the late twentieth-century imperative to manage risk at all costs, except for the very roundedness of all corners and the large number of teenaged lifeguards who managed every possible danger point. The one danger point that such facilities have not been able to contain, however, is water-borne illness. Pool managers have rather successfully used chlorination to combat *E. coli* and other fecal bacteria transmitted by less-than-clean bodies and poorly contained babies, although it is seemingly impossible to keep poop entirely out of the pool. A recent CDC study in the metropolitan Atlanta area showed the presence of *E. coli* in more than half of the pools in the area, a clear "fecal indicator."[58] Even more troubling is the presence of cryptosporidium. Cryptosporidium is a protozoan parasite, also borne in feces, that is easily transmissible through water. The protozoan causes violent gastrointestinal illness and is impervious to chlorine levels tolerated by humans. By the mid-2000s, the Centers for Disease Control had confirmed a number of cryptosporidiosis outbreaks involving water parks. Parks have a way to go yet in controlling a disease that is so resistant to conventional water treatment and filtration.[59] The authors of a recent study of a large statewide increase in cryptosporidiosis in Colorado found that "recreational water" was the major culprit.[60] Interestingly enough, the children just kept coming to the water parks. Until a child became ill, it was hard to convince parents of the seriousness of a threat that they literally could not see.

What did it mean when parks and recreation districts across the United States began abandoning their time-tested, serviceable swimming pools for the watery equivalent of the amusement park? Adults appeared yet again to be containing and directing children's and teens' behavior. The water parks were a further refinement of the efforts of adults to confine children's water play. The municipal swimming pools of the mid-twentieth century, according to historian Jeff Wiltse, were "intended . . . to combat crime and juvenile delinquency by giving idle youths something constructive to do during the summer."[61] But rather than leaving them to invent their activities, as the unadorned municipal pool required, the water park scripted children's play for them.

Although water parks varied from place to place and designer to designer, their features evolved into a somewhat regular form over time, allowing entertainment for a range of children. If they were young enough, children could entertain themselves with the equivalent of a playground play structure, with climbing areas and small slides. These play areas often included special water features, such as buckets dumping or fountains squirting water, and a zero-entry, beach-like approach to the water. Older children made use of the large, fast water slides, walking up stairs and riding down to the point of exhaustion. Once that point had been reached, it was time to relax, gliding along on an inner tube on the lazy river. No doubt the whole experience was fun, even exhilarating, which would explain why no one aside from the occasional swimmer who craved a quiet lap or two seemed to

mourn the passage of the simple, outdoor pool.[62] As one Midwesterner reacted to the passage of the old in her community, "I don't begrudge the kids
any, but I wish (the city would) consider the adults too."[63] Clearly, city parks
and recreation directors intended water parks for children and their parents, looking for a safe place to play on long summer afternoons. To evaluate
the water park in Bill Bryson's terms, an afternoon there might be insanely
physical, but it was neither unsupervised nor unregulated. Reflecting on his
own childhood experiences, Jeff Wiltse remembered the joy of free play at
the swimming pool and commented, "It would be a shame if future generations did not have the same opportunity to create their own vivid childhood
memories." He doubted the ability of "water theme parks" to deliver that
same experience, saying "There was something special about the pool."[64]
Children had lost yet another opportunity to take a simple structure and use
their imaginations to make it more than the sum of its parts. Bigger, fancier
and more exciting was not necessarily better.

Parents organized their children's interactions with the world in other
ways as well. In the post–World War II era, one of the chief features of the
lives of suburban children was the incredible array of organized youth activities available to them. Families could choose from a plethora of offerings:
scouting and Camp Fire, church choirs and youth groups, ballet lessons,
piano lessons and a whole range of youth sports activities, from gymnastics
to swimming and skating to football, softball and baseball. In the 1970s (or
a bit before or after, depending upon geography) the youth soccer craze hit
suburban America, gobbling up children's (and their parents') after-school
hours in practices and their Saturdays with games. Thousands of parents
who had never seen or played the game themselves either yelled from the
sidelines or got onto the field as coaches and referees. No wonder children
seemed to have no time for and little interest in free, unsupervised outdoor
play. They were too tired, having given their all at Boy Scouts, choir practice
and soccer—or Camp Fire, ballet and piano lessons. The age of the "over
programmed child" had arrived.

As mentioned in Chapter Five, parental anxiety about the safety of children in public spaces grew considerably from the 1970s onward. It was even
there at the breakfast table, in the form of milk carton appeals to keep an
eye out for abducted youngsters.[65] Parents responded in predictable ways,
limiting their children's freedom of movement. Outdoor activities would be
restricted and controlled. This was not a new impulse in the late twentieth
century, but it did reach new heights. As early as the 1920s, child development experts were admonishing urban parents to control their children's

outdoor play. While farm children could safely enjoy the out-of-doors, urban children needed greater care.[66] Across the twentieth century, parents' limitations on their children's activities mushroomed to the point that many youngsters born in the late 1970s and early 1980s would go through their entire childhoods without themselves organizing their time or their relationship to their environment. They would not be sent out to play. As journalist David Brooks commented about these youngsters in 2001, "They are the most honed and supervised generation in human history. . . . We have devoted our prodigious energies to imposing a sort of order and responsibility on our kids' lives that we never experienced ourselves."[67] This kind of supervision extended backwards into early childhood, as "upscale parents fill their kids' datebooks with structured play sessions. And they want to make sure not only that the children will be occupied at somebody's house but also that the activities undertaken will be developmentally appropriate, enriching, and safe."[68] From play dates to soccer games to piano and Girl Scouts, youngsters lived in a carefully organized world, and the points on their personal maps were connected by mini-van or SUV.[69]

As the outdoors grew more boring and restricted, youngsters turned their focus toward the indoors. By the beginning of the twenty-first century, American homes were bigger than ever, with more room than ever for children and their individual pursuits. Other factors made the home appealing as well. As researchers have admitted, the allure of the indoors was strong. A National Science Foundation study pointed to a key group of facts: "98% of U.S. homes have television, 42% have computers, and over 70% have air conditioning."[70] These statistics help to highlight the ways in which the appeal of the indoors versus the outdoors had changed. In earlier decades, television reception was often unreliable, and the choice of programming quite limited. Parents often limited the choices even more by allowing only a few carefully chosen hours of viewing during the day. There was no computer to turn to when the viewing was grim. At best, a youngster might resort to a transistor radio or phonograph for alternative passive entertainment. In an era before widespread air-conditioning, the outside, especially on summer evenings, was often preferable to inside, in terms of air temperature and entertainment choices. And, as Bill Bryson's memoirs remind us, everyone else was outside, too.

In the 1980s, 1990s and 2000s, everyone seemed to be inside. Changes in the spatial arrangement of cities and towns, with more children living in suburban areas with dispersed, low-density housing patterns led to far fewer children exploring their communities on foot. Between 1977 and 2001, the number of children's "walking trips" declined by 60 percent.[71] Children no longer walked to school or to the store, and parents instead chauffeured their children to these destinations. Patterns within children's leisure also changed. While the numbers of hours children spent in organized sports activities were significant, the number of hours they spent outside in unscripted pursuits was pitifully small. In the late 1990s, the average child, including youngsters of all ages up to twelve, spent 4:40 hours per week engaged in sports. Children pursued some of those activities indoors (gymnastics, basketball) and others outside (soccer, football, baseball). Children spent far more limited time outdoors: on average, only thirty-four minutes per week. The variations by age were minimal. Very small children, age two and under, spent twenty-five minutes per week outside, other preschoolers thirty-seven minutes, early grade-schoolers twenty-nine minutes, and nine-to-twelve-year-olds forty-two minutes. Youngsters of all ages, on average, spent more than fifteen hours per week in front of the television.[72] Another study found that by the late 1990s, the average child's "screen time," including both television and computers, had grown to nearly five hours per day.[73] Queried about his activities, a sixteen-year-old commented "I really want to move to Antarctica—I'd want my cat and Internet access and I'd be happy."[74] The most important environment for most youngsters was no longer a vacant lot or a park across the street, but the interior of their homes—specifically the space including themselves and a screen.

By the early years of the twenty-first century, however, children's access to even the tame space in their backyards had become quite constricted. While not choosing to comment on whether or not this was a good or bad development, researchers at the University of California–Los Angeles's Center on Everyday Lives of Families spent the years from 2001 to 2005 studying the daily lives of thirty-two Los Angeles households in minute detail. They collected 20,000 images, made dozens of maps and spent 1,500 hours videotaping activities. The results confirm the overwhelming orientation of children and their families toward the interior spaces of their homes. The researchers found that these middle-class L.A. families seemingly embraced the 1950s ideal of outdoor living, providing their families pools, hot tubs, trampolines, swing sets and all of the accoutrements of outdoor family play and sociability. The great irony is that no one used these expensive acquisitions. "Parents simply do not find time for outdoor leisure, and most children spend no time at all outside at home. . . . Leisure is indoors."[75] Parents, apparently, were too busy to go outside, and their children preferred to remain inside. The researchers photographed and described the luxurious,

14,850-square-foot backyard belonging to "Study Family 18," a mother and father with three children, ages nine to twelve. During the course of the study, the sumptuously appointed yard, which included a pool, swing set, trampoline, batting cage, patio and dining table, "went unused."[76] Although this study focused exclusively on the Los Angeles area, its implications for the rest of the country were troubling. Families spent the vast majority of their time indoors, or in structured activities outside their homes. As the researchers noted, "This is a striking finding in a city where the mild climate allows for outdoor activity year round. Such a pronounced indoor orientation is probably greatly magnified in the colder regions of the U.S."[77]

Forces had collided, making the interior of the home the most attractive venue for children, from the perspective of both adults and children. Given the fears and doubts plaguing parents, they preferred their children to remain in controlled space, either inside or out. Changes making the indoor environment more comfortable coincided with technological developments, such as improved television reception, video games and home computers that expanded children's entertainment options within the home. The growing size of American homes made it less imperative for parents to send children outside to get them out from under foot. A child planted in front of a computer in his or her own room was just as quiet, and far more contained, than a child on a bicycle in the neighborhood.[78] Whether such changes were actually good for children is another discussion, reserved to psychologists, educational reformers and pediatricians. Suffice it to say that the environments with which children were most familiar had changed, and changed radically, and sometimes on the basis of parental concerns that had a fairly shaky basis in fact.

As discussed in Chapter Five, the world outside of most children's homes was not actually all that dangerous. Across the twentieth century, children became more likely to live to adulthood, rather than less. They were more likely to arrive at adulthood with all of their faculties, digits and limbs intact. And even in a world where parents were highly aware of stranger-danger, the likelihood of an unsupervised child facing an unknown kidnapper or molester was exceedingly slim. This low level of danger, however, cannot be universalized to all children. In some places in the United States, the levels of danger facing children spiked in the 1980s and 1990s, as a result of gang activity and the trade in illicit drugs. Children were literally caught in the crossfire between rivals for inner-city territory. Unlike relatively well-to-do urban and suburban children who moved indoors because of their parents' (ill)-perceived fears of the world outside their doors, poor urban children faced very real threats on the corner, across the street and even inside of their own buildings.

That inner-city children would increasingly move their activities indoors was entirely understandable. By the 1980s, conditions in many impoverished urban neighborhoods had deteriorated to the point where it was no longer safe to play outside. In his 1992 book, *There Are No Children Here: The Story of Two Boys Growing Up in the Other America*, journalist Alex Kotlowitz described the urban jungle where many poor children lived. The two boys Kotlowitz followed in his research, Pharoah and Lafeyette, lived with their mother and siblings in the Henry Horner Homes, a high-rise Chicago Housing Authority (CHA) public housing project. Their mother had moved to the Henry Horner Homes as a child in the 1950s, when the project was new and well maintained. In her early years, the Henry Horner Homes had boasted a child-friendly playground, a grassy baseball diamond and flower beds. As she commented about her childhood, "We had it all. I really thought this was it. And I never knew, until I lost it all, that it wasn't."[79] By the time her own children were growing up, the place barely resembled the home of her youth.

The buildings' disintegration was inevitable, having been cheaply built and poorly maintained. In a cold climate, the city had constructed the Henry Horner Homes with open breezeways or galleries, and the elevator cables froze regularly. The trash chutes were inadequate to the job. In the 1970s, the CHA no longer had the funds for paint, and the walls looked shabbier and shabbier. The wet basements of the buildings were littered with rodents, rotting animal carcasses and garbage. The stench, and sometimes sewage, made its way into the floors above.[80] The playgrounds, too, had disintegrated. The swings and slides were the same ones that the CHA had installed when the project was first built and were in a terrible state of disrepair. The baseball diamond no longer existed, and the basketball courts were hardly usable. Four thousand children lived in the Henry Horner Homes; the CHA, essentially, provided them no place to play.[81]

At the Henry Horner Homes, some parents were so worried about the neighborhood that they would not have allowed their children out to play anyway. As Kotlowitz noted, "One mother moved her living room furniture to make an open and safe place where her children could frolic."[82] Her concerns were not unreasonable. The threats lurking outside were significant. Parents feared speeding cars, stray bullets and the dangers and complexity of navigating in and around gang territory.[83] The fact that the Henry Horner Homes was a high-rise project further complicated the situation for parents. Given thirteen stories of apartments, thousands of resident children and

The great distance between children and parents on playgrounds of the high-rise Victor Olander Homes housing projects is apparent in this view. Photograph by Mildred Mead, Special Collections Research Center, University of Chicago Library. By permission of the University of Chicago Library.

limited and often broken elevators, supervising children's play was problematic at best. Unlike earlier low-rise public housing, the distance between a child on the playground and a mother in an apartment was significant.[84]

This, too, created another problem that no one had considered when the project was in the planning and building stage—access to bathrooms. Children in high-rises, playing outside, were a distressing distance from bathroom facilities, often with inadequate or nonfunctioning elevators in between. The resulting (literal) mess further degraded the environment for all, and discouraged children who wanted to venture outdoors. The situation was so dire that in 1966, Reverend Martin Luther King, Jr., presented the problem in a list of complaints to Chicago Mayor Richard Daley, demanding that the CHA provide more adequate bathroom facilities, especially in proximity to children's play areas.[85]

Children being children, however, still wanted to play outside. Pharoah and Lafeyette longed to find places in the out-of-doors to call their own. Going in search of the railroad tracks provided a sense of adventure. As Kotlowitz described, "To reach the tracks the children had to scale a steep mound of earth shoved against one side of the aging concrete viaduct. Bushes and small trees grew in the soil alongside the tracks; in some places the brush was ten to fifteen feet thick."[86] The boys liked the tracks, because they were a vantage point for observing the downtown skyline in the distance and for encountering wildflowers and butterflies. They even dug for snakes in the hard earth. The tracks gave the boys a perspective on their city and on wild things that were unavailable in the Henry Horner Homes.[87] The boys, however, eventually gave up on the tracks. Teens assaulted them on their way, and rumors abounded of the dangers of passing trains. They would have to find other places of refuge.[88] For Pharoah, that place would be a condominium complex three blocks from home. Damen Courts, with "Its manicured lawns and graffiti-free walls" offered him a reprieve from the world of the projects. "The grass carpet offered a quiet resting place; it was like going to the beach. Pharoah found a shady place on the lawn and shot marbles or read a *Captain America* or *Superman* comic. Or, if the mood fit him, he just sat and daydreamed."[89] Pharoah had found a small corner of Chicago to call his own. Lafeyette, on the other hand, retreated further indoors. "He didn't trust going outside. Too much going on, he'd say. Too many wrongheaded people."[90] For too many children in the 1980s and 1990s, Lafeyette's experience was typical.

A few miles away, at the CHA's Robert Taylor Homes, the situation was all too similar. The housing authority built the Robert Taylor Homes in the late 1950s and early 1960s, and the massive project included twenty-eight buildings, each sixteen stories tall, divided into 4,500 apartments. Built in the heart of the city's black ghetto, planners intended the project to provide a habitable alternative to a downtrodden slum neighborhood. In the beginning, it was a potentially attractive site with "trees, gardens, and decorative flower beds interspersed amid the startling high-rises." "External galleries on the buildings gave thousands a remarkable view of the city's South Side, a clear day revealing the downtown skyline." An early observer would have seen "only signs of life and vitality: throngs of children climbed on new playground equipment, men and women colonized parking lots and alleyways with music and festivities, and softball and basketball games filled the park areas."[91] This potential, however, went unfulfilled. The project was never able to overcome its site, in the midst of an impoverished neighborhood, cut off from better neighborhoods by a multilane highway.[92]

All too soon, the Robert Taylor Homes lost their shine, and the insufficiencies of the facilities became glaringly apparent. Although the buildings covered only 7 percent of the land upon which the project sat, planners made very little use of the space, covering most of it with concrete and asphalt.[93] While one early resident described the Robert Taylor Homes of his youth as a "giant black playground," his aunt was struck by the difficulties of raising children in this environment. She commented, "Playground? Yeah, well, you *made* it into playground . . . for me, it was a chore trying to keep up with these kids. Empty lots, and those train tracks! Ooh! You had to watch everywhere 'cause there wasn't no parks or nothing like that, just a lot of open space that [kids] would mess around in."[94] Planned space for children's play was sorely lacking. A CHA report on the Robert Taylor Homes noted "'children lined up seven and eight deep just waiting to use a piece of play equipment [and] . . . upwards of 2,000 children may be cramped into one or two relatively small play spaces."[95] With approximately 20,000 children in all of the project's buildings, and very few accommodations made for them, children spilled over into other public spaces.

Children claimed as their own a built environment that adults had designed for other purposes. Kenny Davenport, an early resident, described the uses of stairwells: "You could slide down those long metal railings, and you tried not to fall in between 'cause you'd die right quick."[96] Children made elevators central to their play. One man remembered, "We used to ride them like we was at Great America. . . . Popping them buttons, loading as many kids as we could, trying to climb out of them if we could."[97] The elevators became some of the most dangerous locations in high-rise projects and unfortunately some of the most appealing to children. In 1956, an

Housing in Chicago's "black belt" could be primitive, as this 1948 photograph demonstrated. Photograph by Mildred Mead, Special Collections Research Center, University of Chicago Library. By permission of the University of Chicago Library.

elevator crushed a nine-year-old boy playing tag. Across the city's projects, Chicago Housing Authority records from the 1970s reported 417 elevator injuries and 15 deaths. A maintenance chief commented, "'With so many kids, the elevators are just $80,000 playtoys.'"[98] As historian D. Bradford Hunt has argued, the most significant problem within the project may very well have been the high concentration of children, relative to the number of adults and relative to the available schools and play spaces. They over-whelmed the resources of their surroundings and their caregivers.[99] The CHA began demolishing the dilapidated structures in the mid-1990s, after

Low-rise housing limited the distance between playing children and their parents. Photograph by Mildred Mead, Special Collections Research Center, University of Chicago Library. By permission of the University of Chicago Library.

a federally mandated viability study found that many of the buildings were no longer fit for human habitation.[100]

It had not always been so. In the 1930s when Chicago first built public housing, people's perceptions and experiences of the projects were considerably different. Researchers at the University of Chicago had for years canvassed the city's tenement districts, cataloguing the myriad ills of families forced to live in drastically substandard housing. African American families, in particular, lived crowded into disintegrating neighborhoods with few if any alternatives. In the middle years of the twentieth century, Chicago had some of the most rigidly segregated housing in the northern United States. Conditions in the city's "black belt" were grim, with most families living in very expensive, yet very poor-quality housing.[101] Not surprisingly, reformers welcomed the advent of public housing, built under the auspices of the New Deal's Public Works Administration. The CHA meant its projects not for the poorest of the poor, but for upwardly mobile working families the authority anticipated would live in public housing for a time before moving on to home ownership.[102]

In the early years the aesthetics of public housing were important. The authority planned to build comfortable, modern buildings and to frame them with careful landscaping.[103] The first of these projects, called the Jane Addams Houses and the Julia C. Lathrop Homes, were model developments, designed with the needs of families in mind. Although the apartments were of interest to housing reformers, the surroundings at the Jane Addams Houses received special note. In describing the landscape, a writer noted "The rest of the area will be left open; a part of it will be planted with trees, shrubbery, and grass; and parts will be reserved for playgrounds and gardens." An artist's rendering showed broad streets, shady courtyards and a degree of cleanliness and order generally unknown in chaotic slum neighborhoods.[104]

Interviews done in the 1980s confirmed that early residents of the housing projects found their new homes to be a substantial improvement over their former residences. Before moving to Altgeld Gardens in 1944, Andrew Greenlee's family moved from rural Mississippi to a crowded ghetto neighborhood. In particular he remembered the coal-fired furnaces and the resulting dust that polluted the family's rooming house. "Every time you touched anything, it was dirty." He described the year his family spent waiting to get into Altgeld Gardens as "devastating."[105] For many families, moving to public housing was a relief. The housing projects were new, clean and chock-full of luxuries that residents had never before enjoyed, such as central heating and refrigerators. Bertrand Ellis lived in the Ida B. Wells Homes from 1941 until 1955. He remembered the amenities provided for the children:

> Three buildings formed a triangle, and in the middle of that triangle was a playground. We grew up playing football, baseball, hockey, every sport you could imagine. We had a little yard, it was a pretty good sized yard, on the front side of the building I lived in, and after some time they put up a basketball court there. . . . And then, of course, Madden Park also had a swimming pool. So we could swim in the summer, and in the winter they would freeze a smaller playground—that's where I learned to ice-skate. We were poor kids in the community, but we didn't really know we were poor, really. We had everything kids could ever want.[106]

Ellis was not alone in his appreciation for the Ida B. Wells Homes. Leon Hamilton, who lived there at roughly the same time, exclaimed, "We had new facilities! Central heat! The apartments were new and clean! Everything! Refrigerators and modern stoves! . . . we were like little rich kids."[107]

Gwendolyn Duncan Alexander, who grew up in the Mother Cabrini Homes (which predated high-rise Cabrini Green), loved the freedom that existed in the early years. "Cabrini was ideal because I was free to go anywhere I wanted. There was a sand lot between the row houses where kids could play, and there were jungle gyms. I used to sleep on the back porch. I would bring my pillows and sleep out on the back porch all night!" In part, her nostalgia stemmed from the contrast between then and now: "You can't even sleep with the windows open today."[108] Children who grew up in CHA facilities in the forties and fifties remembered public housing that was safe, comfortable and even luxurious.

The CHA achieved this order and attractiveness at the cost of strictly controlling the behavior of youngsters. Keeping the projects beautiful entailed keeping the children off the grass and out of the bushes. In 1940, Melvin Wilson moved into the Ida B. Wells Homes with his family. He remembered "You had to maintain the house, the hallways had to be clean, and they would rotate that kind of duty between the two families that were living across from one another. And the same would apply to the landscaping and groundskeeping. So children didn't play on the grass."[109] Nelvia Brady grew up in the Henry Horner Homes with strict rules about how to use the buildings and grounds. "From a child's perspective, the standards were fairly rigorous and rigid—in terms of the laundry facilities, in terms of the use of elevators, in terms of where children played. We were very familiar with what we could do and should do, and what we should *not* do." To her, the standards made sense, because her family lived with many others in a thirteen-story building, which had only two elevators.[110]

Again and again, individuals recounted the stiff penalties for breaking the rules. James Fletcher, who lived in the Ida B. Wells Homes, mused about the trouble he got into for misusing public grounds. "I remember having one heck of a couple days because I swung on a tree and broke a limb. A janitor saw me, and of course he came over that night and told my mother. Then my father came home from work, and I didn't swing again in the trees for a long time."[111] William Shaw, who lived in Altgeld Gardens, also knew the penalties for disturbing the carefully cultivated landscaping. "No one would step on those flowers. And you never stepped on the grass. There was a guy by the name of Mr. Rothings, he was a security guard. If he caught you on the grass, you got a whipping. And the whipping you'd take was no problem. You didn't go home and talk about it."[112] Many former residents described CHA housing projects in their early years as villages. "If you were throwing rocks, somebody would say, 'I'm going to tell your mother on you!'"[113] Security guards, janitors and the ever-present eyes of parents enforced community standards.

By the time Lafeyette and Pharoah were growing up, much of this community feeling and cooperation within Chicago's housing projects was gone, and the environment for children had disintegrated significantly. There was no longer any place to play safely, and little of public housing's early attractiveness remained. In such an extreme situation, children were trapped within their homes. They had little choice about how they would experience their environment. As British historian Colin Ward commented in the 1970s, in regard to high-rise housing projects,

> The relatively affluent, with the freedom of choice that money can buy, select the suburban street, where their children can be, at will, indoor or outdoor kids. The poor of the inner city, who over the generations, have evolved a code of practice which seeks to make life tolerable for themselves or their offspring, have been the victims of the decisions of others whose values do not include a consideration of the psychic damage they inflict.[114]

Families crowded into high-rise, low-income housing had lost the saving grace of being able to send their children out to play. Given a choice, families wanted low-rise housing. They wanted to be able to supervise their children at play and have safe places out-of-doors to which they could send children. In many of the poorest neighborhoods in places like Chicago, families, however, had no choice.[115]

High-rise housing projects offered limited indoor space for children and distanced mothers and other caregivers from children making use of outdoor spaces. Planners hoped that the small footprint of the buildings would leave more space for play, but plans for the green, park-like expanses of the architect's drawings never really came to fruition. Elizabeth Wood, who began her career as a social worker and ended as a prominent housing administrator, recognized the problems inherent in their plans: "When architects and planners lay out a low coverage high-rise project, they almost immediately will lay out a large and beautiful mall and other fenced and grassed areas, all of which will promptly be labeled with 'keep off the grass signs.'"[116] Although planners worried from a very early date that the design of high-rise projects such as the Henry Horner Homes, the Robert Taylor Homes and Cabrini Green were incompatible with the needs of children, the CHA built them as a low-cost solution to a high-density problem.[117] Designers attempted to remedy the problem of distance from playgrounds and limited outdoor space by constructing galleries or "sidewalks in the air," in which small children could play, but ultimately the galleries had to be enclosed with wire fences to keep people below from being injured or killed by those throwing objects from above. The buildings looked like prisons, from the inside and from without. Residents of the Robert Taylor Homes, after the installation of fencing, referred to the project as "Stateville," or "Stateville Homes," a reference to the Illinois State Penitentiary by the same name.[118]

In the 1980s and 1990s, many inner-city urban spaces had become extremely dangerous. The CHA responded to the conditions of the era with evictions of disruptive tenants and renovations of various projects. Some projects, such as Rockwell Gardens, gained new security guards, playground equipment and landscaping.[119] By the mid-1990s, however, high-rise housing projects were falling to the wrecking ball, and the CHA was dispersing their residents throughout the Chicago area. In 1996, the city began tearing down projects such as the Robert Taylor Homes. The Henry Horner Homes and Cabrini Green faced the same fate, as did some low-rise projects, like the dilapidated Ida B. Wells Homes.[120] The CHA's sixty-year experiment with environmental engineering of disadvantaged communities had come to an unfortunate pass and demanded new solutions. Chicago began planning for a new era in public housing, and one that would hopefully avoid the pitfalls of the enormous high-rise, gallery-style projects of the past. For Lafeyette, Pharoah and their siblings, change came entirely too late. At the time when this chapter was researched and written, Lafeyette, Pharoah and their younger brother, Timothy, were no longer housed by the CHA, but by the Illinois Department of Corrections.[121]

The point of this chapter, however, is not to promote environmental determinism. Children growing up on depressed midwestern farms did not all grow up to raise their own children on equally depressed acreages, permanently scarred by their childhood experiences. Children growing up in turn-of-the-century slum neighborhoods went on to live adult lives in many different locations and in many different sets of social and economic circumstances. Late twentieth-century children growing up in poor Southern California neighborhoods made the best of what they had. Researchers found little girls improvising upon their limited environments, made smaller by the dangers of the surrounding neighborhood. Although their parents had restricted the scope of their play, a researcher found that "Katie and her friend spent their days pretending that their scooters were horses and making the 100 feet of sidewalk they were allowed to ride along into an imaginary kingdom."[122] Imaginary kingdoms, of course, have unlimited boundaries.

The canyons created by high-rise housing dwarfed the playground and children below. Special Collections Research Center, University of Chicago Library. By permission of the University of Chicago Library.

Other difficult environments, such as the CHA's housing projects, did not have to destroy the lives of children who lived within them. Children were not simply the product of the place in which they lived. The environment parents created within the home might counterbalance the challenges facing children when they stepped out of the family's door. Parents, grandparents, teachers and other supportive adults helped mentor some youngsters out of the projects and into more hopeful surroundings.[123] The point is, however, that in a reasonably affluent, post–World War II America, the kind of environments that shaped children like Lafeyette and Pharoah placed them at an increasing disadvantage, relative to children growing up in other, more affluent Americas. The same Southern California study that found little girls making the most of a hundred feet of sidewalk also found that youngsters growing up in less dangerous, middle-class neighborhoods had far more opportunities to get to know the larger environment, playing outside and riding bikes. Their parents allowed them greater freedom of movement, because they believed that their neighborhoods, in general, were safe. A higher family income generally translated into a world with less restrictive spatial boundaries.[124]

In the latter years of the twentieth century, however, boundaries increasingly defined the world of American children. This is not to say that the children of the second half of the nineteenth century and the early years of the twentieth had lived without boundaries, but their parents had drawn the boundaries of those decades much more loosely. Although the practices in individual families varied, and girls sometimes experienced greater restrictions than boys, many children ranged across the countryside and across their cities in the way Bill Bryson described midcentury child-life in Des Moines. Bryson and his friends not only had the run of their neighborhood, but also the run of the city, from parks and urban wild spaces to the buildings downtown. His parents, busy with their own lives, expressed little concern about the ramblings of their adventurous progeny. He was, to use today's terminology, a "free-range kid," a condition that no one found exceptional in 1950 or 1960 or even in 1970. What was common at midcentury was increasingly unlikely in its last decades. The story of Lafeyette and Pharoah and their struggle to find a place in their world is a much more dramatic and drastic version of the struggles going on in many homes and neighborhoods. It was no longer clear where children belonged. Adult fears, both founded and unfounded, limited children's independent access to the larger world. New amenities increased the appeal of indoor environments to new decades of children. Children, sometimes reluctantly and sometimes willingly, exchanged a remarkable degree of freedom for greater confines. An outpouring of activity, comment and hand-wringing would mark the realization that this state of affairs was apparently here to stay.

CHAPTER SEVEN

RECONNECTIONS AND RECONSIDERATIONS

I began this book with the comment that the world we live in today is not the world that existed at the close of the Civil War. In so many ways, that is the case. Sheer growth in the population has changed the way the nation looks, sounds and feels. Changes in technology have given people new ways to alter the environment in which they live. People and their machines, for example, are responsible for mechanical noises that had no counterpart 150 years ago. The landscape is filled with the artifacts of human occupation, from houses to golf courses to asphalt. The smells are certainly different. In most places, the odor of exhaust has replaced those of the barnyard and outhouse. And while there are more people, there are proportionally fewer children, and those children are less visible than they would have been in the past. Children have a different place in the landscape than they did 150, 100 or 50 years ago, and the vast majority have far less familiarity with the landscapes within which they live than their grandparents or great-grandparents had. This, too, changes the environment. Think about a summer evening in the 1950s, 1960s or 1970s. During those decades, in any city or town, the atmosphere of a summer evening would not have been complete without the sounds of children playing outside, ringing bicycle bells, clacking along on roller skates or skateboards, all the while shrieking back and forth to each other. Today, there is the hum of traffic and the click of air conditioners cycling on and off. The outdoors no longer belongs to the children.

To whom does the outdoors belong in the twenty-first century? A little bit of observation in outdoor public spaces will quickly confirm that the grown-ups are in charge. There are certainly exceptions to this rule, but there are very few, if any, unattended children in most parks, playgrounds and wild spaces. Mothers and fathers watch their children as they play on swings and slides, keeping an eye out for their children's safety. It is rare to see a young child out alone on a bicycle. There are almost always parents within sight, usually on their own bicycles. In secluded places, such as bike and walking

The Skunk River in Ames, Iowa, is no longer a playground for local children. Photograph by author.

paths through woods and along watercourses, there are few adults and fewer children taking advantage of the space. The adults wear the determined look of those exercising to improve their health, and the children look as if they are being dragged along against their will. In the thirteen years I have lived near the Skunk River in central Iowa, I have seen precisely one unattended child playing in or near the water. I was so surprised, seeing him there, that I have remembered it for more than a decade. Children go chaperoned in the outdoors, with very few opportunities to experience the world on their own terms, without adult interference. Instead, they spend the majority of their time indoors, and the outdoor time that they have tends to be scripted and managed by the adults in their lives.

Adult observers began noting this change in the late years of the twentieth century and began reacting with dismay to what they perceived to be a significant cultural loss. In the 1990s, Robert M. Pyle was a leading voice for naturalists who believed that the world had been diminished when children went inside and began to experience nature largely from a distance. He, after all, attributed his career as a naturalist to important formative experiences along the High Line Canal. Pyle believed that the indoor orientation of the nation's children would have dire consequences for the state of scientific knowledge in the United States, not to mention the health and well-being of the nation's children. He argued that a series of losses had accompanied the reduction in both wild land and children's free time. These changes deprived children of the benefits provided by the important developmental activity of outdoor play. They lost what he called "nature literacy." They also lost "literacy's partner, intimacy."[1] He feared that children raised in the late twentieth century would never have the kind of relationship with the natural world that he had enjoyed and that had inspired him to become a scientist.

One of Pyle's worries, often overlooked by others, was that our modern media culture, combined with children's increasing orientation toward the indoors, would extinguish their interest in the world next door. Television, computers and movies gave children access to the most unusual of wildlife, right there on the screen. Zoos, with their exotic occupants, also had the capacity to overwhelm children with creatures of amazing color, size and majesty. These displays, both on the screen and in the zoo, had the potential to tarnish youngsters' interest in the common, everyday, but equally interesting wildlife around them, such as moths, squirrels and rabbits. Pyle wrote, "Displays of extravagant animals behaving dramatically in captivity and on television can spoil the young for the real thing outside their door. Those big, brilliant blue morphos [butterflies] in the tropical house should not excite more fascination than the equally bright but tiny spring azures among the dogwoods in the ditch."[2] Pyle's autobiographical work, *The Thunder Tree: Lessons from an Urban Wildland* is a love story about a reverence for nature cultivated in an urban wild place that still exists, but has become largely inaccessible to twenty-first-century children.[3]

Very similar, but very different, was the call embedded within Janisse Ray's autobiography, *Ecology of a Cracker Childhood*. Ray's reminiscences provided an additional corrective to the idea that only in dramatic and wild places could a child find beauty and a landscape worth knowing. Her words about rural south Georgia were both plain and evocative. "The creation ends in south Georgia, at the very edge of the sweet earth. Only the sky, widest of the wide, goes on, flatness against flatness. The sky appears so close that, with a long-enough extension ladder, you think you could touch it, and sometimes you do, when clouds descend in the night to set a fine pelt of dew on the grasses, leaving behind white trails of fog and mist."[4] Raised in a junkyard, Ray became a naturalist like Pyle, nurtured by her unusual surroundings. Ray played in and around the remnants of automobiles, and became immersed in the flora and fauna of the American South. Ray and her siblings were free to explore the junkyard and bore the marks of their experience; Ray grew up "among piles of scrap iron and glittering landmines of broken glass that scattered ivory scars across my body, among hordes of rubber tires that streaked my legs black, among pokeweed and locust."[5] In the midst of this potentially dangerous chaos, however, she found her calling. She remembered, "I attribute the opening of my heart to one clump of pitcher plants that still survives on the backside of my father's junkyard."[6] Even though a 4-H project featuring the carnivorous plant failed to impress the judges, it taught her many lessons, such as a joy in rain and a deep dislike for "artificial bouquets of plastic and silk." The plant taught her an appreciation of nature alien to her mechanically minded father and helped her to find her own passion for the southern landscape and particularly the long-leafed pine.[7] For Ray, her father's junkyard worked as effectively as Pyle's High Line Canal in inspiring and nurturing a lifelong interest in the workings of the natural environment. In Ray's and Pyle's experiences, a place did not need to be a pristine wilderness, or even particularly aesthetically pleasing, in order to inspire a child's interest in nature or its remnants. An untamed or partially tamed place simply had to exist, available to children for exploration.

While the untamed and partially tamed places still exist, parental fears and youthful preferences have limited their availability to children. Well-meaning, concerned adults, perceiving the lives of today's children as deprived and diminished, have attempted to name the problem and resolve it. The clearest manifestation of this concern is in the "No Child Left Inside" or "Leave No Child Inside" movement, which has popularized the idea of reintroducing children to nature and curing their "nature deficit disorder." Richard Louv, author of *Last Child in the Woods: Saving Our Children from Nature-Deficit Disorder*, has urged parents to allow every child to spend free and unstructured time in wild places, while conceding that some adaptations to the conditions of the twenty-first century, such as maintaining cell-phone contact, might now be a necessity. Without nature, Louv argued, the mental, spiritual and physical health of the nation's children was at risk. Louv wrote that by immersing themselves in nature, children could learn a hyper-awareness of their surroundings that would keep them safe in the face of danger. Louv even argued for the creation of defense funds to protect summer camps and other outdoor venues against lawsuits arising from injuries and deaths of young visitors.[8] He was at the center of the creation of an umbrella organization, the Children & Nature Network, which brought together programs and organizations from across the United States, and in some cases, the world, to promote the idea of returning children to the out-of-doors.

One of the most common ways in which organizations, both public and private, have participated in the No Child Left Inside movement has been in the generation of documents titled "children's outdoor bill of rights." The organizations creating these statements are attempting to distill out of the many ways in which children could interact with their environments the essential ways in which all children should experience the outdoors. The California Roundtable on Recreation, Parks and Tourism established a "California Children's Outdoor Bill of Rights," which, like the U.S. Bill of Rights, set out ten basic principles. According to the California Children's Outdoor Bill of Rights, "every child should have the opportunity to Discover California's Past, Splash in the water, Play in a safe place, Camp under the stars, Explore nature, Learn to swim, Play on a team, Follow a trail, Catch a fish [and] Celebrate their heritage."[9] The document's sponsors claimed that each of these activities was integral to a well-rounded, fulfilling life and backed up those claims with an array of studies. Camping under the stars, for example, might lead youngsters to a positive self-image, better teamwork, and self-reliance. Exploring nature, the writers argued, resulted in better grades, less stress and greater environmental awareness.[10]

Bills of rights from different states are all fairly similar, but still tailored to the unique concerns and values of their people. The Oregon Recreation and Park Association created a document quite similar to California's, urging that "every Oregon child should have the opportunity to 1. Follow a trail 2. Go boating 3. Camp out under the stars 4. Learn to swim 5. Walk barefoot on the beach 6. Climb a tree 7. Observe animals in their habitat 8. Catch a fish 9. Play in a nearby park 10. Celebrate Oregon's Culture & History."[11] The Indiana and North Carolina documents revealed their states' somewhat different demographics by asserting that children should have the right to visit farms and raise a plant of some sort themselves. Indiana added hunting, in addition to fishing, to its list of rights. The authors of Indiana, North Carolina and Maryland's documents all emphasized knowing nature as part of a learning process, stressing that children should share their experiences with friends, teachers or other mentors.[12]

Other efforts to reconnect children with their surrounds have been much more informal, carried out by individual parents. Parents have access to a plethora of reading material on the topic, which they can bestow on their reluctant children. One example of such literature is the *Daring Book for Girls*, authored by Andrea J. Buchanan and Miriam Peskowitz.[13] The book, published in 2007, came quite self-consciously out of a nineteenth-century literary mold, providing girls with page after page of ideas for interesting activities, indoors and out. Consciously or not, Buchanan and Peskowitz probably meant the preface of their book for parents, rather than their young readers. They wrote,

> We were girls in the days before the Web, cell phones, or even voicemail. . . . we did daring things like walk to school ourselves. Ride our banana-seat bikes to the local store. Babysit when we were still young enough to be babysat ourselves. Spent hours on our own, playing hopscotch or tetherball, building forts in our rooms, or turning our suburban neighborhoods into the perfect setting for covert ops, impromptu ball games, and imaginary medieval kingdoms. . . . Consider the *Daring Book for Girls* a book of possibilities and ideas for filling a day with adventure, imagination—and fun. The world is bigger than you can imagine, and it is yours for the exploring—if you dare.[14]

Buchanan and Peskowitz were remembering a type of childhood that seems to have disappeared and were suggesting that girls find again an outdoor world they and others their age had known.

The outdoor activities suggested by Buchanan and Peskowitz were really not all that daring: building a campfire, singing campfire songs, paddling a canoe and hiking. What a child might find novel was their suggestion that they should experience the out-of-doors unadulterated. The point of camping out, the authors wrote, was to really be out of doors. "Whether you are in your backyard or the Rocky Mountains, remember the whole point of sleeping out is to breathe in the night air, listen to nature's songs, and drift off to sleep under the stars."[15] They discouraged bringing along the conveniences of the modern home, preferring roughing it. Unlike many parents, the authors encouraged tree climbing, although preceded by appropriate practice: "Tree climbing doesn't necessary [sic] cause injury, but falling out of one surely does. Climb with caution. . . . Climbing walls at gyms are a great place to practice. Keep climbing, but remember once you go up, you still have to figure out how to safely get down."[16] In their discussion of hiking, the authors also, surprisingly, touted the benefits of getting lost. "Getting lost and finding your way home is part of the journey and a compass should help you figure out how to get back on the path. Match the dial on the compass so it reads north wherever the needle points, and turn the map, too, to line up with the compass' north. Start early in the day and bring a whistle along if you're worried."[17] The book bore a great resemblance to a midcentury Girl Scout handbook, minus the pledge and badges.[18]

Much of what Buchanan and Peskowitz encouraged would have seemed familiar to Lina and Adelia Beard, writing a little less than a century earlier in *On the Trail: An Outdoor Book for Girls*. The sisters exhorted their readers to prepare and to get out and explore the world around them. The clear give-away that *The Daring Book* was a modern publication, however, was tucked away, inside the front cover: "NOTE TO PARENTS: This book contains a number of activities which may be dangerous if not done exactly as directed or which may be inappropriate for young children. All of these activities should be car-ried out under adult supervision only. The authors and publishers expressly disclaim liability for any injury or damages that result from engaging in the activities contained in this book."[19] Unsurprisingly, the authors disclaimed responsibility for "daring girls" getting themselves into trouble. The Beards would be confused, and probably dismayed. An important assumption in their world was that part of growing up was becoming responsible for one's own actions. Although their writings assumed a good deal of skill building, they described very little if any adult supervision and encouraged girls to encounter the world responsibly, yet bravely. In their time and place, more than a hundred years ago, the Beards had little fear of being held liable for any of the scrapes into which their suggestions might lead girls.[20]

Books were just one item parents could buy to try to coax their children into experiencing the outdoor world they were missing. Old standbys such as ant farms, butterfly nets and microscopes were still available, but so were a whole host of "science and discovery" toys unheard of in the 1950s and 1960s. Manufacturers had found a multitude of ways to improve on the ant farm, and now children could observe a "light up ant farm and gel colony," or a "Geo Safari Ant Zone." For the squeamish child, there was the "backyard safari bug catcher and vacuum," which made insect study possible without anyone actually having to touch one. Instead of having children deposit captured insects in a discarded jam jar with holes punched in the lid, parents could purchase a set of bug jars with magnifying lids at considerably greater cost. A radio-controlled tarantula or scorpion, avail-able from Animal Planet, vastly increased the ability of children to torment their siblings or parents with their bug obsessions. In 2013, Toys R Us sold sixty-eight items in the "ant farms and bug science" category alone.[21] Nature sells, and there is money to be made from adults' guilty feelings about their indoor-oriented offspring.

If books and toys provided one avenue to increased outdoor activity, enforced daily trips out of the house was another. In 2007, the National Wildlife Federation launched its "Green Hour" program. The organization encouraged parents to give their children a Green Hour every day, or an hour spent outside in recreational activities. The description was flexible. The Green Hour could take place "in a garden, a backyard, the park down the street, or any place that provides safe and accessible green spaces where children can learn and play."[22] The National Wildlife Federation encouraged sensory exploration: seeing, hearing and smelling the outdoors. The organization encouraged parents to be partners with their children in the business of exploration. Their literature also promised that the results would be amazing:

> Twenty years from now, your child may not remember every piano lesson or soccer practice. But you can bet they'll remember climbing a tree with you! You have tremendous influence as a role model. If you are squeamish about worms or spiders or rain or mud, your child is likely to follow suit. On the other hand, if you're the first one to fall over and make a snow angel or wade bravely into the pond to catch a bug, your child will probably be eager to try it too.[23]

Green parenting promised a lifetime of memories.

The appeal of the Green Hour program was obvious, but the ease with which it could be accomplished was less so. The parents of fifty years ago would have found providing their children a daily hour of unstructured outdoor play laughably easy, since mothers routinely sent children out the door, insisting that they not return until dinner time. Fewer mothers, too, worked outside the home and might have been more readily available for joint adventures. Times, however, have changed. Mothers rarely just send their children out to play anymore, especially to see, hear and smell uncontrolled outdoor spaces. Parents, on the whole, are afraid of who or what might be lurking out there. If a child needs a "green hour," then a parent or other caregiver must have a green hour, too. Busy working parents have a hard time finding that hour in their day.[24] Another factor is at play here as well. With more women working, there are fewer adults home during the day keeping an informal eye on the neighborhood's children. Busy working parents, too, are often very short with their time, and not looking out for roaming children in the same way that their parents and grandparent were in the middle years of the century. Given this situation, it feels easier, and safer, to keep children indoors.

Overwhelming worries, conjured up by some truly horrible events, mock parents' efforts to change their children's relationship with the out-of-doors. Parents of a certain age remember Etan Patz, who as a six-year-old in 1979, walked for the first time alone to a New York City school bus stop and was never seen again. In 2001, he was declared dead.[25] Midwestern parents remember the 1982 disappearance of Johnny Gosch, and the 1984 disappearance of Eugene Martin, two Des Moines, Iowa, paperboys presumably kidnapped while making their rounds. Neither has ever been found.[26] In the summer of 2011, a horrified nation learned of the results when eight-year-old Leiby Kletzky, of Borough Park, Brooklyn, walked home from day camp alone for the first time. A stranger abducted, drugged, killed and dismembered the boy after he turned in the wrong direction, only seven blocks from home.[27] Incidents like these are, thankfully, quite rare. Children, sadly, are at far more risk from their nearest and dearest than from strangers, but that is of little comfort when a rare event happens in one's own community or family. As historian Steven Mintz has commented, "During the last quarter of the twentieth century there was a tendency to generalize about young people's well-being on the basis of certain horrific but isolated events." He continued, "The literary term *synecdoche*—confusing a part for a whole—is helpful in understanding how late twentieth-century Americans constructed an image of youth in crisis, as shocking episodes reinforced the impression that childhood was disintegrating."[28]

Given this tendency to confuse the part with the whole, parents even find it a scary proposition to send a child off to a camp, presumably well supervised by trained teens and adults. Children, after all, are injured and die in these places. A highly developed national media assured that parents in all parts of the country knew about the deaths of four Boy Scouts when a tornado hit the Little Sioux camp in western Iowa, for example. The most recent scholarly treatment of the Boy Scouts, Jay Mechling's *On My Honor*, does not do a great deal to help parents feel better about the safety of scouting. His description of time spent camping with a Boy Scout troop includes a vivid description of a summer thunderstorm, accompanied by hail and nearby lightning strikes. Mechling wrote, "The pleasing aroma of burnt pine belied the danger we were all sensing, the terror we were all sharing, as we listened to the thunder and joked nervously about how close it sounded." As evocative as this description was, and as interesting as Mechling's book is, few parents wish to be reminded that something that sounds as safe and supervised as scouting actually entails a certain amount of danger, as does any outdoor activity.[29]

Another kind of fear dogs parents as well: the fear of judgment. The parenting advice written in the last three decades strongly warns against allowing children to roam freely. In fact, it demands constant, careful supervision. Parents worry that their friends, neighbors and family will judge their parenting deficient if they do not keep a steady eye on their offspring. Less economically secure parents fear social services as much or more than they fear this other, informal judgment. Failure to supervise their children might result in a visit from the police and the loss of those children to foster care. As sociologist Markella B. Rutherford has noted, "The fact that as a society we have increasingly individualized parents' responsibility for children's safety is apparent in parents' fears, whether justified or not, that they could be charged with child endangerment for allowing their children to do things that the parents judge as safe and the parents and children in past generations considered routine."[30] Parental fears are not just for their children's safety, but for their own standing within their communities.

Fear has made parents unwilling to set their children free. Modern American mothers, according to one recent study, attribute their children's limited exposure to the outdoors to their own limited time to supervise them there.[31] Outdoors, unless one is talking about a safe, fenced backyard, is not a place for children to explore without supervision. Or is it? Lenore Skenazy thinks it is. This New York City mother of two horrified (or alternately encouraged) legions of parents nationwide when she admitted to allowing her nine-year-old son to ride the subway alone. As she wrote in the aftermath of the uproar that followed: "The media dubbed me 'America's Worst Mom.' (Go ahead—Google it.) But that's not what I am."[32] Since that experience, Skenazy has written a book entitled *Free-Range Kids: Giving Our Children the Freedom We Had without Going Nuts with Worry* and has led a "free-range kids" movement from her ongoing blog under the same name. In her book and blog, she encourages parents to allow their children the same freedom that they had as youngsters, countering the common belief that "an unwatched child is a tragedy waiting to happen!"[33] Skenazy argues that

> a lot of parents today are really bad at assessing risk. They see no difference between letting their children walk to school and letting them walk through a firing range. When they picture their kids riding their bikes to a birthday party, they see them dodging Mack trucks with brake problems. To let their children play unsupervised in a park at age eight or ten even thirteen seems about as responsible as throwing them in the shark tank at Sea World with their pockets full of meatballs.[34]

The overwhelming fear parents feel about letting their children play outside, unattended, or even walk to school alone, she writes, stems from made-for-TV movies, news programs and milk carton campaigns. She quotes statistics from the National Center for Missing and Exploited Children, showing that the number of children abducted and murdered by strangers in the United States is roughly 1 in 1.5 million, essentially what it was in her own youth. "Put yet another, even better way, by British author Warwick Cairns, who wrote the book *How to Live Dangerously*: if you actually *wanted* your child to be kidnapped and held overnight by a stranger, how long would you have to keep her outside, unattended, for this to be statistically likely to happen? About seven hundred and fifty thousand years."[35]

Crime against children, Skenazy argues, is actually falling, due to a confluence of forces, such as less tolerance of child abuse, better prosecution, improved psychiatric medication and cell phones. "Let's hear it for society working," she writes. "But of course, you never do. Hear about society working, that is. 'Mellowed-out criminal uninterested in snatching local child, and even if he did, greater police presence would probably prevent it' is just not a ratings grabber. At least not compared to 'Child snatched off scooter!'"[36] There are (statistically) far bigger risks to children's lives, she points out, such as automobile accidents, house fires and drowning. "Things that we're familiar with, like driving, don't scare us," she comments, "despite the odds. Meanwhile the stranger danger fear is so gruesome and out of the ordinary, it dominates our parenting lives even though it doesn't deserve to."[37]

So, according to Skenazy and her free-range kids movement, what is the solution? Parents, she says, need to turn off the TV, train their children how to react to the unlikely situation of encountering a predator and trust that they will be safe. "Childhood independence," she writes, "has become taboo, even though our world is no less safe than twenty or thirty years ago. The ground has not gradually gotten harder under the jungle gym. The bus stops have not crept further from home. Crime is actually lower than it was when most of us were growing up."[38] In the face of Leiby Kletzky's abduction and murder, she reaffirmed her stance. "People will blame the parents for letting their son walk even a few blocks on his own. I've already read some of those comments. They are like knives. . . . It is really hard to even suggest that life continue on as normal, but that is truly what I believe is the only response to this crime. . . . I'm shaken. I'm sad. I'm so sorry for what has happened. And I will send my sons out again."[39] Another commentator agreed: "While we mourn the death of young Leiby, we must remember that safety is more than just the absence of danger. It's the presence of a full and happy life—a life that's not dominated by fear. . . . Perhaps it is a good time to remember how much we love our children and let them know, but it's not a time to lock them up, keep them from the world, prevent them from exploring or fill them with fear."[40]

A quick look at the electronic responses to these two commentaries indicates that parental opinion was decidedly mixed. While some agreed that the time had come for children to have more freedom and more opportunities to go unaccompanied into the world, other parents vehemently disagreed. What would you think, they asked, if your child was the 1 child in 1.5 million who encountered the murderous predator? Any risk at all, no matter how small, seemed too great to bear. Fears such as these have led to a brisk business in GPS tracking devices for children, which parents can conveniently place inside hats, coats and backpacks. Such devices not only pinpoint a child's location, but let parents know when a child has strayed outside of a self-selected safe zone.[41] Safety, like nature, also sells. This is a far different world than the one in which mothers and fathers told their children to go outside and play and to not come back until dark. Struggle as they might with their own doubts, the grown-ups have allowed their fears to overcome them, and the indoor child has become the norm.

If, in the last few chapters, you have noticed a drift away from discussion of the concerns and desires of children toward a discussion of the concerns and desires of adults, you are not imagining things. The shape of my discussion has taken on the shape of predominating societal pressures. At one time, because parents had so many other more pressing concerns, children to a large extent managed their own relationships with the environment outside their homes. Children ventured out in pursuit of their own interests, and the resulting narrative was one of action and adventure, even if quite a bit of it was imaginary. In the last twenty to thirty years, the management of the outdoors has shifted to worried adults, and the relationship of children to that world has constricted. The tale is no longer so exciting. For large numbers of children (although admittedly not all), the outdoor script is being written by adults, and the increasingly indoor script, written by children, is one about their relationships to screens, whether on a television, a computer, or a cell phone.

The voices expressing concern about these developments are not those of children. They are the voices of adults, people like Richard Louv and Robert Pyle. They are also the voices of parents. Parents are left with a real dilemma. One hundred years ago, fifty years ago, thirty years ago, children could get what was good for them from the outdoors without parents necessarily making a significant personal investment in the process. If exposure to the outdoors is good for children, as the experts tell us, and independent exploration is even better, the children of 1900, or even 1970, could generally get their fill without a mother or father making a commitment to (or even thinking about) getting them outside. Children went outside of their own free will, or their mothers happily chucked them out of the house for significant periods of time, without really worrying about what they were doing. Children then had the opportunity to explore the world around them, whether they actually knew that was what they were doing or not. Youngsters like Robert Pyle found butterflies, moths, trees and freedom in the urban wildlands beyond their backyards. In more exotic cases, children like Janisse Ray found carnivorous pitcher plants outside their junkyard homes and learned invaluable lessons about the natural world in the most unlikely of places. Their parents made no more commitment to this process than to issue a few cautions and wave as their offspring went out of the door. If parents wanted-to add more structured outdoor experiences to their children's lives, they signed them up for various youth organizations and camps, run by the Girl Scouts, Boy Scouts, Campfire, the Y.M.C.A. or 4-H. Midcentury children could easily accumulate hours and hours of structured and unstructured adventures outside. Parents, remembering youthful adventures outdoors in free play, feel a real sense of loss, even grief, over their own children's experiences.[42] The children, having been raised in a different time and place, feel something completely different. As Richard Louv reflected in 1990, "Curiously, children are not nearly as worried as their parents about their loss of physical freedom." Instead, for them, and their parents, "nature . . . is becoming something to wear, to watch, to consume."[43]

These developments should not come as a surprise to anyone. To return again to Elliott West's observations about children's experiences on the far western frontier, pioneer parents worried about the negative effects of a raw, western environment on their children. Children growing up in that environment had nothing with which to compare their experiences. That landscape was simply their home, and they embraced it in ways that adults often could not and did not. Likewise, it would be a fairly meaningless exercise to ask today's children if they share their parents' concerns or preferences. A child cannot miss a freewheeling, independent relationship with the out-of-doors if he or she has never had that experience, and a growing number of youngsters are in that category.

Shifting the emphasis back to the children, what do they have to say about the environments in which they live? Even researchers who argue strongly for children experiencing more outdoor activities have had to acknowledge that "today's children are choosing not to play outdoors. Some children may actually prefer sitting and watching events unfold on television to playing outdoors and creatively thinking of ways to entertain themselves."[44] For some children, this is not so much a choice as a necessity. Not all children live in the kind of neighborhoods where going outside might be appealing, or even desirable. Dangerous environments in some communities keep children indoors and even have the potential to negatively affect children's every perception of the world outside their doors. An educational researcher examining poor, inner-city children's attitudes about nature noted that the danger of the world in which the children lived colored their beliefs about the safety of fields and forests where they had never even been. As the author of the 1994 publication noted, "students associate nature with dangerous people hiding behind trees." He also noted "in the suburban interviews this issue does not emerge even once."[45] Children's reactions to pictures of forests with hikers were startling. One thirteen-year-old girl commented that she would never go to a forest alone at night. This, in itself, was not all that surprising, but her reasoning, perhaps, was. She said, "There ain't no way of you surviving because there are killers out there . . . there are killers everywhere in this world." Another adolescent girl, viewing the same picture, commented that it looked like "a nice spot for someone to go camping." She qualified her observation, however, by stating "these trees keep people from seeing what goes on because the murderers and the rapists use the trees to block what they're doing."[46] Youngsters who lived day in and day out in unpredictable and dangerous urban locations associated trees, bushes, parks and open space with bodily, physical peril, reflecting their fears of city environments.

In other places, the outdoors is considerably less scary, but also terribly unappealing. Grown-ups and their ways of thinking have helped to create this situation. Some children may avoid outdoor exploration simply because they believe that there is very little that is fun or exciting out there. Many of the opportunities that their parents had to muck about and explore are simply not available to young people today. Fears of liability have led many a municipality to limit access to many natural features within parks and other open spaces. A sign, posted in Bittersweet Park in Greeley, Colorado, says it all. Although there is a small lake and a large marshy area teeming with possibilities, children and all others are forbidden from getting too close. Large red and white signs loudly proclaim, "FOR SAFETY STAY OUT OF WATER." Even though the pond is adjacent to a play area, posted with suggestions for par-

This sign in Bittersweet Park, Greeley, Colorado, warns children away from the fun they might have playing in the water. Photograph by author.

ents about fun, nature-oriented activities for their children, drowning risks and concerns about water contamination place strict limits on children's explorations. Children and parents who choose to follow the directions are confined to a considerably less interesting playground. Operating under these constraints, why would a ten- or eleven-year-old want to play outdoors?

Many children lack the intense familiarity with the outdoors world that leads to attachment and a desire to be there on a regular basis. Compared to the children of the past, children today rarely walk or bicycle through their neighborhoods. In 2001, the U.S. Department of Transportation surveyed American households and found that the number of daily "walking trips" that people made had declined by 40 percent since 1977. Fully 70 percent of all trips taken by children were made in cars. Fifty percent fewer children walk or bike to school than did in 1969.[47] On the one hand, this means that children are getting less exercise. On the other, it has serious implications for children's relationships with the wider environment. Children who spend little time out and about in their neighborhoods have fewer opportunities for finding intriguing places and making them their own. A 1990 study of the ways in which children claimed ownership of places in their environments points out the real problems today's children must have in attaching themselves to particular pieces of earth. The study's author found that "special places" had certain characteristics. "Special places are *found or constructed by children on their own*. . . . Special places are *secret*. Children do not want other people to know where they are. . . . Special places are *owned by their creators*. . . . Special places are *safe*. A feeling of calm and repose comes over children when they are in their special places [emphasis in original]."[48] Very few children are being allowed to find those special spots, root about in the dirt and have quiet, alone moments in places they call their own. Studies with adults emphasize the longer-term importance of experiences like these. People who lack frequent, positive experiences with the out-of-doors in childhood tend to have fewer such experiences in adulthood. They don't feel confident and at home in those places, and avoid them as adults.[49] We have helped to create a world where children would prefer to stay indoors, and indeed are often encouraged to stay indoors, and will be afraid or uncomfortable with the space outside their homes as adults.

The perspective from other vantage points, however, is considerably less bleak. A unique project undertaken at a Wisconsin grade school allows a much less declensionist view of children's activities in the twenty-first century to emerge. During the 2000–2001 school year, the fourth-grade students at Levi Leonard Elementary School in Evansville, Wisconsin, sat down to record stories about their lives. They wrote about a number of topics: their families, pets and activities, among others. They did this at the request of archivists at the Wisconsin Historical Society, who wanted to create a "Kids Archive," chronicling child-life in turn-of-the-twenty-first-century Wisconsin. The historical society envisioned a large sample of Wisconsin children writing "in [their] own words, their thoughts and feelings about themselves and the world in which they live."[50] Even though the larger project failed to come to fruition, Evansville teacher Gail Guenther enlisted her class in the project. In writing about their lives, the students exhibited real interest in activities outside of their homes and the natural world in many forms. Writing essays involved the students picking and choosing those elements in their lives about which to reflect. Clearly, their teacher provided some guidance, asking the students to think about their favorite activities, their most recent vacations and their hopes and dreams for the future.

If parents' and reformers' fears about the future of child life were entirely founded, these essays should have been replete with references to computers, television and the world inside four walls. These elements did, of course, appear in the students' essays. But what also appeared were thoughtful and interesting discussions of children's interactions and fascination with nature. In one essay, young Cheyenne Alisankus identified her interests in the out-of-doors. "My favorite Out door activities are looking at nanture and helping the frogs and the flowers." She described both the built and naturally occurring elements in her hometown with which she interacted. "It has a lot of trees and flowers. It also has a Mcdonels and a roller rinck. . . . I live in a cul-de-sac that is a circl part of the Street This is good because I have a lot of place to ride my bike and work with side walk chalk. there is more room in my back yard because we can play on our swing set!"[51] Outdoor activities actually featured more extensively in Cheyenne's descriptions than indoor activities, such as visiting McDonald's or the roller rink.

Cheyenne was not alone in her focus on the outdoors. Nikki Marie Arndt's essay brimmed with discussion of outdoor activities. "My favrot sport is riding horses in the woods. My least favort thing owr snakes. In winter my favoret thing to do is to have a snowball fight. In summer I like to go swimming in a pool." She identified a number of animals that intrigued her, such as "deer, skunks, frogs, cats, and more. . . . Sometimes there are gees, wild gees, ducks, and fish." Nikki's parents shared and encouraged her interests. The last family vacation had been a fishing trip to Minnesota. She wrote, "One time I caught a 12 pound cat fish off the dock with a brown fake worm. In Minnesota, you are most likely to catch the big fish by the weeds." The trip to Minnesota afforded the opportunity to observe new and different wildlife. "In Minnesota the cotteges is in the woods and there are black bears in Minnisota by the cottages." Her wildlife observing ambitions extended even farther afield, though. If she was rich, she stated, she would "Go to florida, and go swimming in a pool with dolphins."[52]

Shane Gardener's parents also encouraged ventures into the outdoors. He wrote, "My last vacation was to Govenor Dodge which is a place to camp. I got my own tent which is like a portable house and I made my own breakfast of bacon an egg sandwitch with jelly on it. When I went to the beach I swam to the other side of the lake. There was a rope tied to a branch there, so I swung off it into the water a couple of times and swam back. As luck would have it I caught a water snake. . . . Then I let it go back into the lake."[53] His adventures at Governor Dodge State Park would have seemed entirely normal and familiar to children decades earlier. Camping, swimming, cooking over a campfire and capturing snakes would have appealed to the boys of 1900, just as they appealed to Shane in 2000.

Some of the children's descriptions neatly juxtaposed their fascination with the wild and their interests in modern indoor kid culture. Elisabeth Brummond had high hopes: "When I grow up I think I will be an ocean-ographer. that is a person who studies the ocean. . . . My goal when I get older is to discovor a new animal so I can be rich. Maybe even one day I'll swim with dolphins in the ocean." She also dabbled in computer games. "My favorite toys are computer games. One of my favorite computer games is The Sims."[54] Like Elisabeth, Mary Luchsinger also moved back and forth between her interest in popular culture and the natural world. "If I could have 3 wishes one would be that Pokemon were real, So that people could be Pokemon masters if they wanted to. My second wish would be that there was no more hunting in the world. I don't have to worry about dead animals that have been shot. My third wish is that animals can talk and tell people what they want. That way we could get them what they want. I also like it because they could listen to us and talk back to us."[55] Being conversant with modern kid culture did not preclude an active interest in animals. Margaret O'Brien would have been right at home with many a midcentury child. "My favorite summer activity is to go swimming in the ocean. My favorite winter activity is to make snow forts. My favorite outdoor activity is to climb trees and roofs. My favorite indoor activities are to play on the computer and to watch T.V."[56] Once common (although probably not encouraged), climb-ing trees and roofs had presumably gone by the wayside by 2000. Monica Pelkey also climbed trees: "I like . . . climbing trees because I can climb high higher than my sister can." She, however, eschewed computer games for other activities. "I like to run so I can get some exersize and muscles so I can help my dad split wood, load it up load it bring it to my dads friends house."[57]

There is no tale of woe here. These youngsters were conversant with tele-vision, computer games and Pokemon, but they were also intrigued with wild animals, tree climbing and science. They caught fish and dreamed of swimming with dolphins. While some vacationed at the Mall of America, others travelled to Minnesota lakes and Wisconsin state parks. Their ex-periences may or may not have been typical. Some of this familiarity and comfort with the out-of-doors may have derived from their residence in a small Wisconsin town, home to less than 5,000 people. Their parents may have felt comfortable allowing them experiences that worried parents in larger communities. Or perhaps Cheyenne, Nikki and Shane were not ter-ribly unusual in their enjoyment of a wide variety of activities, including a reasonable dose of those experienced in the out-of-doors.

Have observers exaggerated the degree to which children have abandoned the outdoors in favor of their televisions and computers? This is a difficult question to answer, particularly in the absence of historical perspective and more data. What appears to be a long-term and permanent divorce between children and the out-of-doors may just be a relatively short-term phenomenon. More than likely it is a partial and incomplete phenomenon, with children in different communities in different regions experiencing it to varying degrees. Today's poor children may spend more time inside than those from wealthier backgrounds because of their parents' concerns about the dangers lurking in their neighborhoods.[58] Research indicates that working-class children often have greater freedom to roam than middle-class or poor children. Boys also have more freedom to come and go than girls. One researcher found that parents allowed their boys to ride their bicycles farther away from home, and with considerably less supervision, than their girls.[59]

Geography and population density also play a role in the freedoms that parents grant children. Children in Alaskan villages and small midwestern towns most assuredly have different opportunities on a day-to-day basis to experience the outdoors than those growing up in Los Angeles, Chicago or midtown Manhattan. Many small heartland communities advertise themselves to potential newcomers as places where "their kids have smaller classes at the school and they can walk or bike anywhere without the parents having to worry about them."[60] The anecdotal evidence suggests that in these places families are more relaxed about stranger danger than in urban and suburban neighborhoods. There are still small towns where on summer afternoons children ride their bicycles all over and wander out to see who is home and available to play. There are even places where people leave their houses unlocked at night. These communities, and these children, are far harder to find than they were thirty years ago, and unfortunately, we often learn of their existence after something unfortunate has happened to change children's and parents' attitudes and behavior.[61] To return to Evansville, Wisconsin, if the evidence provided by that community's children can be generalized, it may be that youngsters are not as divorced from the out-of-doors as the media frenzy might suggest. Without a larger sample of the nation's children, rural and urban, from small towns and large, it is difficult to draw conclusions, either dire or hopeful.

Where do today's children play? Most often, they play indoors, or on tended soccer fields. They are there because of a combination of their own desires and their parents' fears. Children born in the last decades of the twentieth century, and the first decade of the twenty-first, are far more conversant with indoor environments than those available outside. Once upon a time, houses were small and crowded, and mothers dealt with their own environmental crisis by sending all but the tiniest of their offspring, and all but the most immediately useful, off to amuse themselves in the world out-of-doors. On washing day, with fires burning and water boiling, there was more to fear for a child under foot than a child outside, exploring independently.

The contours of our world, however, have shifted. Homes became larger and more comfortable, indoor entertainment options widened, and Americans became far more connected than ever before to news—news that had the capacity to bring isolated tragedies happening hundreds or thousands of miles away into every family's home. Parents imagine the 1 in 1.5 million children abducted and killed by a stranger as their own far more readily, because they know the stories and faces of Etan Patz, Johnny Gosch and Leiby Kletzky. Had the climate of parental fear pervading the last thirty years coincided with the technology and the homes of the 1930s or 1950s, the children would have been in revolt by now, and perhaps we would have already found a way to get them back outside. The tide of fear, and the tide of technological change, however, came together. Parents could confine their children indoors, and those children could find ways to entertain themselves, even if parents have ultimately become uneasy with that solution. Struggle as they might with their own doubts, the grown-ups have allowed their fears to overcome them, and the indoor child has carried the day.

NOTES

INTRODUCTION: THE ENVIRONMENTAL CHILD

1. For an excellent discussion of the many meanings of natural in the landscape, see Mark Fiege, *Irrigated Eden: The Making of an Agricultural Landscape in the American West* (Seattle: University of Washington Press, 1999), 3–10.

2. Bernard Mergen, *Play and Playthings: A Reference Guide* (Westport, Conn.: Greenwood Press, 1982), 86.

3. Environmental health has been ably examined in several different books including Charles R. King, *Children's Health in America: A History* (New York: Twayne Publishers, 1993), and Peter C. English, *Old Paint: A Medical History of Childhood Lead-Paint Poisoning in the United States to 1980* (New Brunswick, N.J.: Rutgers University Press, 2001). Elliott West's chapter on environmental health on the frontier is also excellent. Elliott West, *Growing Up with the Country: Childhood on the Far Western Frontier* (Albuquerque: University of New Mexico Press, 1989), 213–244.

4. West, *Growing Up with the Country*, 21.

5. John R. Gillis, "The Islanding of Children—Reshaping the Mythical Landscapes of Childhood," in Marta Gutman and Ning de Coninck-Smith, *Designing Modern Childhoods: History, Space and the Material Culture of Children* (New Brunswick, N.J.: Rutgers University Press, 2008), 316.

6. Among the many definitions of "nature" in *The American Heritage Dictionary* are "3. The world of living things and the outdoors. . . . " and ". . . . A primitive state of existence, untouched and uninfluenced by civilization or artificiality." *The American Heritage Dictionary of the English Language*, 3rd ed. (Boston: Houghton Mifflin, 1996), 1204.

7. Helena Karella, "Work and Play Club," *The Nebraska Farmer*, July 3, 1907, 593.

8. Amrys O. Williams, "Head, Heart, Hands, and Health: 4-H, Ecology, and Conservation in Wisconsin, 1930–1950," Master's Research Essay, History of Science Department, University of Wisconsin–Madison, April 9, 2007.

9. Howard P. Chudacoff, *Children at Play: An American History*. (New York: New York University Press, 2007), 108–109.

10. Chudacoff, *Children at Play*, 115.

11. David Danbom, *Born in the Country: A History of Rural America* (Baltimore: Johns Hopkins University Press, 1995), 66–67.

12. Alex Kotlowitz, *There Are No Children Here: The Story of Two Boys Growing Up in the Other America* (New York: Anchor Books, 1991).

13. Robert Michael Pyle, *The Thunder Tree: Lessons from an Urban Wildland* (Boston: Houghton Mifflin, 1993).

14. See, for example, Richard Louv, *Last Child in the Woods: Saving Our Children from Nature-Deficit Disorder* (Chapel Hill, N.C.: Algonquin Books, 2008).

CHAPTER ONE: THE ENVIRONMENT AND THE FARM CHILD

1. Louise Fassacht, "Summer and Winter," *Prairie Farmer*, June 18, 1921, 18.

2. As Charles R. King notes in *Children's Health in America*, the problem largely consisted of a lack of sanitation and the close proximity of people to each other in crowded urban areas. Charles R. King, *Children's Health in America* (New York: Twayne Publishers, 1993), 98–99.

3. Mamie Griswold, Manuscript Diaries, 1878–1883, Henry A. Griswold Family Papers, Box 4, Illinois State Historical Library, Springfield, Illinois, January 1, 22, February 1, April 1, 20, June 12, 17, 20, July 17, September 5, 1878, January 18, 1879.

4. Hermann C. Benke, Manuscript Diary, Manuscripts Division, Kansas State Historical Society, Topeka, Kansas, January 3, 1886.

5. Benke, Manuscript Diary, April 10, 14, May 8, June 28, September 10, 1886.

6. "The Opposum," *The Atchison Daily Globe*, April 9, 1885, Issue 2, 286, column C.

7. Benke, Manuscript Diary, January 3, 1886.

8. Benke, Manuscript Diary, February 28, 1886.

9. Elliott West, *Growing Up with the Country: Childhood on the Far Western Frontier* (Albuquerque: University of New Mexico Press, 1989), 101–104.

10. "Boys and Girls Write the Editor," *Prairie Farmer*, June 1, 1912, 18.

11. "Prairie Farmer Boys and Girls," *Prairie Farmer*, February 26, 1921, 30; "Boys and Girls Write the Editor," *Prairie Farmer*, February 23, 1918, 34.

12. Benke, Manuscript Diary, March 14, 1887.

13. Bird T. Baldwin, Eva Abigail Fillmore, and Lora Hadley, *Farm Children: An Investigation of Rural Child Life in Selected Areas of Iowa* (New York: D. Appleton, 1930), 150–151.

14. Anonymous, "Life on the Farm," ca. 1898–1900, John E. Brown Papers, Special Collections, State Historical Society of Iowa, Iowa City, Iowa.

15. Washington Lafayette McClary, Manuscript Diary, December 3, 1910, MS 3775, Manuscripts Collection, Nebraska State Historical Society, Lincoln, Nebraska.

16. Lewellyn Amos Gushee, Letter to Brother Frank, March 1, 1875, Lewellyn Amos Gushee Papers, 1861–1892, MS 3972, Manuscripts Collection, Nebraska State Historical Society, Lincoln, Nebraska.

17. Nellie Crow Bedford, "The Blizzard I Remember," Iowa Commission on the Aging, Essay Contest, 1976, Ms. 89, State Historical Society of Iowa, Iowa City, Iowa.

18. August Schulz, Manuscript Diary, Manuscripts Division, Kansas State Historical Society, Topeka, Kanas, July 11, 1877.

19. Emily V. Culek, "Young People," *The Nebraska Farmer*, July 5, 1916, 753.

20. Charles M. Turner, Typescript Reminiscence, 12, RS 1478.AM, Box 1, Manuscripts Collection, Nebraska State Historical Society, Lincoln, Nebraska.

21. Maude Baumann Arney, Manuscript Diary, April–July 1900, Manuscripts Department, Minnesota Historical Society, St. Paul, Minnesota, June 5, 1900.

22. There is some question from the way in which Ise wrote the story if Nebraska Stevens died as a result of his illness, or as a result of a mercy killing, since the men of the community who were attending him knew that he could not survive rabies and did not want him or his mother to suffer further. John Ise, *Sod and Stubble* (Lawrence: University Press of Kansas, 1996), 56–60.

23. Opal Watson, "Young People," *The Nebraska Farmer*, April 21, 1915, 495.

24. Walker D. Wyman, "Boyhood Recollections of Dogs, Ponies, Trapping, Even Flying Off the Hen House Roof," Manuscript reminiscence, used by permission of the holder, Mark Wyman, Normal, Illinois.

25. Laura Ingalls Wilder explored both of these scenarios in her children's stories. Not surprisingly, given the audience, these encounters with nature ended happily. For other children, such as one mentioned in the Gitchel correspondence below, the results could be tragic. See Laura Ingalls Wilder, *By the Shores of Silver Lake* (New York: Harper Trophy, 2007), 277–280, and *The Long Winter* (New York: Harper Trophy, 1971), 20–22.

26. Jack Temple Kirby, *Rural Worlds Lost: The American South, 1920–1960* (Baton Rouge: Louisiana State University Press, 1987), 186–187. For a discussion of hook-worm eradication efforts, see William A. Link, "Privies, Progressivism and Public Schools: Health Reform and Education in the Rural South, 1909–1920," *Journal of Southern History* 54, 4 (November 1988): 623–642. The lack of privies is documented in sources such as Charles E. Gibbons, *Child Labor among the Cotton Growers of Texas* (New York: National Child Labor Committee, 1925), 86.

27. Link, "Privies, Progressivism and Public Schools," 627–630.

28. Mary Gitchel, letter to "Friends," August 6, 1894, Gitchel-Larsen Family, MS 3622, Manuscripts Collection, Nebraska State Historical Society, Lincoln, Nebraska.

29. Edna S. Rapp, "Sod House Letters, 1957–1958," to the *Nebraska Farmer*, MS 721, Manuscript Collections, Nebraska State Historical Society, Lincoln, Nebraska.

30. "'Tis Only a Grasshopper," *American Young Folks* III, 3 (March 1877): 38.

31. Frederick B. to Governor Cushman Davis, May 13, 1875, as quoted in Gilbert C. Fite, "Some Farmers' Accounts of Hardship on the Frontier," *Minnesota History*, 37, 5 (March 1961): 209.

32. Despite popular impressions, there were not, in fact, grasshoppers, but Rocky Mountain locusts. See A. S. Packard, Jr., *Report on the Rocky Mountain Locust and Other Insects Now Injuring or Likely to Injure Field and Garden Crops in the United States* (Washington, D.C.: U.S. Geological Survey, Department of the Interior, 1877).

33. Julie Courtwright, "'When We First Come Here It All Looked Like Prairie Land Almost': Prairie Fire and Plains Settlement," *Western Historical Quarterly* 38, 2 (Summer 2007): 166–170.

34. Mrs. W. O. Bishop, "Sod House Letters, 1957–1958," to the *Nebraska Farmer*, MS 721, Manuscripts Collection, Nebraska State Historical Society, Lincoln, Nebraska.

35. Benke, Manuscript Diary, March 12, 1887.

36. Courtwright, "'When We First Come Here,'" 170.

37. Sanora Babb, *An Owl on Every Post* (Albuquerque: University of New Mexico Press, 1994), 48–50.

38. Babb, *An Owl on Every Post*, 59.

39. Liberty Hyde Bailey, *The Training of Farmers* (New York: Century, 1909), 91.

40. Ibid., 102–104.

41. Baldwin, Fillmore, and Hadley, *Farm Children*, 151.

42. Bailey, *The Training of Farmers*, 124.

43. Ibid., 126–134.

44. Ibid., 120.

45. Charles Loring Brace, *The Dangerous Classes of New York and Twenty Years' Work among Them* (New York: Wynkoop & Hallenbeck, 1872), 95, 223–245.

46. Cheryl Lee Carpenter, "The Social Production of Fresh Air Charity Work, 1870–1930," PhD diss., Syracuse University, 1994, 122.

47. Marilyn Irvin Holt, *The Orphan Trains: Placing Out in America* (Lincoln: Bison Books, 1992), 27.

48. Ibid., 48.

49. Ibid., 31.

50. Ibid., 118–155.

51. Ibid., 158.

52. "The Children's Garden," *The Atchison Daily Globe*, March 12, 1886, Issue 2, 575, column F.

53. Anna Stanley, Memoir, Archives Collection, Wisconsin Historical Society, Madison, Wisconsin, 3.

54. George B. Thompson, "Pioneering on the Nebraska Prairies," MS 1463, Manuscripts Collection, Nebraska State Historical Society, Lincoln, Nebraska, 2.

55. Frank J. Engles, "Reminiscence," MS 0482, Manuscripts Collection, Nebraska State Historical Society, 1–4.

56. Curtis Harnack, *We Have All Gone Away* (Garden City, N.Y.: Doubleday, 1973), 85.

57. Laura Ingalls Wilder, *On the Banks of Plum Creek* (New York: Harper Trophy, 1971), 280–281, 286–292.

58. Laura Ingalls Wilder, *Little House in the Big Woods* (New York: Harper Trophy, 1971); *Little House on the Prairie* (New York: Harper Trophy, 1971); *On the Banks of Plum Creek* (New York: Harper Trophy, 1971); *By the Shores of Silver Lake* (New York: Harper Trophy, 1971); *Little Town on the Prairie* (New York: Harper Trophy, 1971); *These Happy Golden Years* (New York: Harper Trophy, 1971).

59. Wilder, *The Long Winter*, 225.

60. Doan Robinson, *History of South Dakota*, vol. 1 (Logansport, Ind.: B. F. Bowen, 1904), 306–309.

61. Wilder, *The Long Winter*, 334.

62. Wilder, *By the Shores of Silver Lake*, 164–165.

63. Ibid., 168.

64. This line of inquiry was inspired by discussion with Dr. Roberta Trites, after her class lecture and discussion of *By the Shores of Silver Lake*. Lecture, "English 470: Studies in Children's Literature: Narrative, Gender, History," Illinois State University, February 10, 2010.

65. Helena Karella, "Work and Play Club," *The Nebraska Farmer*, July 3, 1907, 593.

66. Pamela Riney-Kehrberg, *Rooted in Dust: Surviving Drought and Depression in Southwestern Kansas* (Lawrence: University Press of Kansas, 1994), 32–33.

67. David B. Danbom, *Born in the Country: A History of Rural America* (Baltimore: Johns Hopkins University Press, 1995), 167.

68. U.S. Senate, *Report of the Country Life Commission: Special Message from the President of the United States Transmitting the Report of the Country Life Commission* (Washington, D.C.: Government Printing Office, 1909), 53–55.

69. Kevin C. Armitage, *The Nature Study Movement: The Forgotten Popularizer of America's Conservation Ethic* (Lawrence: University Press of Kansas, 2009), 185–189.

70. Clyde O. Bye, "A Study of the Sources of Material Available for Use in an Elementary Course in Nature-Study for Rural School Children, with Especial Reference to Animals, Birds, and Insects," M.S. thesis, Vocational Education, Iowa State College, Ames, Iowa, 1923, 1–2.

71. Melvin W. Strong, "A Study of the Sources of Material Available for Use in an Elementary Course in Nature Study for Rural School Children with Especial Reference to Inorganic Nature," M.S. thesis, Vocational Education, Iowa State College, Ames, Iowa, 1923, 1.

72. Even though the organization was called the Farm *Boy* Cavaliers, the organization invited girls to join existing units or form their own. While most of the troops enlisted only boys, four girls belonged to Troop No. 1 in Fergus, North Dakota. Troop No. 2 of Clearfield, South Dakota, and Troop No. 2 of Belvidere, Illinois, were composed entirely of girls. While the boys were Esquires and Knights, the girls were Home Cavaliers, with the ranks of Novice, Damoiselle and Lady. Dexter D. Mayne Papers, Farm Boy Cavaliers of America, Manuscripts Collection, Minnesota Historical Society, St. Paul, Minnesota, Folder 3, File 3, Miscellaneous Papers. This material about the Farm Boy Cavaliers appeared originally in *Agricultural History*, and is used with journal's permission. See Pamela Riney-Kehrberg, "Farm Youth and Progressive Agricultural Reform: Dexter D. Mayne and the Farm Boy Cavaliers of America," *Agricultural History* 85, 4 (Fall 2011): 437–459.

73. David I. MacLeod, *Building Character in the American Boy: The Boy Scouts, YMCA, and Their Forerunners, 1870–1920* (Madison: University of Wisconsin Press, 1983), 227–228; "Boys and Girls," *Prairie Farmer*, November 18, 1916, 24.

74. *Preliminary Announcement of Farm Boy Cavaliers: An Organization of Farm Boys Mounted on Horses*, 2–3. Undated pamphlet, Folder 1, Printed Materials, Dexter D. Mayne Papers, Manuscripts Collection, Minnesota Historical Society, St. Paul, Minnesota.

75. Baldwin, Fillmore, and Hadley, *Farm Children*, 150–151.

76. See Pamela Riney-Kehrberg, *Childhood on the Farm: Work, Play and Coming of Age in the Midwest* (Lawrence: University Press of Kansas, 2005), 136–142.

77. *Preliminary Announcement*, 5.

78. Ibid., 12–28.

79. R. R. Olmstead, "Bird Study," *Farm Boy Cavalier News* 2, 11 (January 1918): 4.

80. "Work and Play," *Farm Boy Cavalier News* 2, 6 (August 1917): 1.

81. "The Boy Problem in the Country," *The Charities and the Commons* 17 (December 1906): 332–333.

82. Edwina Mary Layman, "The Boys' and Girls' Clubs," *Farm Home*, February 1, 1916, 10.

83. Alfred E. Ross, *Graded Games for Rural Schools* (New York: A. S. Barnes, 1926), ix.

84. James Edward Rogers, *The Child and Play, Based on the Reports of the White House Conference on Child Health and Protection* (New York: Century, 1932), 104–106.

85. Thomas Wessell and Marilyn Wessell, *4-H: An American Idea, 1900–1980* (Chevy Chase, Md.: National 4-H Council, 1982), 43–49.

86. I want to express my particular thanks to Amrys Williams for introducing me to Wakelin McNeel at the June 2008 Agricultural History Society meeting in Reno, Nevada.

87. Wakelin McNeel, Sr., "Lessons from Nature," *Bulletin of the Wisconsin State Board of Health* (December 1951): 21.

88. Wakelin McNeel, Sr., *Forestry Club 4-H Work*, Circular 4-H20 (Madison: Extension Service of the College of Agriculture, Revised, February 1940; First published January 1936), cover.

89. Ibid.

90. Ibid., 14.

91. Ibid., 14–15.

92. Amrys O. Williams, "Head, Heart, Hands, and Health: 4-H, Ecology, and Conservation in Wisconsin," Master's Research Essay, Department of History of Science, University of Wisconsin–Madison, April 9, 2007, 29–30.

93. Ibid., 33–34.

94. Wakelin McNeel, Sr., "School Forests and Why They Grow," *National Waltonian* (May 1934): 4–5.

95. Ibid., 5.

96. Story Matkin-Rawn, "'Afield with Ranger Mac': Conservation Education and School Radio during the Great Depression," *Wisconsin Magazine of History* 88, 1 (Autumn 2004): 5.

97. Ibid., 9.

98. Williams, "Head, Heart, Hands, and Health," 19. There is some dispute over the beginning date of "Afield with Ranger Mac." Matkin-Rawn places it in 1933, Williams in 1932. I am using the 1932 date.

99. Pupils of Homiston School, Fond du Lac, Wisconsin, to Ranger Mac, October 22, 1941; Fifth Grade, Washington School, Marshfield Wisconsin, to Ranger Mac, January 8, 1942; Beverly Nedorski, Wilson, Wisconsin, to Ranger Mac, March 4, 1943; Gaston School Pupils, Cottage Grove, Wisconsin, to Ranger Mac, February 9, 1945; Ranger Mac to Gaston School Pupils, February 16, 1945, Wakelin McNeel Papers, Correspondence File, Mss 150, Archives and Manuscripts Division, Wisconsin Historical Society, Madison, Wisconsin.

100. Pupils of the Stone School, Omro, Wisconsin, to Ranger Mac, October 8, 1945; M. J. Bangert to Ranger Mac, October 19, 1942; Ranger Mac to M. J. Bangert, October 26, 1942; Wakelin McNeel Papers, Correspondence File.

101. Vincent Kuharic, "I Plough a Straight Black Furrow," *From the Fields* (Madison: Farm Folk School, College of Agriculture, University of Wisconsin, 1940), 2.

CHAPTER TWO: URBAN ENVIRONMENTS, URBAN CHILDREN

1. Historian Bernard Mergen commented, "The choice of preferred play sites is to a large extent a matter of sex, family size, and economics. Almost without exception, girls are more restricted in both time and space to play." Bernard Mergen, *Play and Playthings: A Reference Guide* (Westport, Conn.: Greenwood Press, 1982), 81–82.

2. Helen M. Scheetz, "Beside the Still Waters," Manuscript Memoir, Iowa Women's Archives, University of Iowa Libraries, Iowa City, Iowa, 30.

3. Charles Honce, "Lost in Yesterday: Adventures in Nostalgia Spun on a White Peach," Typescript Memoir, 1957, BL 240, State Historical Society of Iowa, Iowa City, Iowa, 38–39.

4. Ibid., 40.

5. Mrs. John Folsom, "The Main Street I Remember," Iowa Commission on Aging Essay Contest, 1976, Ms. 89, State Historical Society of Iowa, Iowa City, Iowa.

6. Honce, "Lost in Yesterday," 61.

7. "The Joys of Coasting Told in Rhyme by One Who Does Not Care for Thumps or Bumps So He Can Have a Good Time," Young Folks' Column, *Atchison Daily Globe*, January 16, 1889, Issue 4, 467, column E.

8. Honce, "Lost in Yesterday," 63.

9. Ibid.

10. Maxine Teele, "The Main Street I Remember," Iowa Commission on Aging Essay Contest, 1976, Ms. 89, State Historical Society of Iowa, Iowa City, Iowa.

11. Ruth Barkley, "The Main Street I Remember," Iowa Commission on Aging Essay Contest, 1976, Ms. 89, State Historical Society of Iowa, Iowa City, Iowa.

12. Sanford Gaster, "Public Places of Childhood, 1915–1930," *Oral History Review* 22, 2 (1995), 8.

13. Interview with Dorothy Menkin, in Jeff Kisseloff, *You Must Remember This: An Oral History of Manhattan in the 1890s to World War II* (New York: Harcourt Brace Jovanovich, 1989), 222. (Hereafter cited as "Kisseloff.")

14. Interview with Stanley Marx, in Kisseloff, 222–223.

15. Interview with Freddy Tarzian, in Gaster, "Public Places of Childhood," 11.

16. Ibid., 14.

17. Ibid., 15–19.

18. Ibid., 29.

19. David Nasaw, *Children of the City: At Work and at Play* (Garden City, N.Y.: Anchor Press/Doubleday, 1985), 9.

20. Alvin K. Lukashok and Kevin Lynch, "Some Childhood Memories of the City," *Journal of the American Institute of Planners* 22, 3 (Summer 1956): 143.

21. Lukashok and Lynch, "Some Childhood Memories," 145.

22. Howard Chudacoff, *Children at Play: An American History* (New York: New York University Press, 2007), 78.

23. Ibid.

24. Philip Davis and Grace Kroll, *Street-Land: Its Little People and Big Problems* (Boston: Small, Maynard, 1915), 122.

25. Interview with Blanche Lasky in Kisseloff, 29.

26. Interview with Marty Cohen, in Kisseloff, 29–30.

27. Interview with Ed McGee, in Kisseloff, 567.

28. Davis and Kroll, *Street-Land*, 14.

29. Nasaw, *Children of the City*, 19.

30. Interview with Robert Leslie, in Kisseloff, 19.

31. Interview with Joe Henry, in Kisseloff, 128.

32. Interview with Joe Henry, in Kisseloff, 132.

33. Interview with Mary Thompson, in Kisseloff, 497.

34. Nasaw, *Children of the City*, 28–32.

35. Interview with Anna Murphy, in Kisseloff, 268.

36. Nasaw, *Children of the City*, 32–34.

37. Interview with Hannah Vance, in Kisseloff, 501.

38. Interview with Olga Marx, in Kisseloff, 185.

39. Interview with Columbia Altieri, in Kisseloff, 357.

40. Reginald Robinson, "Leisure-Time Activities of the Children of New York's Lower West Side," *Journal of Educational Sociology* 9, 8 (April 1936): 484–486.

41. Davis and Kroll, *Street-Land*, 124.

42. Nasaw, *Children of the City*, 29–30.

43. Viviana A. Zelizer, *Pricing the Priceless Child: The Changing Social Value of Children* (Princeton, N.J.: Princeton University Press, 1985), 52.

44. Una Hunt, *Una Mary: The Inner Life of a Child* (New York: Charles Scribner's Sons, 1914), 24–25.

45. Interview with Peter Pascale, in Kisseloff, 349.

46. Nasaw, *Children of the City*, 21–22.

47. Interview with Ed McGee, in Kisseloff, 571; see also interview with Bud Burns, in Kisseloff, 573.

48. Zelizer, *Pricing the Priceless Child*, 34–35.

49. Ibid., 32.

50. Bernard Mergen, "The Discovery of Children's Play," *American Quarterly* 27, 4 (October 1975): 412–413.

51. Chudacoff, *Children at Play*, 108–109.

52. "Doctoring the Poor for 35 Years," *New York Times (1857–Current file)*; March 15, 1914; ProQuest Historical Newspapers, The New York Times (1851–2005), pg. SM5.

53. "Boys Win Tom Johnson," *New York Times (1857–Current file)*; August 19, 1906; ProQuest Historical Newspapers, The New York Times (1851–2005), pg. 1.

54. U.S. Department of Labor, Children's Bureau, *Facilities for Children's Play in the District of Columbia*, Miscellaneous Series no. 8, Bureau Publication no. 22 (Washington, D.C.: U.S. Government Printing Office, 1917), 14.

55. Edward Barrows, quoted in "Child Crime in New York Is Due to Street Play," *New York Times (1857–Current file)*; February 15, 1914; ProQuest Historical Newspapers, The New York Times (1851–2005), pg. SM6.

56. Ibid.

57. Dominick Cavallo, *Muscles and Morals: Organized Playgrounds and Urban Reform, 1880–1920* (Philadelphia: University of Pennsylvania Press, 1981), 40.

58. U.S. Department of Labor, Children's Bureau, *Facilities for Children's Play*, 11.

59. Interview with Joe Henry, in Kisseloff, 128; interview with Olga Marx, in Kisseloff, 185.

60. Roy Rosenzweig and Elizabeth Blackmar, *The Park and the People: A History of Central Park* (Ithaca, N.Y.: Cornell University Press, 1992), 393.

61. Interview with John Bainbridge, in Kisseloff, 405.

62. Interview with Stanley Marx, in Kisseloff, 222.

63. Interview with Ludwig Kottl, in Kisseloff, 126.

64. Interview with Robert Leslie, in Kisseloff, 19.

65. Interview with Peter Pascale, in Kisseloff, 350.

66. Interview with Roman Alvarez, in Kisseloff, 418.

67. Interview with Bill Bailey, in Kisseloff, 567.

68. Interview with Florence Willison, in Kisseloff, 404.

69. Interview with Bresci Thompson, in Kisseloff, 489.

70. Interview with Marty Cohen, in Kisseloff, 31.

71. Nettie McGill, *Child Workers on City Streets*, Children's Bureau Publication no. 188 (Washington, D.C.: U.S. Government Printing Office, 1928), 2.

72. McGill, *Child Workers*, 2–9, 11–12.

73. Ibid., 18.

74. Ibid., 17–21; Nasaw, *Children of the City*, 103–104.

75. McGill, *Child Workers*, 31.

76. Nasaw, *Children of the City*, 198.

77. Frisby Leonard Rasp to John and Lavina Rasp, May 13, 1888, Folder 1, Frisby Leonard Rasp Collection, MS 0635, Manuscripts Collection, Nebraska State Historical Society, Lincoln, Nebraska.

78. Frisby Leonard Rasp to John and Lavina Rasp, May 6, 1888.

79. Frisby Leonard Rasp to John and Lavina Rasp, May 13, 1888.

80. Frisby Leonard Rasp to John and Lavina Rasp, May 19, 1888.

81. Frisby Leonard Rasp to John and Lavina Rasp, May 9, 1888.

82. Ibid.

83. James Marten, *Childhood and Child Welfare in the Progressive Era: A Brief History with Documents* (Boston: Bedford/St. Martin's, 2005), 3.

84. Robert W. DeForest and Lawrence Veiller, eds., *The Tenement House Problem Including the Report of the New York State Tenement House Commission of 1900*, vol. 1 (New York: Macmillan, 1903), 10.

85. Ibid., 5.

86. Ibid., 12–19.

87. Ibid., 47.

88. "Report of the Small Parks Committee of 1897," in DeForest and Veiller, *The Tenement House Problem*, vol. 2, 7.

89. C. A. Mohr, "Tenement Evils as Seen by an Inspector," in DeForest and Veiller, *The Tenement House Problem*, vol. 1, 430.

90. Lawrence Veiller, "Parks and Playgrounds for Tenement Districts" in DeForest and Veiller, *The Tenement House Problem*, vol. 2, 6.

91. DeForest and Veiller, *The Tenement House Problem*, vol. 2, 9–12.

92. Edith Abbott, *The Tenements of Chicago, 1908–1935* (Chicago: University of Chicago Press, 1936), 150.

93. Ibid., 171–173, 177.

94. Ibid., 190.

95. Ibid., Map 5.

96. Ibid., 121.

97. Abbott, 479–491. The author endorsed Chicago's new housing projects, which

were being built in the mid-1930s, as an important part of the solution to the city's environmental problem, and particularly noted the Jane Addams Houses and the Julia Lathrop Homes with their parks and playgrounds for the development's children.

98. James Edward Rogers, *The Child and Play, Based on the Reports of the White House Conference on Child Health and Protection* (New York: Century, 1932), 27.

99. Ibid., 28–31.

100. Ibid., 101.

101. "For Playgrounds for Poor Children," *New York Times (1857–Current file)*; ProQuest Historical Newspapers, The New York Times (1851–2005), pg. 9.

102. Cavallo, *Muscles and Morals*, 23–25.

103. Ibid., 25.

104. Chudacoff, *Children at Play*, 111–113.

105. Mergen, *Play and Playthings*, 89.

106. Davis and Kroll, *Street-Land*, xvi, 258, 18.

107. Cavallo, *Muscles and Morals*, 4.

108. Ibid., 6.

109. Luther H. Gulick, "Fewer 'Little Savages,'" *New York Times (1857–Current file)*; ProQuest Historical Newspapers, The New York Times (1851–2005), pg. 12.

110. Chudacoff, *Children at Play*, 112.

111. Will R. Reeves, "Report of the Committee on Street Play," *Journal of Educational Sociology* 4, 10 (June 1931): 613, 614.

112. Ibid., 614.

113. R. M. Fleming to C. O. Sherrill, August 4, 1927, as reproduced in Reeves, "Report of the Committee on Street Play," 615.

114. Ibid.

115. Reeves, "Report of the Committee on Street Play," 613.

116. Chudacoff, *Children at Play*, 114.

117. Helen Bullitt Lowry, "Child Gamblers of Our Noisy Streets," *New York Times (1857–Current file)*; August 29, 1920; ProQuest Historical Newspapers, The New York Times (1851–2005), pg. BRM3.

118. Nasaw, *Children of the City*, 117–120.

119. Chudacoff, *Children at Play*, 114.

120. Clifford Edward Clark, Jr., *The American Family Home, 1800–1960* (Chapel Hill: University of North Carolina Press, 1986), 29–30.

121. Chudacoff, *Children at Play*, 114–115.

122. U.S. Department of Labor, Children's Bureau, *Home and Play Equipment for the Preschool Child*, Bureau Publication no. 238 (Washington, D.C.: U.S. Government Printing Office, 1937), 2.

123. Clark, *The American Family Home*, 167.

124. Bernard Mergen noted that even before the 1950s, middle-class children often played indoors, making use of all of the home's elements, from floors to furniture to "secret spaces within spaces." Mergen, *Play and Playthings*, 83.

125. U.S. Department of Labor, Children's Bureau, *Home and Play Equipment*, 8.

126. Ibid., 8–9.

127. Zelizer, *Pricing the Priceless Child*, 51.

128. Ibid., 53.

129. Interview with Harold Gates, in Kisseloff, 437.

130. Jeff Wiltse, *Contested Waters: A Social History of Swimming Pools in America* (Chapel Hill: University of North Carolina Press, 2007), 10–11.

131. Ibid., 12.

132. Ibid., 26.

133. Ibid., 29.

134. Ibid., 32–34, 43.

135. Ibid., 48.

136. Ibid., 45.

137. Ibid., 61–62.

138. Ibid., 92–93.

139. Madison's lakes and beaches, accessible to nearly every neighborhood in town, discouraged the building of municipal swimming facilities (outside of the schools) until 2007, when the city opened its first pool.

140. Cora Bussey Hillis Papers, MS 72, Box 2, Folder 2 (1901–1913), photocopies from scrapbooks, State Historical Society of Iowa, Iowa City, Iowa.

141. For a description of the genesis and evolution of open-air schools in Europe, see Anne Marie Chatelet, "A Breath of Fresh Air: Open-Air Schools in Europe," in Marta Gutman and Ning de Coninck-Smith, *Designing Modern Childhoods: History, Space and the Material Culture of Children* (New Brunswick, N.J.: Rutgers University Press, 2008), 107–127.

142. Walter E. Kruesi, "The School of Outdoor Life for Tuberculous Children," *Charities and the Commons* 21 (December 19, 1909): 448.

143. Leonard P. Ayres, *Open-Air Schools* (New York: Doubleday, Page, 1910), 52.

144. Ibid., 45–72.

145. David L. Ellison, *Healing Tuberculosis in the Woods: Medicine and Science at the End of the Nineteenth Century* (Westport, Conn.: Greenwood Press, 1994), 181.

146. Mergen, "The Discovery of Children's Play," 403.

147. Bernard Mergen, *Snow in America* (Washington, D.C.: Smithsonian Institution Press, 1997), 83.

CHAPTER THREE: TEACHING NATURE APPRECIATION

1. Jacob A. Riis, *How the Other Half Lives* (New York: Hill and Wang, 1957), 134–138.

2. Theodore Roosevelt, "The American Boy," in *The Strenuous Life* (New York: Century, 1901), 155–157.

3. See Gail Bederman, "'Teaching Our Sons to Do What We Have Been Teaching the Savages to Avoid': G. Stanley Hall, Racial Recapitulation, and the Neurasthenic Paradox," in Gail Bederman, ed., *Manliness and Civilization: A Cultural History of Gender and Race in the United States, 1880–1917* (Chicago: University of Chicago Press, 1995), 77–120.

4. G. Stanley Hall, *Adolescence: Its Psychology and Its Relations to Physiology, Anthropology, Sociology, Sex, Crime, Religion and Education*, vol. 2 (New York: D. Appleton, 1905), 229.

5. Leslie Paris, *Children's Nature: The Rise of the American Summer Camp* (New York: New York University Press, 2008), 28–29.

6. Hall, *Adolescence*, 231.

7. Dominick Cavallo, *Muscles and Morals: Organized Playgrounds and Urban Reform, 1880–1920* (Philadelphia: University of Pennsylvania Press, 1981), 57–58.

8. David I. MacLeod, *Building Character in the American Boy: The Boy Scouts, YMCA, and Their Forerunners, 1870–1920* (Madison: University of Wisconsin Press, 1983), 32, 52, 227.

9. William Byron Forbush, *The Boy Problem*, 6th ed. (Boston: The Pilgrim Press, 1907), 144.

10. Ibid., 168.

11. Ibid., 146.

12. James Edward Rogers, *The Child and Play, Based on the Reports of the White House Conference on Child Health and Protection* (New York: Century, 1932), 26.

13. "Outing Clubs," *Midland Schools* 13, 10 (June 1899): 315.

14. Kevin C. Armitage, "Bird Day for Kids: Progressive Conservation in Theory and Practice," *Environmental History* 12, 3 (July 2007): 4.

15. Kevin C. Armitage, *The Nature Study Movement: The Forgotten Popularizer of America's Conservation Ethic* (Lawrence: University Press of Kansas, 2009), 113.

16. Neighborhood House Records, Box 4, Folder 3, Junior Better Homes and Gardens Club Records, May 1936 Report, Archives and Manuscripts Division, Wisconsin Historical Society, Madison, Wisconsin.

17. Armitage, "Bird Day," 1.

18. Armitage, *The Nature Study Movement*, 101–102.

19. Robert Baden-Powell, *Scouting for Boys: A Handbook for Instruction in Good Citizenship* (Oxford: Oxford University Press, 2004), 20.

20. Ibid., 21.

21. For a comprehensive history of the Boy Scouts of America to 1920, see David I. MacLeod, *Building Character in the American Boy: The Boy Scouts, YMCA, and Their Forerunners, 1870–1920* (Madison: University of Wisconsin Press, 1983).

22. Ibid., 10–11, 19–27, 47.

23. Boy Scouts of America, *The Official Handbook for Boys* (Garden City, N.Y.: Doubleday, Page, 1916), x.

24. Ibid., 4.

25. Ibid., 8.

26. Ibid., 9.

27. Boy Scouts of America, *Scoutmaster's Troop Program Note Book* (N.P.: Boy Scouts of America, 1935), 21.

28. Ibid., 50.

29. Ibid., 98.

30. Susan A. Miller, *Growing Girls: The Natural Origins of Girls' Organizations in America* (New Brunswick, N.J.: Rutgers University Press, 2007), 1–4.

31. For a description of the somewhat contentious creation of the Girl Scouts, see Miller, *Growing Girls*, 23–31.

32. W. J. Hoxie, *How Girls Can Help Their Country*, Sixtieth Anniversary Facsimile Edition (New York: Girl Scouts of the U.S.A., 1972), 19.

33. For a full description of appropriate camping activities, see Hoxie, *How Girls Can Help Their Country*, 19–65.

34. Ibid., 21.

35. Ibid., 10.

36. Leslie Paris, "The Adventures of Peanut and Bo: Summer Camps and Early Twentieth Century American Girlhood," *Journal of Women's History* 12, 4 (2001): 54.

37. Miller, *Growing Girls*, 170.

38. Ibid., 21.

39. Ibid., 6, 7.

40. Lina Beard and Adelia Belle Beard, *The Original Girl's Handy Book* (New York: Black Dog and Leventhal Publishers, 2007; facsimile of *The American Girl's Handy Book*, 1887), preface.

41. Ibid., 13, 159.

42. Ibid., 201–224, 334.

43. Ibid., 335.

44. Lina Beard and Adelia B. Beard, *Girl Pioneers of America Official Manual*, 3rd ed. (New York: Girl Pioneers of America, 1918), 11.

45. Ibid., 139, 134, 127.

46. Ibid., 41.

47. Ibid., 42.

48. Lina Beard and Adelia B. Bird, *On the Trail: An Outdoor Book for Girls* (New York: Charles Scribner's Sons, 1922), 3.

49. Ibid., 4.

50. Ibid., 6–7.

51. Ibid., 119.

52. Ibid., 178.

53. Michael B. Smith, "'The Ego Ideal of the Good Camper' and the Nature of Summer Camp," *Environmental History* 11, 1 (2006): 6.

54. Abigail A. Van Slyke, *A Manufactured Wilderness: Summer Camps and the Shaping of American Youth, 1890–1960* (Minneapolis: University of Minnesota Press, 2006), 4.

55. Paris, *Children's Nature*, 52.

56. Miller, *Growing Girls*, 130–131.

57. Leslie Paris, *Children's Nature*, 29.

58. Smith, "'The Ego Ideal of the Good Camper,'" 2.

59. Ibid., 6.

60. L. G. Schneller, "The Complete Story of Camp Mishawaka," ca. 1925, 27, 28, 81–89. Manuscripts Collection, Minnesota Historical Society, St. Paul, Minnesota.

61. Ibid., 39–40, 42, 61.

62. Ibid., 94–100.

63. Ibid., 23.

64. Ray Wallace "Mishawaka Bred," in Schneller, "The Complete Story of Camp Mishawaka," 116.

65. Paris, "Adventures of Peanut and Bo," 55.

66. Camp Kiwadinipi Promotional Materials, 1933, 2, Alice Gortner Johnson Papers, Manuscripts Collection, Minnesota Historical Society, St. Paul, Minnesota.

67. Ibid., 3.

68. Ibid.

69. Louise W. Goodwin Rankin, "Gypsying," *Everygirl's Magazine*, May 1923, 280.

70. Ibid., 281.

71. Alice Gortner, "Record of Trips—Trip in Northern Minnesota, 1933," Entry for Monday, Alice Gortner Johnson Papers, Manuscripts Collection, Minnesota Historical Society, St. Paul, Minnesota.

72. Gortner, "Record of Trips," Tuesday.

73. Gortner, "Record of Trips," Saturday.

74. American Girl Camp Promotional Materials, 1929, 1, Mildred Sebo Papers, Minnesota Historical Society, St. Paul, Minnesota.

75. Ibid., 2.

76. Ibid., 2–5.

77. American Girl Camp Scrapbook, 1934.

78. Letter, "The American Girl Island Camp for Junior Girls, 1932."

79. Paris, "The Adventures of Peanut and Bo," 57–58.

80. Boys Camping Scrapbook, 1941, 4, Neighborhood House Papers, Box 2, Wisconsin Historical Society, Madison, Wisconsin.

81. Ibid., 1–2, 4.

82. Ibid., 13.

83. Ibid., 14–17.

84. Ibid., 27.

85. Boys Camping Scrapbook, 1942, 29–31, Neighborhood House Papers, Box 2, Wisconsin Historical Society, Madison, Wisconsin.

86. America Williams Camp brochure, Neighborhood House Papers, Box 2, Wisconsin Historical Society, Madison, Wisconsin.

87. Boys Camping Scrapbook, 1942, 99.

88. "Our Teenage Boys and Girls," in "Talks and Reports of Neighborhood House from 1919–1932," vol. 1, 65–67, Neighborhood House Papers, Wisconsin Historical Society, Madison, Wisconsin.

89. Paris, "Adventures of Peanut and Bo," 57.

90. "Hosteling from Neighborhood House, Madison, Wisconsin," American Youth Hostel Scrapbook, Neighborhood House Papers, Box 3, Wisconsin Historical Society, Madison, Wisconsin.

91. Ibid.

92. "First Hostel Trip," American Youth Hostel Scrapbook.

93. Charles F. Schwartz, "Trip to Mount Horeb and Blue Mounds June 10–11, 1947," American Youth Hostel Scrapbook.

94. "Overnight Hike to Hoyt Park, July 1–2, 1947," American Youth Hostel Scrapbook.

95. Ibid., "Eagles Overnight Trip to Arboretum," and "Second Overnight Hike to the Arboretum," American Youth Hostel Scrapbook.

96. "Eagles Overnight Trip to Arboretum," American Youth Hostel Scrapbook.

97. Paris, *Children's Nature*, 57–58.

98. "The Children's Excursions," *New York Times*, July 11, 1872, ProQuest Historical Newspapers, The New York Times, 5.

99. The Fresh Air Fund was not alone, or even the first, in such endeavors. In 1876, a Swiss pastor, Wilhelm Bion, began taking children from Zurich to the Alps. In the 1880s, the French adopted the model, creating *colonies de vacances* to improve the health and well-being of urban children. See Laura Lee Downs, *Childhood in the Promised Land: Working Class Movements and the Colonies de Vacances in France, 1880–1960* (Durham: Duke University Press, 2002); Jacob A. Riis, *Children of the Poor* (New York: Charles Scribner's Sons, 1902), 152–155; "Fresh Air Fund, at 112, Contends with Change," *New York Times*, May 1, 1988, ProQuest Historical Newspapers, The New York Times, 56.

100. Editorial, *New York Times*, July 27, 1892, ProQuest Historical Newspapers, The New York Times, 4.

101. Lawrence Wright, *City Children, Country Summer* (New York: Charles Scribner's Sons, 1979), 15.

102. "Fresh Air Fund, at 112," 56.

103. Riis, *Children of the Poor*, 155; Kari Haskell, "After 125 Years, Idea Still Changes Lives," *New York Times*, June 2, 2002, ProQuest Historical Newspapers, The New York Times, 40.

104. Haskell, "After 125 Years," 40.

105. "The Daily Papers Often Suggest Powerful Moral Lessons by the Juxtaposition of Matter in Their Columns," *The Congregationalist*, September 4, 1940, 4.

106. "'I Had Never Heard Such Silence,'" *New York Times*, May 7, 1989, ProQuest Historical Newspapers, The New York Times, E26.

107. Grace Frank, "Visiting the Barnyard Creatures Can Outshine TV," *New York Times*, June 30, 2002, ProQuest Historical Newspapers, The New York Times, 26.

108. Robert M. Vanderbeck, "Inner-City Children, Country Summers: Narrating American Childhood and the Geographies of Whiteness," *Environment and Planning* 40 (2008): 1140.

109. Riis, *Children of the Poor*, 156–158.

110. Vanderbeck, "Inner-City Children, Country Summers," 1133–1134.

111. Wright, *City Children, Country Summer*, 191–200.

112. Vanderbeck, "Inner-City Children, Country Summers," 1147.

113. Walter S. Ufford, *Fresh Air Charity in the United States* (New York: Bonnell, Silver, 1897), 86.

114. Riis, *Children of the Poor*, 160–161. The idea of teaching the children so that the children could change the parents' behavior was not unique to the Fresh Air Fund. Many Progressive Era programs, the 4-H program included, intended to reform the family and its practices from the bottom up. Even in the 1970s, this type of emphasis persisted. A 1976 article recruiting families to host Fresh Air Fund children noted, "The Fresh Air Fund's Friendly Town experience broadens their horizons and gives them a motivation they would have never known otherwise." "Host Homes Needed for Fresh-Air Kids," *Lancaster Farming*, April 24, 1976, 74.

115. Wright, *City Children, Country Summer*, 202.

116. Vanderbeck, "Inner-City Children, Country Summers," 1147.

117. C.E.D., "Fresh Air for the Children," *The North American*, July 21, 1887, column B.

118. Ufford, *Fresh Air Charity*, 10–11.

119. Julia M. Brown, "Early Organized Camping in Wisconsin," Papers, American Camping Association, Wisconsin Section, File 17, Wisconsin Historical Society, Madison, Wisconsin.

120. "The Railway World: Half-Fare Charity Rates East of Chicago to Be Continued," *The Daily Inter Ocean*, May 3, 1896, issue 40, column F, 16.

121. To understand the many aspects of Mennonite fresh-air work, see Tobin Miller Shearer's work, and particularly, Tobin Miller Shearer, "More Than Fresh Air: African American Children's Influence on Mennonite Religious Practice, 1950–1979," *Journal of Race, Ethnicity and Religion* 2, 7 (May 2011), http://www.raceandreligion.com/JRER/Volume_2_%282011%29_files/Shearer%202%207.pdf, and "'Chickens, Crops and Tractors': The Use of Machines as a Sacred Resource in Mennonite Fresh Air Hosting Programs," *Journal for the Study of Religion, Nature and Culture* 4, 3 (Fall 2010): 153–181.

122. North Madison Happy Pals 4-H Club, Box 2, 1968 Scrapbook, Iowa Women's Archives, University of Iowa Libraries, Iowa City, Iowa.

123. "The Long, Long Trail from Camp to School," *Everygirl's Magazine* 10, 1 (September 1922): frontispiece.

CHAPTER FOUR: THE ENVIRONMENTALLY AWARE CHILD AT MIDCENTURY

1. Roger G. Barker and Herbert F. Wright, *One Boy's Day: A Specimen Record of Behavior* (North Haven, Conn.: Archon Books, 1966. Reprint of New York: Harper and Row, 1951), 117–118.

2. Ibid., 166–169.

3. Ibid., 184–185.

4. Ibid., 205.

5. Ibid., 335–345.

6. Ibid., 415–416.

7. Sociologist Markella Rutherford's research shows that in midcentury America, parenting advice literature encouraged an enormous amount of freedom among children, even toddlers and other very young children. Markella B. Rutherford, *Adult Supervision Required: Private Freedom and Public Constraints for Parents and Children* (New Brunswick, N.J.: Rutgers University Press, 2011), 65–68.

8. Nancy Norg to Molly Fisher, January 8, 1944, Molly Fisher Collection, Archives and Manuscripts Collection, Wisconsin Historical Society, Madison, Wisconsin.

9. Norg to Fisher, January 20, 1944.

10. Alberna Herrick to Molly Fisher, February 2, 1946.

11. Alberna Herrick to Molly Fisher, June 6, 1947.

12. Robert S. Lynd and Helen Merrell Lynd, *Middletown: A Study in Modern American Culture* (New York: Harcourt Brace Jovanovich, 1957), 270–271.

13. Reginald Robinson, "Leisure-Time Activities of the Children of New York's Lower West Side," *Journal of Educational Sociology* 9, 8 (April 1936): 486.

14. Ibid., 488.

15. Ibid., 486, 490.

16. Ibid., 492.

17. Steven Mintz and Susan Kellogg, *Domestic Revolutions: A Social History of American Family Life* (New York: Free Press, 1988), 190; Evelyn I. Banning, "Social Influences on Children and Youth," *Review of Educational Research* 25, 1 (February 1955): 37.

18. Banning, "Social Influences," 36.

19. Robert D. Hess and Harriett Goldman, "Parents' Views of the Effect of Television on Their Children," *Child Development* 33, 2 (June 1962): 411.

20. Constance M. McCullough, "A Log of Children's Out-of-School Activities," *Elementary School Journal* 58, 3 (December 1957): 158.

21. Ibid., 158–159.

22. Raymond Jung, "Leisure in Three Cultures," *Elementary School Journal* 67, 6 (March 1967): 288.

23. Ibid., 293; see also McCullough, "A Log of Children's Out-of-School Activities," 164.

24. Hess and Goldman, "Parents' Views," 411.

25. Peter Wyden, *Suburbia's Coddled Kids* (Garden City, N.Y.: Doubleday, 1962), 1.

26. Ibid., 5.

27. Ibid., 6–7.

28. Ibid., 14.

29. Ibid., 35–38.

30. John D. Woolever, "Animals and Why Children Fear Them," *American Biology Teacher* 15, 5 (May 1953): 121.

31. Ibid., 122.

32. Ibid., 123.

33. Ibid.

34. Ruth Schwartz Cowan discusses this particular addition to mothers' chores in her book, *More Work for Mother: The Ironies of Household Technology from the Open Hearth to the Microwave* (New York: Basic Books, 1983): 201.

35. Steven Mintz, *Huck's Raft: A History of American Childhood* (Cambridge, Mass.: Belknap Press of Harvard, 2004), 282; Steven Mintz and Susan Kellogg, *Domestic Revolutions: A Social History of American Family Life* (New York: Free Press, 1988), 184–185.

36. *Boys' Life*, January 1950, 17, 37–38.

37. *Boys' Life*, January 1950.

38. Frank Cetin, "Operation Snowbound," *Boys' Life*, January 1960, 14.

39. *Boys' Life*, January 1960, 47.

40. Camp Fire Girls, *The Book of the Camp Fire Girls* (New York: Camp Fire Girls, Inc., 1960), frontispiece, 54.

41. Ibid., 154.

42. Ibid., 154–162.

43. Ibid., 167–169.

44. Girl Scouts of the United States of America, *Annual Report, 1950* (New York: Girl Scouts of the United States of America, 1950), 32.

45. Ibid., 32–33.

46. Girl Scouts of the United States of America, *Cadette Girl Scout Handbook* (New York: Girl Scouts of the United States of America, 1963), 153–154.

47. Ibid., 156–183, 292–306.

48. Ibid., 306.

49. Girl Scouts of the United States of America, *Senior Girl Scout Handbook* (New York: Girl Scouts of the United States of America, 1963), 164.

50. Ibid., 167.

51. Girl Scouts of the United States of America, *Annual Report, 1950*, 38.

52. Susan Sessions Rugh, *Are We There Yet? The Golden Age of American Family Vacations* (Lawrence: University Press of Kansas, 2008), 120.

53. Ibid., 120–123.

54. Ibid., 130.

55. Ralph H. Lutts, "The Trouble with Bambi: Walt Disney's *Bambi* and the American Vision of Nature," *Forest & Conservation History* 36, 4 (October 1992): 160. This also explains why I did not see this movie until I was doing the research for this book. My father and his father, like many men with western and midwestern rural and small-town backgrounds, were hunters. My father boycotted Disney nature films for many reasons, but in particular, their anthropomorphized animal characters. Wild animals, he liked to say, were wild, and should never be depicted as otherwise. *Charlie the Lonesome Cougar*, treated later in this chapter, would have come in for particular criticism.

56. All references are to David D. Hand, director, *Bambi*, Walt Disney Studios, 1942; 2011 DVD version.

57. Lutts, "The Trouble with Bambi," 165.

58. Lutts, "The Trouble with Bambi," 169.

59. Gregg Mitman, "Cinematic Nature: Hollywood Technology, Popular Culture, and the American Museum of Natural History," *Isis* 84, 4 (December 1993): 653.

60. Derek Bouse, Review of "The Bear by Jean-Jacques Annaud," *Film Quarterly* 43, 3 (Spring 1990): 32.

61. Jan-Christopher Horak, "Wildlife Documentaries: From Classical Forms to Reality TV," *Film History* 18, 4 (2006): 467.

62. Ibid.

63. All references to James Algar, director, *Walt Disney's True-Life Adventures: The Living Desert*, Walt Disney Studios, 1953.

64. All references to James Algar, director, *Walt Disney's True-Life Adventures: The Vanishing Prairie*, Walt Disney Pictures, 1954.

65. Nicholas Sammond, *Babes in Tomorrowland: Walt Disney and the Making of the American Child, 1930–1960* (Durham, N.C.: Duke University Press, 2005), 202.

66. All references to James Algar, director, *Walt Disney's True-Life Adventures: The African Lion*, Walt Disney Pictures, 1955.

67. James Algar, director, *Walt Disney's True-Life Adventure: Secrets of Life*, Walt Disney Pictures, 1956.

68. All references to N. Paul Kenworthy Junior and Ralph Wright , directors, *Perri: The First True-Life Fantasy*, Walt Disney Pictures, 1957.

69. Hank Schloss, director, *Walt Disney Presents: Flash, the Teen-Age Otter*, Walt Disney Films, 1961.

70. This was the kind of Disney production that made my father froth at the mouth. It showed people behaving badly around animals and did not adequately discuss the

consequences of that bad behavior. In *Yellowstone Cubs*, people get away with feeding, petting and even kissing the bears. Hank Schloss, director, *Yellowstone Cubs*, Walt Disney Studios, 1963. For a discussion of the dangers posed by the park's wildlife and the high incidence of dangerous human-bear encounters in this era, see Rugh, *Are We There Yet?*, 144–146.

71. *The Jungle Book* was an interesting choice of a double feature. In the *Jungle Book*, Mowgli, the man cub, unlike Charlie the cougar, must be sent from the wild into civilization. Just like Charlie, however, he was seduced into his proper home by a female of the species. *The Jungle Book* was a riot of anthropomorphism, animal rights, family values and British colonial imagery. Wolfgang Reitherman, director, *The Jungle Book*, Walt Disney Pictures, distributed by Buena Vista, 1967; viewed in 2007 40th anniversary DVD version.

72. All references to Walt Disney Films, *Charlie, the Lonesome Cougar*, 1967.

73. Horak, "Wildlife Documentaries," 467.

74. Derek Bouse, Review of "The Bear, by Jean-Jacques Annaud," 31.

75. "Mutual of Omaha's Wild Kingdom," http://www.wildkingdom.com/nostalgia/history.html; http://www.wildkingdom.com/nostalgia/perkins_bio.html; http://www.wildkingdom.com/nostalgia/fowler_bio.html.

76. *Mutual of Omaha's Wild Kingdom*, "The Definitive 50 Episode Collection: Designs for Survival, Pilot Episode," 1963, Disc 7, Side A.

77. *Mutual of Omaha's Wild Kingdom*, "The Definitive 50 Episode Collection: Strange Ways of the Wild," Episode 2, 1963, Disc 7, Side A.

78. *Mutual of Omaha's Wild Kingdom*, "The Definitive 50 Episode Collection: Strange but True," Episode 4, 1963, Disc 6, Side A.

79. *Mutual of Omaha's Wild Kingdom*, "The Definitive 50 Episode Collection: The Polar Bears of Churchill," 1967, Disc 4, Side A.

80. *Mutual of Omaha's Wild Kingdom*, "The Definitive 50 Episode Collection: Wildfire Part 1," 1972, Disc 6, Side B.

81. *Mutual of Omaha's Wild Kingdom*, "The Definitive 50 Episode Collection: Wildfire Part 2," 1972, Disc 6, Side B.

82. William Grigg, "The Bear That Stops Fires," *Science News Letter* (October 1, 1955): 218; Ellen Earnhardt Morrison, *Guardian of the Forest: A History of the Smokey Bear Program* (Alexandria, Va.: Morielle Press, 1989), 7–8. This is a very slim book. There is most assuredly more to be written about the Smokey Bear phenomenon.

83. Morrison, *Guardian of the Forest*, 25. Even some scholars get it wrong. In a 2002 article, Roberta Robin Dods commented on the live bears representing Smokey and Winnie the Pooh: "Each had a remarkable road to public recognition, and each ended as an iconic figure eventually achieving cartoon fame." While that may have been true of the Pooh-bear, it most certainly was not true of Smokey, who was a cartoon before he was a cub. Roberta Robin Dods, "The Death of Smokey Bear: The Ecodisaster Myth and Forest Management Practices in Prehistoric North America," *World Archaeology* 33, 3, Ancient Ecodisasters (February 2002): 475.

84. Grigg, "The Bear That Stops Fires," 218.

85. Hal K. Rothman, *Saving the Planet: The American Response to the Environment in the Twentieth Century* (Chicago: Ivan R. Dee, 2000), 130.

86. Grigg, "The Bear That Stops Fires," 218.

87. Morrison, *Guardian of the Forest*, 95.

88. Ibid., 96.

89. Grigg, "The Bear That Stops Fires," 218.

90. Morrison, *Guardian of the Forest*, 97–98.

91. This I know from experience. My mother was an adolescent in the 1950s, and in the 1970s when she told her children about the Smokey Bear story, her eyes still welled up with tears at the thought of the burned and orphaned bear cub.

92. Roberta Robin Dods notes the flatness of the message embedded in Smokey Bear. "The Smokey campaign was remarkably successful. It represents a mindset associated with mythic forest of the past in which the wilderness was unmanaged, and in which forest fires were an unmitigated ecodisaster. With few exceptions and until quite recently, it obscured the recognition that the past and present 'wilderness' comprised many types of managed, cultural landscape." Dods, "The Death of Smokey Bear," 476.

93. Thomas B. Allen, *Guardian of the Wild: The Story of the National Wildlife Federation, 1936–1986* (Bloomington: Indiana University Press, 1987), 81–82.

94. Ibid., 84.

95. Ibid., 86–87.

96. Arlene Plevin, "Still Putting Out 'Fires': Ranger Rick and Animal/Human Stewardship," in Sidney Drobin and Kenneth B. Kidd, eds., *Wild Things: Children's Culture and EcoCriticism* (Detroit: Wayne State University Press, 2004), 169.

97. Allen, *Guardian of the Wild*, 88.

98. Plevin, "Still Putting Out 'Fires,'"169.

99. Judy Braus, "Environmental Education," *BioScience* 45, Supplement: Science and Biodiversity Policy (1995): S-51.

100. Plevin, "Still Putting Out 'Fires,'" 170.

101. Morrison, *Guardian of the Forest*, 65–66.

102. Forest Service, U.S. Department of Agriculture, "Woodsy Owl, A Short History," http://www.fs.usda.gov/Internet/FSE_DOCUMENTS/stelprdb5193740.pdf.

103. Many Americans have never heard the new slogan. Rick Shefchik, a columnist for the *St. Paul Pioneer Press*, referred to the new slogan as "vapid and undefined." Rick Shefchik, "Kids Need New Anti-Litter Lesson," *Beaver County Times*, April 4, 2002, 81.

104. This was a particularly successful ad, garnering millions of dollars in donated time and many awards. In fact, *TV Guide* named it the sixteenth-greatest television commercial of all time. Robert B. Cialdini, "Crafting Normative Messages to Protect the Environment," *Current Directions in Psychological Science* 12, 4 (August 2003): 105.

105. "Hollywood Star Walk: Iron Eyes Cody," *Los Angeles Times*, Entertainment section, http://projects.latimes.com/hollywood/star-walk/iron-eyes-cody/. "Iron Eyes Cody, Memorable Indian Actor, Dies at 94," *Los Angeles Times*, January 5, 1999, http://articles.latimes.com/1999/jan/05/local/me-60544. There has been long and heated discussion about Cody's heritage, authenticity and ability to speak for Native Americans. This is a discussion better carried out elsewhere. Suffice it to say that most Americans watching his memorable advertisement believed him to be Native American.

106. David Rich Lewis, "Still Native: The Significance of Native Americans in the

History of the Twentieth-Century American West," *Western Historical Quarterly* 24, 2 (May 1993): 221, 223. Hal Rothman also comments on this in *The Greening of a Nation*. "The symbolism of the man dressed as a mythic Indian chief conveyed many things: the passing of the obligation from the so-called first ecologists to modern people, who had clearly abdicated their responsibility; the reverence in which Americans were beginning to regard the Native American past, and the simply disastrous condition of the American landscape. The appropriation of this symbol played an important role in bringing environmental issues closer to the mainstream." Hal K. Rothman, *The Greening of a Nation? Environmentalism in the United States since 1945* (Fort Worth, Tex.: Harcourt Brace College Publishers, 1998), 105–106.

107. Rothman, *Saving the Planet*, 146–148.

108. "Area Schools Conduct Earth Day Activities," *Ames Tribune*, April 23, 1970; "Environmental Week to Feature Sen. Hughes," *Iowa State Daily*, April 16, 1970, 2.

109. "AHS Combats Pollution," *Ames High School Web*, April 22, 1970; "Environmental Week to Feature Sen. Hughes," *Iowa State Daily*, April 16, 1970, 2.

110. "Churches on the Environment," *Iowa State Daily*, April 16, 1970, 5.

CHAPTER FIVE: ALONG THE HIGH LINE

1. William H. Whyte, *The Last Landscape* (Garden City, N.Y.: Doubleday, 1968), 260.

2. Howard Chudacoff, *Children at Play: An American History* (New York: New York University Press, 2007), 114.

3. Whyte, *The Last Landscape*, 265.

4. Ibid., 263.

5. Adventure playgrounds were a mid-twentieth-century Danish invention. These essentially undeveloped play sites allowed children great latitude to explore and create, making use of building materials, water, dirt, and imagination. Youngsters used the playgrounds to build, cook and generally mess about. Paid adults supervised these playgrounds, but very lightly. Although widely admired by recreational professionals in the United States, very few were ever built here, largely due to concerns about safety and liability. Vance Packard, *Our Endangered Children: Growing Up in a Changing World* (Boston: Little, Brown, 1983), 231.

6. Robert Michael Pyle, *The Thunder Tree: Lessons from an Urban Wildland* (Boston: Houghton Mifflin, 1993), xvii. Pyle was not the only observer to note the ability of children to absorb a love of natural history from somewhat unlikely landscapes. Janisse Ray received her early education as a naturalist from the junkyard in which she grew up. Janisse Ray, *Ecology of a Cracker Childhood* (Minneapolis: Milkweed Editions, 1999).

7. America's developers built 15 million new homes during the 1950s. New developments had considerably less acreage in parks than earlier developments. Adam Rome, "William Whyte, Open Space, and Environmental Activism," *Geographical Review* 88, 2 (April 1998): 260.

8. Adam Rome, *The Bulldozer in the Countryside: Suburban Sprawl and the Rise of American Environmentalism* (New York: Cambridge University Press, 2001), 122.

9. This letter appeared in U.S. Department of Interior, *The Race for Inner Space* (Washington, D.C.: U.S. Government Printing Office, 1964), 19, as quoted in Rome, *The Bulldozer in the Countryside*, 128.

10. Alvin K. Lukashok and Kevin Lynch, "Some Childhood Memories of the City," *Journal of the American Institute of Planners* 22, 3 (Summer 1956): 152.

11. Margo Tupper, *No Place to Play* (Philadelphia: Chilton Books, 1966), 1.

12. Samuel P. Hays, *Beauty, Health, and Permanence: Environmental Politics in the United States, 1955–1985* (Cambridge: Cambridge University Press, 1987), 91–92.

13. David Skari, *High Line Canal: Meandering through Time* (Denver: C & M Press, 2003), 8–11.

14. Richard H. Johnson, ed., *Guide to the High Line Canal Trail* (Denver: Denver Water Board, 1999), 77.

15. Skari, *High Line Canal*, 31.

16. Johnson, *Guide to the High Line Canal Trail*, 4.

17. John Bowen, letter to the author, May 20, 2009. Source note: In order to gather memories of individuals who had used the canal as children in the mid-years of the twentieth century, I sent out inquiries by way of the High Line Canal Preservation Association, several electronic bulletin boards and the *Denver Post*. This resulted in e-mail communications from just over forty individuals who used the canal as children for recreational purposes between the 1930s and 1990s, or adults whose children had done so in the same time frame. Their memories are highlighted in this chapter.

18. Although his family's story detailed the problems of a different irrigation project, Ralph Moody's autobiographical account, *Little Britches*, provides an excellent first-hand account of the chaos ensuing when water was insufficient to farmers' needs along Colorado's front range. Ralph Moody, *Little Britches* (New York: W. W. Norton, 1950).

19. Skari, *High Line Canal*, 31–32.

20. Frances Melrose, "Drought Left Canal Backers Dry," *Rocky Mountain News*, March 22, 1992, 14M.

21. Pyle, *The Thunder Tree*, 9.

22. Richard Wensley and A. P. Gumlick to George E. Cranmer, September 20, 1935. Denver Board of Water Commissioners, Box # 392825673, Folder 10, Correspondence, 1935–1975.

23. See Pyle, *The Thunder Tree*, 18–39, for a thorough description of the watercourse as it currently is, including flora and fauna. Skari also provides an excellent description of the canal trail. See also Frances Melrose, as cited in the *Rocky Mountain News* above.

24. Mae Swan Woodruff, e-mail communication with author, June 20, 2009.

25. Craig Barnes, *Growing Up True: Lessons from a Western Boyhood* (Golden, Co.: Fulcrum Publishing, 2001), 30.

26. Ibid., 41–43.

27. Ibid., 49.

28. Ibid.

29. Ibid., 70–71.

30. Ibid., 172–173.

31. Ibid., 178–179.

32. Ibid., 181–184, 187.

33. Pyle, *The Thunder Tree*, xv–xvi.

34. Ibid., 4, 7, 9.

35. Ibid., 9.

36. Robert Michael Pyle, "Eden in a Vacant Lot," in Peter H. Kahn, Jr., and Stephen R. Kellert, eds., *Children and Nature: Psychological, Sociocultural, and Evolutionary Investigations* (Cambridge, Mass.: MIT Press, 2002), 308.

37. Pyle, *The Thunder Tree*, 152.

38. Pyle, "Eden in a Vacant Lot," 306.

39. Ibid., 322.

40. David Von Drehle, e-mail communication with author, August 3, 2009.

41. Joseph E. Taylor III commented on the same type of community building around shared outdoor fun in his book *Pilgrims of the Vertical: Yosemite Rock Climbers and Nature at Risk* (Cambridge, Mass.: Harvard University Press, 2010).

42. Dan Hoglund, e-mail communication with author, May 24, 2009.

43. Kathy Clark, Janis Hansen, and Kerrie Dreher, e-mail communication with the author, August 30, 2009.

44. This is my own High Line Canal memory, probably encouraged by my voracious reading of Laura Ingalls Wilder's books, and the wild plum bushes that grew on the canal, directly across from my home. The canal was my own "banks of plum creek."

45. Deborah Spencer, e-mail communication with author, August 3, 2009.

46. Ibid.

47. Andrea Labak, e-mail communication with author, May 29, 2009.

48. Steven Perry, e-mail communication with author, May 10, 2009.

49. Dustan Osborn, e-mail communication with author, May 11, 2009.

50. Mothers took part in these activities, too. My brother and I picked plums and chokecherries with our mother. L. Earl Lehrer collected asparagus with his mother. L. Earl Lehrer, e-mail communication with author, May 13, 2009; Scott Riney, e-mail communication with author, May 4, 2010.

51. Hoglund, May 24, 2009.

52. My brother, Scott Riney, and his friend, Stacy Norton, ate their crawdads with my mother's assent and to Stacy's mother's horror.

53. Stacy Norton Wareham, e-mail communication with author, February 15, 2009.

54. Joan Chiang, e-mail communication with author, March 30, 2009.

55. Scott Riney, e-mail communication with author, May 4, 2010.

56. Susan Wenaas, e-mail communication with author, January 22, 2009.

57. Fern Marston, e-mail communication with author, August 4, 2009.

58. Doug Miller, e-mail communication with the author, May 8, 2009.

59. Von Drehle, August 3, 2009.

60. Darryl Harris, e-mail communication with author, May 13, 2009.

61. Osborn, May 11, 2009.

62. Kim Bierman, e-mail communication with author, May 19, 2009.

63. Benjamin Fitzpatrick, e-mail communication with author, April 22, 2009.

64. Spencer, August 3, 2009.

65. Michael J. Austin, "Claim against the South Suburban Parks and Recreation District," 1978, Denver Board of Water Commissioners, Box # 392825673, Folder 17, South Suburban Metropolitan Recreation and Park District Correspondence, 1970–1986.

66. "Teen Falls Off Horse, Drowns in Canal," *Rocky Mountain News*, July 1, 1980,

n.p. Denver Board of Water Commissioners, Box # 392825673, Folder 19, Newspaper Articles.

67. Eleanor C. Foley, "Forty-Nine Years on the High Line Canal: A Colorado Memoir of Houses, Horses and Land," unpublished manuscript, used by permission of the High Line Canal Preservation Association, 44.

68. Ibid., 44–45.

69. Spencer, August 3, 2009.

70. Don Drake, e-mail communication with author, March 24, 2009.

71. Donna Judish, e-mail communication with author, March 24, 2009.

72. Labak, May 29, 2009.

73. Stacy Norton Wareham, e-mail communication with author, March 15, 2009.

74. Von Drehle, August 3, 2009.

75. The teens of the 1950s and beyond had a great need to find spaces of their own. As historian Clifford Clark noted in his book, *The American Family Home, 1800–1960*, new suburban spaces were not designed with teenagers in mind. They were intended instead for young children. He wrote, "The winding street patterns and lack of neighborhood stores were seen as a major drawback." Steven Mintz has also noted, "Lacking spaces to call their own, adolescents engaged in frequent battles with adults as they sought space at shopping malls, fast-food restaurants and public streets." Clifford Edward Clark, Jr., *The American Family Home, 1800–1960* (Chapel Hill: University of North Carolina Press, 1986), 233; Steven Mintz, *Huck's Raft: A History of American Childhood* (Cambridge, Mass.: Belknap Press, 2004), 348.

76. Fitzpatrick, April 18, 2009.

77. Bierman, May 19, 2009.

78. Clark, Hansen, and Dreher, August 30, 2009.

79. Rachel Myron, e-mail communication with author, August 9, 2009.

80. Barbara Pothier, e-mail communication with author, July 21, 2009.

81. Pyle, *The Thunder Tree*, 106.

82. Von Drehle, August 3, 2009.

83. John Prescott, e-mail communication with author, July 24, 2009.

84. Aleta Labak, e-mail communication with author, May 29, 2009.

85. Pyle, *The Thunder Tree*, 107.

86. Willard Mounts, correspondence with author, March 20, 2009.

87. Noel Congdon to the Denver Water Board, Denver Board of Water Commissioners, Box # 392825673, Folder 16, South Suburban Metropolitan Recreation and Parks District Correspondence, 1966–1969.

88. Mary Whitney to the Denver Water Board, Denver Board of Water Commissioners, Box # 392825673, Folder 16, South Suburban Metropolitan Recreation and Parks District Correspondence, 1966–1969.

89. Klasina VanderWerf, *High on Country: A Narrative History of Cherry Hills Village* (N.P.: The Cherry Hills Land Preserve), 13.

90. Scott Riney, e-mail communication with author, February 23, 2009.

91. Glen Stenson to Bob Panesi, April 7, 1967, and R. D. Panesi to Glen Stenson, April 19, 1967, Denver Board of Water Commissioners, Box # 392825673, Folder 10, Correspondence 1935–1975.

92. "Denver Water Board May Again Allow Horse, Bike Riders to Use Highline Road," *Littleton Independent*, November 16, 1967, 1; Donald L. Snyder on behalf of "Property Owners and Objectors" to Gerald Stapp, November 25, 1967, Denver Board of Water Commissioners, Box # 392825673, Folder 10, Correspondence 1935–1975.

93. John G. Bowen to Denver Water Board, December 4, 1967, Denver Board of Water Commissioners, Box # 392825673, Folder 15, South Suburban Metropolitan Recreation and Parks District Correspondence 1966–1969.

94. "The Highline—Let's Use Its Potential," *Arapahoe Herald* 66, 44 (March 4, 1969), 1.

95. Robert M. Pyle, Notice, August 2, 1967, Denver Board of Water Commissioners, Box # 392825673, Folder 16, South Suburban Metropolitan Recreation and Park District Correspondence, 1966–1969.

96. Skari, *High Line Canal*, 32.

97. Agreement between the Board of Water Commissioners and the South Suburban Metropolitan Recreation and Park District, March 24, 1970, 2, Denver Board of Water Commissioners, Box # 392825673, Folder 17, South Suburban Metropolitan Recreation and Park District Correspondence, 1970–1986.

98. Alfred J. Nielsen to George Zoellner, August 10, 1977; Memo from G. A. Wilson to R. D. Panesi, August 16, 1977; Alfred J. Nielsen to R. D. Panesi, August 23, 1977, Denver Board of Water Commissioners, Box # 392825673, Folder 17, South Suburban Metropolitan Recreation and Park District Correspondence, 1970–1986.

99. Mark E. Barber to Ray Printz, October 13, 1971, Denver Board of Water Commissioners, Box # 392825673, Folder 10, Correspondence 1935–1975.

100. Memo to William Miller, June 25, 1974; Clifford D. Fales to W. H. Miller, June 25, 1974; W. H. Miller to Clifford D. Fales, July 1, 1974, Denver Board of Water Commissioners, Box # 392825673, Folder 10, Correspondence 1935–1975.

101. Roy E. Upthegrove to Bob Panesi, October 1, 1975, Denver Board of Water Commissioners, Box # 392825673, Folder 11, Correspondence 1976–1977.

102. R. D. Panesi to C. S. Coward, June 30, 1976, Denver Board of Water Commissioners, Box # 392825673, Folder 11, Correspondence 1976–1977.

103. The rules also only allowed careful horseback riding. Racing and galloping was not encouraged, as it could lead to accidents like the one that happened in July of 1988, when a horse, uncontrolled by its intoxicated rider, trampled a five year old boy, causing a head injury, two broken legs, and a broken arm. "Horse Trampling of Boy Spurs Suit," *Rocky Mountain News*, July 10, 1990, 98.

104. Interview with Neil Sperandeo, Manager of Recreation and Property Specialist, Denver Water Board, July 29, 2010.

105. Richard Louv, *Childhood's Future* (Boston: Houghton-Mifflin, 1990), 178.

106. Chudacoff, *Children at Play*, 189.

107. Peter Stearns, *Anxious Parents: A History of Modern Childrearing in America* (New York: New York University Press, 2003), 34–35.

108. Mintz, *Huck's Raft*, 337.

109. Guy Kelly, "Coyotes Prey on Cherry Hills Pets," *Rocky Mountain News*, March 21, 1993, 22.

110. "Woman Reports Cougar," *Rocky Mountain News*, May 5, 1992, 8; Tillie Fong,

"Mountain Lion Surprises Trail Users," *Rocky Mountain News*, October 27, 1999, 30A; "Mountain Lion Warnings Planned," *Rocky Mountain News*, November 1, 1999, 21A.

111. John C. Ensslin, "Vanished Child, Diminished Hope," *Rocky Mountain News*, November 3, 1991, 33.

112. Lynn Bartels, "Suspect Faces 5 More Sex Charges," *Rocky Mountain News*, July 21, 1994.

113. "Littleton Student Robbed of Tuition," *Rocky Mountain News*, July 28, 1995, 30A.

114. Ann Carnahan, "'Relax, You're Going to Die Slowly' Pregnant Sex-Assault Victim Recounts Ordeal, and Rescue," *Rocky Mountain News*, July 13, 1999, 5A.

115. Hector Gutierrez, "Cops Hunt Suspect in Stabbing," *Rocky Mountain News*, February 24, 2001, 32A.

116. John Aguilar, "Man Who Abducted, Raped Hiker Gets 65 Years to Life," *Rocky Mountain News*, September 30, 2004, 20A.

117. Owen S. Good, "Users of Canal Trail Don't Let Fear Prevail," *Rocky Mountain News*, September 19, 2003, 35A.

118. Von Drehle, August 3, 2009.

119. Prescott, July 24, 2009.

120. Joseph Brookshire, e-mail communication with author, June 4, 2009.

121. High Line Canal Partners, *High Line Canal Future Management Study*, July 16, 2002, Appendix C, 10.

122. High Line Canal Partners, Appendix C, 11.

123. Tupper, *No Place to Play*, 5.

124. Position yourself to watch a park or playground and see how many unsupervised children come to play. (Unobtrusively, so no one takes you for a lurking predator.) In all likelihood, you could watch for days—or weeks—before seeing an unsupervised child playing. I have lived across the street from a large park for more than a decade, and in all those years, I have seen exactly one child playing there without parents, sitters or teachers. School playgrounds are sometimes a bit different, with children living directly adjacent coming after hours to play.

CHAPTER SIX: CHILDHOOD MOVES INDOORS

1. Bill Bryson, *The Life and Times of the Thunderbolt Kid* (New York: Broadway Books, 2006), 36.

2. Ibid., 37.

3. For a discussion of the importance of "doing nothing," see Stuart C. Aitken, *Geographies of Young People* (New York: Routledge, 2001), 17.

4. Bryson, *The Life and Times*, 263.

5. Sandra L. Hofferth and John F. Sandberg, "How American Children Spend Their Time," *Journal of Marriage and Family* 63, 2 (May 2001): 300–301.

6. Aitken, *Geographies of Young People*, 17.

7. Susan M. McHale, Ann C. Crouter, and Corinna J. Tucker, "Free Time Activities in Middle Childhood: Links with Adjustment in Early Adolescence," *Child Development* 72, 6 (November-December 2001): 1770, 1774–1775.

8. Clifford Edward Clark, Jr., *The American Family Home, 1800–1960* (Chapel Hill: University of North Carolina Press, 1986), 215.

9. See "Square Feet of Floor Area in New One-Family Houses Completed," United States Census Bureau, 2007, http://www.census.gov/const/C25Ann/sftotalsqft_2007.pdf. Accessed on October 14, 2010.

10. Viviana A. Zelizer, *Pricing the Priceless Child: The Changing Social Value of Children* (Princeton, N.J.: Princeton University Press, 1985), 34–35.

11. Melodee Martin Helms, "Suburbia's Fortress Mentality," *Christian Science Monitor*, June 1, 2007, http://www.csmonitor.com/2007/0601/p09s03-coop.html, accessed May 15, 2009.

12. Setha M. Low, "The Edge and the Center: Gated Communities and the Discourse of Urban Fear," *American Anthropologist*, New Series, 103, 1 (March 2001): 54.

13. Janet Elder, "Growing Up Savvy: State-of-the-Art City Kids," *New York Times Magazine*, November 9, 1986, 34.

14. Ibid.

15. Ibid.

16. Research would seem to indicate that parents worried more about girls' safety than boys'. Indoor commercial facilities were particularly important to their recreational activities. James F. Sallis and Karen Glanz, "The Role of Built Environments in Physical Activity, Eating and Obesity in Childhood," *Future of Children* 16, 1 (Spring 2006): 91.

17. Kenneth T. Jackson, "All the World's a Mall: Reflections on the Social and Economic Consequences of the American Shopping Center," *American Historical Review* 101, 4 (October 1996):1114.

18. Lizabeth Cohen, *A Consumer's Republic: The Politics of Mass Consumption in Postwar America* (New York: Vintage Books, 2003), 270.

19. Jackson, "All the World's a Mall," 1118.

20. William Glaberson, "The Heart of the City Now Beats in the Mall," *New York Times*, March 27, 1992, 1. ProQuest Historical Newspapers, The New York Times (1851–2007), pg. A1.

21. Janis Newman Hubschman, "The Mall, a Member of the Family," *New York Times*, January 22, 1989, 26. ProQuest Historical Newspapers, The New York Times (1851–2007), pg. NJ 26.

22. Laurel Shaper Walters, "Stores Build in Perks to Keep Families Coming," *Christian Science Monitor* 90, 83 (March 26, 1998), 14.

23. Keep in mind that all parents do not perceive malls in the same way. In particular, African American parents may not see malls as spaces where children are safe, but spaces where their children may be singled out as suspicious, potentially criminal, intruders. Carol Lawson, "Nurturing Black Children in an Unfriendly World," *New York Times*, June 10, 1993, 1. ProQuest Historical Newspapers, The New York Times (1851–2007), pg. C 1.

24. "Volunteers Begin Effort to Fingerprint Children," *New York Times*, April 8, 1986, 20. ProQuest Historical Newspapers, The New York Times (1851–2007), pg. A20.

25. Julie Bick, "This Halloween, Superheroes Will Head to the Mall," *New York Times*, October 29, 2006, nytimes.com, http://www.nytimes.com/2006/10/29/business/yourmoney/29treat.htm.

26. Although numerous web sources point to Chula Vista as the location of this first Play Place, it is extremely difficult to locate any history on this particular innovation. Even the official McDonald's website does not mark the occasion but does mark the arrival of the Happy Meal. "McDonald's History," http://www.mcdonalds.ca/pdfs/history-final.pdf.

27. Holly Blackford, "Playground Panopticism: Ring-around-the-Children, a Pocketful of Women," *Childhood* 11 (2004): 242.

28. Ibid.

29. Ibid.

30. Ibid., 244.

31. U.S. Consumer Product Safety Commission, "CPSC, McDonald's Corp. Announce Agreement for Firm to Pay $4 Million Damage Settlement," Release # 99-130, June 29, 1999. http:///www.cpsc.gov/CPSCPUB/PREREL/PRHTML99/99130.html.

32. Joe L. Frost, *Play and Playscapes* (Albany, N.Y.: Delmar Publishers, 1992), 198.

33. Roberta Seelinger Trites, e-mail communication with author, November 11, 2010.

34. U.S. Consumer Product Safety Commission, "Soft Contained Play Equipment Safety Review," May 2002, http://www.cpsc.gov/library/foia/foia02/os/scpe.pdf.

35. MaryLou Iverson, "The Staying Power of Soft Contained Playgrounds," *P & R* (April 1999): 55.

36. "Statistics show that 79% of all playground accidents are due to falls. Most of these, 68% are due to falls to the surface and 10% are due to falls to the equipment. Just eliminate falls, and you solve almost 80% of the problem." James A. Peterson, "Eliminate Playgrounds? You Must Be Nuts," *P & R* (April 2002): 95; U.S. Consumer Product Safety Commission, "Soft Contained Play Equipment Safety Review."

37. U.S. Consumer Product Safety Commission, "Soft Contained Play Equipment Safety Review."

38. Susan D. Hudson and Donna Thompson, "Signs of the Times," *P & R* (April 2002): 63.

39. U.S. Consumer Product Safety Commission, "CPSC and Manufacturers Alert Playgrounds to Remove Animal Swings," Release # 95-059, January 12, 1995.

40. U.S. Consumer Product Safety Commission, "Miracle Recreation Equipment Company to Repair 'Flying Gym' Playground Swings," Release #86-38, June 4, 1986.

41. U.S. Consumer Product Safety Commission, "CPSC Finds Lead Poisoning Hazard for Young Children on Public Playground Equipment," Release 97-001, October 1, 1996; U.S. Consumer Product Safety Commission, *Public Playground Safety Handbook*, Publication #325 (Washington, D.C.: USCPSC, 2008), 12.

42. U.S. Consumer Product Safety Commission, *Little Big Kids, for Ages 3–5*, CPSC Document #321 (Washington, D.C.: CPSC, n.d.), ii–4.

43. Ibid., 10.

44. Ibid., 10–12.

45. Ibid., 10.

46. Bernard Mergen, *Play and Playthings: A Reference Guide* (Westport, Conn.: Greenwood Press, 1982), 98.

47. Blackford, "Playground Panopticism," 232, 238.

48. Ibid., 239.

49. Vance Packard, *Our Endangered Children: Growing Up in a Changing World* (Boston: Little, Brown, 1983), 65–66.

50. Blackford, "Playground Panopticism," 231.

51. Frost, *Play and Playscapes*, 138.

52. Ibid., 103.

53. Ibid.

54. Ibid., 155.

55. James Kozlowsky, "Dangerous Playground Poses Problem for Park," *Parks and Recreation* (March 2004): 39–41.

56. Ibid., 41–42.

57. *Clark v. Fair Oaks Recreation and Park District*, 106 Cal. App. 4th 336, 130 Cal. Rptr. 2d 633 (Cal. App. Dist. 3 02/14/2003), quoted in Kozlowsky, 44.

58. Karen Kaplan, "*Ewwww*—Poop in Pools More Common Than You May Think," *Los Angeles Times*, May 16, 2013, http://articles.latimes.com/2013/may/16/science/la-sci-sn-contaminated-pools-fecal-matter-20130516.

59. "Cryptosporidiosis Outbreaks Associated with Recreational Water Use—Five States, 2006," *JAMA*, Morbidity and Mortality Weekly Report, 298, 13 (October 3, 2007): 1507–1509.

60. A. L. Valderrama et al., "Multiple Risk Factors Associated with a Large Statewide Increase in Cryptosporidiosis," *Epidemiology and Infectious Disease* 137 (2009): 1785.

61. Jeff Wiltse, *Contested Waters: A Social History of Swimming Pools in America* (Chapel Hill: University of North Carolina Press, 2007), 181.

62. This discussion owes a great deal to Ames, Iowa's, decision to build a multimillion dollar "aquatic center" to replace the city's Carr Pool, opened in 1929. While local youngsters flocked to the new water park in droves, and it quickly gained hundreds, if not thousands, of satisfied customers, a small band of Ames residents, largely older, campaigned unsuccessfully to try to save Carr Pool. Please note: I am an admirer of the water park, in spite of my caveats, because it does so thoroughly entertain and wear out my son. And I like water slides, too. "Last Day of Carr Pool," *Ames Tribune*, September 8, 2009, http://www.amestrib.com/articles/2009/09/08/ames_tribune/news/doc4aa67e07ca916521397335.txt.

63. Ibid.

64. Wiltse, *Contested Waters*, 213.

65. Peter N. Stearns, *Anxious Parents: A History of Modern Childrearing in America* (New York: New York University Press, 2003), 34.

66. Ibid., 192.

67. David Brooks, "The Organization Kid," *The Atlantic*, April 2001, http://www.theatlantic.com/magazine/archive/2001/04/the-organization-kid/2164/.

68. Ibid.

69. John R. Gillis, "The Islanding of Children—Reshaping the Mythical Landscapes of Childhood," in Marta Gutman and Ning de Coninck-Smith, *Designing Modern Childhoods: History, Space and the Material Culture of Children* (New Brunswick, N.J.: Rutgers University Press, 2008), 316.

70. Mary S. Rivkin, *Outdoor Experiences for Young Children*, ERIC Digest (Charles-

ton, W.Va.: ERIC Clearinghouse on Rural Education and Small Schools, December 2000), 3.

71. Charles W. Schmidt, "Obesity: A Weighty Issue for Children," *Environmental Health Perspectives* 111, 13 (October 2003): A 703.

72. Sandra L. Hofferth and John F. Sandberg, "How American Children Spend Their Time," *Journal of Marriage and Family* 63, 2 (May 2001): 300.

73. Kaveri Subrahmanyam, Robert E. Kraut, Patricia M. Greenfield, Elisheva F. Gross, "The Impact of Home Computer Use on Children's Activities and Development," *Future of Children* 10, 2 (Autumn-Winter, 2000): 125.

74. HomeNet research study participant quoted in ibid., 123.

75. Jeanne E. Arnold, Anthony P. Graesch, Enzo Ragazzini, and Elinor Ochs, *Life at Home in the Twenty-First Century: 32 Families Open Their Doors* (Los Angeles: Cotsen Institute of Archaeology, 2012), 3, 14.

76. Ibid., 77.

77. Ibid., 69.

78. By the late 1990s, an important status marker for middle-class children was to have a computer in their own rooms. Tiffani Chin and Meredith Phillips, "Social Reproduction and Child-Rearing Practices: Social Class, Children's Agency, and the Summer Activity Gap," *Sociology of Education* 77, 3 (July 2004): 199.

79. Alex Kotlowitz, *There Are No Children Here: The Story of Two Boys Growing Up in the Other America* (New York: Anchor Books, 1992), 25.

80. Ibid., 239–241.

81. Ibid., 13, 22, 24–25, 30.

82. Ibid., 13.

83. Ibid., 25–26, 72.

84. For descriptions of the ease of supervising children from a low-rise building versus a high-rise, see J. S. Fuerst, *When Public Housing Was Paradise: Building Community in Chicago* (Urbana: University of Illinois Press, 2005), 46, 48, 61, 165, 174. Historian D. Bradford Hunt argues that problems with costs guaranteed that the CHA would turn to building "high-density elevator buildings." D. Bradford Hunt, "What Went Wrong with Public Housing in Chicago? A History of the Robert Taylor Homes," *Journal of the Illinois State Historical Society* 94, 1 (Spring 2001): 104.

85. Sudhir Alladi Venkatesh, *American Project: The Rise and Fall of a Modern Ghetto* (Cambridge, Mass.: Harvard University Press, 2000), 49.

86. Kotlowitz, *There Are No Children Here*, 4.

87. Ibid., 4–6.

88. Ibid., 52–53.

89. Ibid., 143.

90. Ibid., 267.

91. Venkatesh, *American Project*, 14.

92. Ibid., 19.

93. Ibid., 18.

94. Ottie Davis [pseudonym], quoted in ibid., 22.

95. Hunt, "What Went Wrong," 104.

96. Kenny Davenport [pseudonym], quoted in Venkatesh, *American Project*, 24.

97. Bobby Dowell [pseudonym], quoted in ibid., 26.

98. D. Bradford Hunt, *Blueprint for Disaster: The Unraveling of Chicago Public Housing* (Chicago: University of Chicago Press, 2009), 156.

99. See ibid., 145–181, which details the problems posed by a very high child-to-adult ratio in Chicago's high-rise housing projects.

100. Venkatesh, *American Project*, 4.

101. For a survey of conditions in Chicago's African American neighborhoods, and resident comment on those conditions, see St. Clair Drake and Horace C. Cayton, *Black Metropolis: A Study of Negro Life in a Northern City* (New York: Harcourt, Brace, 1945), 174–212.

102. Fuerst, *When Public Housing Was Paradise*, 3. In the late 1960s, the socioeconomic characteristics of public housing residents began to change radically. Housing that had been largely for working-class, two-parent families became housing for deeply impoverished families reliant on welfare, headed by single women. Hunt, "What Went Wrong," 108–109.

103. Hunt, "What Went Wrong," 99.

104. Edith Abbott, *The Tenements of Chicago, 1908–1935* (Chicago: University of Chicago Press, 1936), 488n.

105. Andrew Greenlee, in Fuerst, *When Public Housing Was Paradise*, 58.

106. Bertrand Ellis, in ibid., 47.

107. Leon Hamilton, in ibid., 52.

108. Gwendolyn Duncan Alexander, in ibid., 105–106.

109. Melvin Wilson, in ibid., 64.

110. Nelvia Brady, in ibid., 69.

111. James Fletcher, ibid., 70.

112. William Shaw, in ibid., 115.

113. Ramsey Lewis, in ibid., 167.

114. Colin Ward, *The Child in the City* (London: Architectural Press, 1978), 34.

115. Hunt, *Blueprint for Disaster*, 207.

116. Elizabeth Wood quoted in Hunt, *Blueprint for Disaster*, 132.

117. Hunt, "What Went Wrong," 106.

118. Hunt, *Blueprint for Disaster*, 127, 132, 167; Venkatesh, *American Project*, 49.

119. Kotlowitz, *There Are No Children Here*, 304.

120. Hunt, "What Went Wrong," 96.

121. Subsequent to the publication of *There Are No Children Here*, Kotlowitz revealed that the surname of the family in his book was not Rivers, but Walton, and readers followed their evolving lives with interest. Lafeyette was in trouble with the police before Kotlowitz finished his project. Pharoah and younger brother Timothy followed. An internet search of the Illinois Department of Corrections records in the fall of 2009 showed that Lafeyette, Pharoah and Timothy were all in custody, for various charges, including possession of controlled substances (Lafeyette, Pharoah and Timothy), felony possession of a firearm (Lafeyette), and second-degree murder (Timothy). A year later, all were still in custody. http://www.idoc.state.il.us/subsections/search/inms, accessed 11/19/2009 and 10/01/2010.

122. Chin and Phillips, "Social Reproduction and Child-Rearing Practices," 202.

123. There is a very interesting literature that examines the ways in which project dwellers, and particularly women, worked to overcome their environment. See Venkatesh, *American Project*; Roberta M. Feldman and Susan Stall, *The Dignity of Resistance: Women Residents' Activism in Chicago Public Housing* (Cambridge: Cambridge University Press, 2004); Rhonda Y. Williams, *The Politics of Public Housing: Black Women's Struggles against Urban Inequality* (Oxford: Oxford University Press, 2004).

124. Chin and Phillips, "Social Reproduction and Child-Rearing Practices," 199.

CHAPTER SEVEN: RECONNECTIONS AND RECONSIDERATIONS

1. Robert M. Pyle, "Eden in a Vacant Lot: Special Places, Species, and Kids in the Neighborhood of Life," in Peter H. Kahn, Jr., and Stephen R. Kellert, eds., *Children and Nature: Psychological, Sociocultural, and Evolutionary Investigations* (Cambridge, Mass.: MIT Press, 2002), 311–312.

2. Pyle, "Eden in a Vacant Lot," 319; see also Susan G. Davis, *Spectacular Nature: Corporate Culture and the Sea World Experience* (Berkeley: University of California Press, 1997).

3. Robert M. Pyle, *The Thunder Tree: Lessons from an Urban Wildland* (Boston: Houghton Mifflin, 1993).

4. Janisse Ray, *Ecology of a Cracker Childhood* (Minneapolis: Milkweed Editions, 2000), 3.

5. Ray, *Ecology of a Cracker Childhood*, 127.

6. Ibid.

7. Ibid., 127–128.

8. See Richard Louv, *Last Child in the Woods: Saving Our Children from Nature-Deficit Disorder* (Chapel Hill, N.C.: Algonquin Books, 2008), 178–188, 243.

9. California Roundtable on Recreation, Parks and Tourism, "California Children's Outdoor Bill of Rights," 2, http://www.calroundtable.org/files/cobr_edit.pdf.

10. Ibid., 5–7.

11. Oregon Recreation and Park Association, "Oregon Children's Outdoor Bill of Rights," http://www.eugene-or.gov/portal/server.pt/gateway/PTARGS_0_228_356531 _0_0_18/Oregon_Childrens_Outdoor_Bill_of_Rights.pdf.

12. An affinity for hunting and fishing as a means to preserve children's connections to the natural world is evident in Richard Louv's *Last Child in the Woods*. While Louv is more an advocate of fishing than hunting, he sees both as valuable in maintaining intimate connections to outdoor spaces and in nurturing individuals who believe in nature preservation. "Remove hunting and fishing from human activity, and we lose many of the voters and organizations that now work against the destruction of woods, fields, and watersheds." Louv, *Last Child in the Woods*, 194; Indiana Department of Natural Resources, "Indiana Children's Outdoor Bill of Rights," http://www.in.gov /dnr/7243.htm; North Carolina Kids Outdoors, "NC Children's Outdoor Bill of Rights," http://www.nckidsoutdoors.org/; Governor, State of Maryland, "Proclamation: Maryland Children's Outdoor Bill of Rights," www.governor.maryland.gov/documents/Out doorBillOfRights.pdf.

13. *The Daring Book for Girls* is part of a whole genre of "let's get the kids outdoors" books, including but not limited to the reissued boys' and girls' *Handy Books, The Dan-*

gerous Book for Boys, My Nature Journal: A Personal Nature Guide for Young People, and *Keeping a Nature Journal: Discover a Whole New Way of Seeing the World around You.*

14. Andrea J. Buchanan and Miriam Peskowitz, *The Daring Book for Girls* (New York: HarperCollins, 2007), viii.

15. Ibid., 118.

16. Ibid., 158.

17. Ibid., 246–248.

18. The description of making a "sit upon," to put between the outdoorsperson's backside and the ground, is just like the description in my late 1960s, early 1970s *Girl Scout Handbook.* I even made one, many years ago.

19. Buchanan and Peskowitz, *The Daring Book,* front matter.

20. A quick look at the reissued *Handy Books* shows no such disclaimer in the front of either book. This is unsurprising in the case of the Beard sisters' *Original Girl's Handy Book,* since most of the material pertains to handicrafts and other fairly sedate activities. The omission of such a statement from *The Original Boy's Handy Book* is a bit more surprising, since the book provides instructions for boys to construct weapons, such as spears (for spear fishing), boomerangs, cross-bows, slingshots and blow-guns. Daniel Beard, *The Original Boy's Handy Book* (New York: Black Dog and Leventhal Press, 2007), 188–202.

21. A quick perusal of the website of any large toy retailer will reveal a whole host of items meant to make study of the outdoors more appealing to children. Toys"R"Us, on-line catalog, http://www.toysrus.com/family/index.jsp?categoryId=2256532&view=all.

22. National Wildlife Federation, "What Is a Green Hour," http://www.nwf.org/Get-Outside/Be-Out-There/Why-Be-Out-There/What-is-a-Green-Hour.aspx.

23. National Wildlife Federation, "'Green Hour' Parents' Guide," http://www.nwf.org/Get-Outside/Be-Out-There/Why-Be-Out-There/Parents-Guide.aspx.

24. Rhonda Clements, "An Investigation of the Status of Outdoor Play," *Contemporary Issues in Early Childhood* 5, 1 (2004): 72, 74.

25. "Police and Neighbors Join in a SoHo Search for Missing Schoolboy," *New York Times,* May 27, 1979, 31, Proquest, Historical New York Times; "Death Declaration Ends Hunt for Etan Patz," *New York Times,* June 20, 2001, Metro Section, B2, Proquest, Historical New York Times.

26. "Des Moines Man Sought in Boy's Disappearance," *New York Times,* August 15, 1984, A 18, ProQuest Historical Newspapers, The New York Times (1851–2007).

27. Joseph Berger and Al Baker, "Brooklyn Eight-Year-Old Was Drugged, Then Suffocated, Medical Examiner Says," *New York Times,* July 20, 2011.

28. Steven Mintz, *Huck's Raft: A History of American Childhood* (Cambridge, Mass.: Belknap Press, 2004), 338.

29. Christopher Maag and Graham Bowley, "Tornado Kills 4 in Iowa Boy Scout Camp," *New York Times,* June 12, 2008; Jay Mechling, *On My Honor: Boy Scouts and the Making of American Youth* (Chicago: University of Chicago Press, 2001), 140.

30. Markella B. Rutherford, *Adult Supervision Required: Private Freedom and Public Constraints for Parents and Children* (New Brunswick, N.J.: Rutgers University Press, 2011), 71, 74.

31. In 2004, Rhonda Clements, education scholar, published a study on children's

outdoor activities, as compared to their mothers'. She distributed e-mail surveys to 830 mothers, to find out how much time the mothers had spent in the out-of-doors as children, compared to their own offspring, and to ascertain the reasons for any differences. Seventy percent of the mothers reported playing outside every day as children, and 56 percent remained outside for three hours or more. Only 31 percent of their children played outside every day, and only 22 percent of their children remained outside for three hours or longer. One of the reasons for this disparity was that mothers had too little time to spend outside monitoring their offspring. Clements, "An Investigation of the Status of Outdoor Play," 72, 74.

32. Lenore Skenazy, *Free-Range Kids: Giving Our Children the Freedom We Had without Going Nuts with Worry* (San Francisco: Jossey-Bass, 2009), xvi.

33. Ibid., xvii.

34. Ibid., 4–5.

35. Ibid., 16–17.

36. Ibid., 182–183.

37. Ibid., 184–185.

38. Ibid., 193.

39. Lenore Skenazy, "Such Sadness. Leiby Kletzky, RIP," Lenore Skenazy, Free-Range Kids, http://freerangekids.wordpress.com/2011/07/13/such-sadness-leiby-kletzky-r-i-p/.

40. Larry Magid, "How Should Parents React to Tragic Murder of 8-Year-Old Boy," http://www.huffingtonpost.com/larry-magid/how-should-parents-react-_b_897915.html.

41. A quick look at the internet will confirm the large variety of available devices. See also Sabra Chartrand, "Patent: A Tracking Device That Can Be Fitted into a Child's Backpack or Ball Cap," *New York Times,* August 5, 2002, C4.

42. Richard Louv, *Childhood's Future* (Boston: Houghton Mifflin, 1990), 12, 33.

43. Ibid., 33, 174.

44. Clements, "An Investigation of the Status of Outdoor Play," 74.

45. Arjen E. J. Wals, "Nobody Planted It, It Just Grew! Young Adolescents' Perceptions and Experiences of Nature in the Context of Urban Environmental Education," *Children's Environments* 11, 3 (September 1994): 20.

46. Wals, "Nobody Planted It," 21–22.

47. Charles W. Schmidt, "Obesity: A Weighty Issue for Children," *Environmental Health Perspectives* 111, 13 (October 2003): A703.

48. David Sobel, "A Place in the World: Adults' Memories of Childhood's Special Places," *Children's Environments Quarterly* 7, 4 (1990): 10.

49. Catharine Ward Thompson, Peter Aspinall, and Alicia Montarzino, "The Childhood Factor: Adult Visits to Green Places and the Significance of Childhood Experience," *Environment and Behavior* 40 (2008):137–138.

50. Press Release, "KIDS 2000–2001," State Historical Society of Wisconsin, http://www.shsw.wisc.edu/oss/press/100100.htm, in Kids Archive Collection, 2000–2001, Manuscripts Collection, M2001-163, Wisconsin Historical Society, Madison, Wisconsin.

51. Cheyenne Alisankus, Kids Archive Collection, 2000–2001.

52. Nikki Marie Arndt, Kids Archive Collection, 2000–2001.

53. Shane Gardener, Kids Archive Collection, 2000–2001.

54. Elisabeth Brummond, Kids Archive Collection, 2000–2001.

55. Mary Luchsinger, in Kids Archive Collection, 2000–2001.

56. Margaret O'Brien, in Kids Archive Collection, 2000–2001.

57. Monica Pelkey, in Kids Archive Collection, 2000–2001.

58. Although many middle-class moms and dads grudgingly supply their offspring the electronic toys they so desperately desire, wishing they would go outside to play instead, there are working-class and poor parents who buy their children the same toys, *hoping* to keep them indoors. Sociologist Allison Pugh, examining the consumer behavior of parents from a variety of socioeconomic backgrounds in Oakland, California, found that concerns about dangerous neighborhoods drove their purchases. She wrote, "Toys had a role to play here. Low-income parents wanted goods that would keep their children enthralled, because they often refused to let the children outside when they got home from school in the afternoon. Those children who may have had bicycles or scooters were severely limited in when they could use them. . . . In this light, toys that kept children inside and happy, especially particularly effective ones like Game Boys or Nintendo, were a boon, and their extensive use was fundamental as a public safety issue." For some children, the dangers outside their doors are far more real than for others. Allison J. Pugh, *Longing and Belonging: Parents, Children and Consumer Culture* (Berkeley: University of California Press, 2009), 3–4, 111.

59. Rutherford, *Adult Supervision Required*, 75.

60. Richard E. Wood, *Survival of Rural America: Small Victories and Bitter Harvests* (Lawrence: University Press of Kansas, 2008), 45.

61. This comment, unfortunately, was inspired by events in Iowa in 2012 and 2103. In the summer of 2012, two girls, Elizabeth Collins and Lyric Cook, disappeared from the small town of Evansdale, while riding their bicycles. Searchers found their bicycles more than a mile from home, but did not find them. In December, hunters found their bodies. In the spring of 2013, in rural Dayton, Iowa, Michael Klunder abducted two girls. One escaped, but the other, Kathlynn Shepard, he killed before killing himself. The investigation into Klunder's crimes is ongoing, because of their possible connection to the Collins and Cook kidnappings and murders. Another similarity between the two cases is the degree to which they highlighted the sense of "otherness" in both Evansdale and Dayton. The reporting in both cases indicated the degree of freedom that parents allowed children in both communities, and the degree of separation community members felt between themselves, and larger places with greater dangers. The reporting also indicated that the kidnappings and murders had changed that perception, probably permanently. "'A Different Summer' after Girls' Disappearance," KCRG-TV 9, Cedar Rapids Iowa, http://www.kcrg.com/news/local/A-different-summer-After-Girls-Disappearance-162826326.html; Barbara Rodriguez, "Kathlynn Shepard Missing: Body of Iowa Girl Believed to Be Found," *Huffington Post*, June 8, 2013, http://www.huffingtonpost.com/2013/06/08/kathlynn-shepard-missing-_n_3407486.html.

BIBLIOGRAPHY

UNPUBLISHED PRIMARY SOURCES

American Camping Association, Wisconsin Section. Papers. Archives and Manuscripts Division, Wisconsin Historical Society, Madison, Wisconsin.

Anonymous, "Life on the Farm," ca. 1898–1900. John E. Brown Papers, Special Collections, State Historical Society of Iowa, Iowa City, Iowa.

Arney, Maude Baumann. Manuscript Diary, April-July 1900. Manuscripts Department, Minnesota Historical Society, St. Paul, Minnesota.

Benke, Hermann C. Manuscript Diary. Manuscripts Division, Kansas State Historical Society, Topeka, Kansas.

Brown, John E. Papers. Special Collections, State Historical Society of Iowa, Iowa City, Iowa.

Denver Board of Water Commissioners. High Line Canal Files. Denver Board of Water Commissioners, Denver, Colorado.

Engles, Frank J. "Reminiscence." MS 0482. Manuscripts Collection, Nebraska State Historical Society.

Fisher, Molly. Manuscripts Collection. Archives and Manuscripts Division, Wisconsin Historical Society, Madison, Wisconsin.

Foley, Eleanor C. "Forty-Nine Years on the High Line Canal: A Colorado Memoir of Houses, Horses and Land." Unpublished manuscript, used by permission of the High Line Canal Preservation Association.

Gitchel-Larsen Family. Correspondence. MS 3622. Manuscripts Collection. Nebraska State Historical Society, Lincoln, Nebraska.

Gortner, Alice Johnson. Papers. Manuscripts Collection. Minnesota Historical Society, St. Paul, Minnesota.

Griswold, Mamie. Manuscript Diaries, 1878–1883. Henry A. Griswold Family Papers, Box 4. Illinois State Historical Library, Springfield, Illinois.

Guenther, Gail. Kids Archive Collection, 2000–2001. Manuscripts Collection, M2001-163, Wisconsin Historical Society, Madison, Wisconsin.

Gushee, Lewellyn Amos. Papers, 1861–1892. MS 3972. Manuscripts Collection, Nebraska State Historical Society, Lincoln, Nebraska.

Herrick, Alberna. Letters in the Molly Fisher Collection. M2001-007. Manuscripts Collection. Wisconsin Historical Society, Madison, Wisconsin.

Hillis, Cora Busey. MS 72. State Historical Society of Iowa, Iowa City, Iowa.

Honce, Charles. "Lost in Yesterday: Adventures in Nostalgia Spun on a White Peach." Typescript Memoir, 1957, BL 240, State Historical Society of Iowa, Iowa City, Iowa.

Iowa Commission on Aging Essay Contest, 1976. Ms. 89. State Historical Society of Iowa, Iowa City, Iowa.

Kids Archive Collection, 2000–2001. Manuscripts Collection, M2001-163. Wisconsin Historical Society, Madison, Wisconsin.

Mayne, Dexter D. Papers. Manuscripts Collection. Minnesota Historical Society, St. Paul, Minnesota.

McClary, Washington Lafayette. Manuscript Diary, MS 3775. Manuscripts Collection, Nebraska State Historical Society, Lincoln, Nebraska.

McNeel, Wakelin Papers. Archives Department, Manuscripts Division, Mss 150. Wisconsin Historical Society, Madison, Wisconsin.

Neighborhood House Papers. Archives. Wisconsin Historical Society, Madison, Wisconsin.

Norg, Nancy. Letters in the Molly Fisher Collection. M2001-007. Manuscripts Collection. Wisconsin Historical Society, Madison, Wisconsin.

North Madison Happy Pals 4-H Club. Scrapbooks. Iowa Women's Archives, University of Iowa Libraries, Iowa City, Iowa.

Preliminary Announcement of Farm Boy Cavaliers: An Organization of Farm Boys Mounted on Horses. Undated pamphlet, Folder 1, Printed Materials, Dexter D. Mayne Papers, Manuscripts Collection, Minnesota Historical Society, St. Paul, Minnesota.

Rasp, Frisby Leonard. Manuscripts Collection. MS 0635. Nebraska State Historical Society, Lincoln, Nebraska.

Scheetz, Helen M. "Beside the Still Waters." Manuscript Memoir. Iowa Women's Archives, University of Iowa Libraries, Iowa City, Iowa.

Schneller, L. G. "The Complete Story of Camp Mishawaka," ca. 1925. Manuscripts Collection, Minnesota Historical Society, St. Paul, Minnesota.

Schulz, August. Manuscript Diary. Manuscripts Division, Kansas State Historical Society, Topeka.

Sebo, Mildred. Papers. Manuscripts Collection. Minnesota Historical Society, St. Paul, Minnesota.

"Sod House Letters" to the *Nebraska Farmer*. MS 721. Manuscript Collections, Nebraska State Historical Society, Lincoln, Nebraska.

Sperandeo, Neil. Interview with author, July 29, 2010, Denver, Colorado.

Stanley, Anna. Memoir. Archives Collection, Wisconsin Historical Society, Madison, Wisconsin.

Thompson, George B. "Pioneering on the Nebraska Prairies." MS 1463. Manuscripts Collection, Nebraska State Historical Society, Lincoln, Nebraska.

Turner, Charles M. Typescript Reminiscence. RS 1478.AM. Manuscripts Collection, Nebraska State Historical Society, Lincoln, Nebraska.

Wyman, Walker D. "Boyhood Recollections of Dogs, Ponies, Trapping, Even Flying Off the Hen House Roof." Manuscript reminiscence, used by permission of the holder, Mark Wyman, Normal, Illinois.

PUBLISHED PRIMARY SOURCES

Abbott, Edith. *The Tenements of Chicago, 1908–1935.* Chicago: University of Chicago Press, 1936.

Babb, Sanora. *An Owl on Every Post.* Albuquerque: University of New Mexico Press, 1994.

Baden-Powell, Robert. *Scouting for Boys: A Handbook for Instruction in Good Citizenship.* Oxford: Oxford University Press, 2004.

Bailey, Liberty Hyde. *The Training of Farmers*. New York: Century, 1909.

Baldwin, Bird T., Eva Abigail Fillmore, and Lora Hadley. *Farm Children: An Investigation of Rural Child Life in Selected Areas of Iowa*. New York: D. Appleton, 1930.

Barker, Roger G., and Herbert F. Wright. *One Boy's Day: A Specimen Record of Behavior*. North Haven, Conn.: Archon Books, 1966. Reprint of New York: Harper and Row, 1951.

Barnes, Craig. *Growing Up True: Lessons from a Western Boyhood*. Golden, Colo.: Fulcrum Publishing, 2001.

Beard, Daniel Carter. *The Original Boy's Handy Book*. New York: Black Dog and Leventhal Publishers, 2007; facsimile of *The American Boy's Handy Book*, 1880.

Beard, Lina, and Adelia B. Beard. *Girl Pioneers of America Official Manual*, 3rd ed. New York: Girl Pioneers of America, 1918.

Beard, Lina, and Adelia Belle Beard. *On the Trail: An Outdoor Book for Girls*. New York: Charles Scribner's Sons, 1922.

Beard, Lina, and Adelia Belle Beard. *The Original Girl's Handy Book*. New York: Black Dog and Leventhal Publishers, 2007; facsimile of *The American Girl's Handy Book*, 1887.

"The Boy Problem in the Country." *The Charities and the Commons* 17 (December 1906): 332–333.

Boy Scouts of America. *The Official Handbook for Boys*. Garden City, N.Y.: Doubleday, Page, 1916.

Boy Scouts of America. *Scoutmaster's Troop Program Note Book*. N.P.: Boy Scouts of America, 1935.

Brace, Charles Loring. *The Dangerous Classes of New York and Twenty Years' Work among Them*. New York: Wynkoop & Hallenbeck, 1872.

Bryson, Bill. *The Life and Times of the Thunderbolt Kid*. New York: Broadway Books, 2006.

Buchanan, Andrea J., and Miriam Peskowitz. *The Daring Book for Girls*. New York: HarperCollins, 2007.

Camp Fire Girls. *The Book of the Camp Fire Girls*. New York: Camp Fire Girls, Inc., 1950.

Camp Fire Girls. *The Book of the Camp Fire Girls*. New York: Camp Fire Girls, Inc., 1960.

Charles, Cheryl, Richard Louv, Lee Bodner, and Bill Guns. *Children and Nature 2008: A Report on the Movement to Reconnect Children to the Natural World*. Santa Fe: Children and Nature Network, January 2008.

"Cryptosporidiosis Outbreaks Associated with Recreational Water Use—Five States, 2006." *JAMA*, Morbidity and Mortality Weekly Report, 298, 13 (October 3, 2007): 1507–1509.

Davis, Philip, and Grace Kroll. *Street-Land: Its Little People and Big Problems*. Boston: Small, Maynard, 1915.

DeForest, Robert W., and Lawrence Veiller, eds. *The Tenement House Problem Including the Report of the New York State Tenement House Commission of 1900*, vol. 1. New York: MacMillan, 1903.

Forbush, William Byron. *The Boy Problem*, 6th ed. Boston: The Pilgrim Press, 1907.

Fuerst, J. S. *When Public Housing Was Paradise: Building Community in Chicago*. Urbana: University of Illinois Press, 2005.

Gibbons, Charles E. *Child Labor among the Cotton Growers of Texas*. New York: National Child Labor Committee, 1925.

Girl Scouts of the United States of America. *Annual Report, 1950*. New York: Girl Scouts of the United States of America, 1950.

Girl Scouts of the United States of America. *Cadette Girl Scout Handbook*. New York: Girl Scouts of the United States of America, 1963.

Girl Scouts of the United States of America. *Senior Girl Scout Handbook*. New York: Girl Scouts of the United States of America, 1963.

Grigg, William. "The Bear That Stops Fires." *Science News Letter* 68, 14 (October 1, 1955): 218–219.

Hall, G. Stanley. *Adolescence: Its Psychology and Its Relations to Physiology, Anthropology, Sociology, Sex, Crime, Religion and Education*, vol. 2. New York: D. Appleton, 1905.

Harnack, Curtis. *We Have All Gone Away*. Garden City, N.Y.: Doubleday, 1973.

High Line Canal Partners. *High Line Canal Future Management Study*. July 16, 2002.

Hoxie, W. J. *How Girls Can Help Their Country*. Sixtieth Anniversary Facsimile Edition. New York: Girl Scouts of the U.S.A., 1972.

Hunt, Una. *Una Mary: The Inner Life of a Child*. New York: Charles Scribner's Sons, 1914.

Ise, John. *Sod and Stubble*. Lawrence: University Press of Kansas, 1996.

Kisseloff, Jeff. *You Must Remember This: An Oral History of Manhattan in the 1890s to World War II*. New York: Harcourt Brace Jovanovich, 1989.

Kuharic, Vincent. "I Plough a Straight Black Furrow." *From the Fields*. Madison: Farm Folk School, College of Agriculture, University of Wisconsin, 1940.

Louv, Richard. *Last Child in the Woods: Saving Our Children from Nature-Deficit Disorder*. Chapel Hill, N.C.: Algonquin Books, 2008.

McGill, Nettie. *Child Workers on City Streets*. Children's Bureau Publication no. 188. Washington, D.C.: U.S. Government Printing Office, 1928.

McNeel, Wakelin, Sr. *Forestry Club 4-H Work*, Circular 4-H20. Madison: Extension Service of the College of Agriculture, Revised, February 1940; First published January 1936.

———. "Lessons from Nature." *Bulletin of the Wisconsin State Board of Health* (December 1951): 21.

———. "School Forests and Why They Grow." *National Waltonian* (May 1934): 4–5.

Miller, William S. *Growing Up in Goose Lake*. N.p.: William S. Miller, 1974.

Moody, Ralph. *Little Britches*. New York: W. W. Norton, 1950.

Packard, A. S., Jr. *Report on the Rocky Mountain Locust and Other Insects Now Injuring or Likely to Injure Field and Garden Crops in the United States*. Washington, D.C.: U.S. Geological Survey, Department of the Interior, 1877.

Pernin, Father Peter. *The Great Peshtigo Fire : An Eyewitness Account*. Madison, Wis.: State Historical Society of Wisconsin, 1971. Reprinted from the *Wisconsin Magazine of History*, 54 (Summer, 1971): 246–272.

Pyle, Robert Michael. *The Thunder Tree: Lessons from an Urban Wildland*. Boston: Houghton Mifflin, 1993.

Ray, Janisse. *Ecology of a Cracker Childhood*. Minneapolis: Milkweed Editions, 1999.

Reeves, Will R. "Report of the Committee on Street Play." *Journal of Educational Sociology* 4, 10 (June 1931): 607–618.

Riis, Jacob A. *Children of the Poor*. New York: Charles Scribner's Sons, 1902.

———. *How the Other Half Lives*. New York: Hill and Wang, 1957.

Robinson, Reginald. "Leisure-Time Activities of the Children of New York's Lower West Side." *Journal of Educational Sociology* 9, 8 (April 1936): 484–493.

Rogers, James Edward. *The Child and Play, Based on the Reports of the White House Conference on Child Health and Protection*. New York: Century, 1932.

Roosevelt, Theodore. *The Strenuous Life*. New York: Century, 1901.

Ross, Alfred E. *Graded Games for Rural Schools*. New York: A. S. Barnes, 1926.

Skenazy, Lenore. *Free-Range Kids: Giving Our Children the Freedom We Had without Going Nuts with Worry*. San Francisco: Jossey-Bass, 2009.

Tupper, Margo. *No Place to Play*. Philadelphia: Chilton Books, 1966.

U.S. Census Bureau. "Square Feet of Floor Area in New One-Family Houses Completed." U.S. Census Bureau, 2007. http://www.census.gov/const/C25Ann/sftotalsqft_2007.pdf.

U.S. Consumer Product Safety Commission. *Little Big Kids, for Ages 3–5*, CPSC Document #321. Washington, D.C.: CPSC, n.d.

———. *Public Playground Safety Handbook*, Publication #325. Washington, D.C.: US-CPSC, 2008.

———. "Soft Contained Play Equipment Safety Review." May 2002, http://www.cpsc.gov/library/foia/foia02/os/scpe.pdf.

———. Various news releases.

U.S. Department of Interior. *The Race for Inner Space*. Washington, D.C.: U.S. Government Printing Office, 1964.

U.S. Department of Labor, Children's Bureau. *Facilities for Children's Play in the District of Columbia*, Miscellaneous Series no. 8, Bureau Publication no. 22. Washington, D.C.: U.S. Government Printing Office, 1917.

———. *Home and Play Equipment for the Preschool Child*, Bureau Publication no. 238. Washington, D.C.: U.S. Government Printing Office, 1937.

U.S. Senate. *Report of the Country Life Commission: Special Message from the President of the United States Transmitting the Report of the Country Life Commission*. Washington, D.C.: Government Printing Office, 1909.

Walt Disney Pictures. *Charlie the Lonesome Cougar*. 1967. Buena Vista Distribution Company.

Wilder, Laura Ingalls. *By the Shores of Silver Lake*. New York: Harper Trophy, 1971.

———. *Little House in the Big Woods*. New York: Harper Trophy, 1971.

———. *Little House on the Prairie*. New York: Harper Trophy, 1971.

———. *Little Town on the Prairie*. New York: Harper Trophy, 1971.

———. *The Long Winter*. New York: Harper Trophy, 1971.

———. *On the Banks of Plum Creek*. New York: Harper Trophy, 1971.

———. *These Happy Golden Years*. New York: Harper Trophy, 1971.

Wild Kingdom, Mutual of Omaha's, 1963, 1967, 1972.

Wyden, Peter. *Suburbia's Coddled Kids*. Garden City, N.Y.: Doubleday, 1962.

NEWSPAPERS/PERIODICALS/TELEVISION STATIONS
American Young Folks
Ames Tribune
Arapahoe Herald
Atchison Daily Globe
The Atlantic
Berkshire World and Corn Belt Stockman
Boys' Life
The Charities and the Commons
Christian Science Monitor
Congregationalist
Daily Inter-Ocean
Everygirl's Magazine
Farm Boy Cavalier News
Farm Home
Iowa State Daily
Lancaster Farming
Littleton Independent
Los Angeles Times
Midland Schools
Nebraska Farmer
New York Times
North American
P & R
Prairie Farmer
Rocky Mountain News
Science News Letter
KCRG-TV 9, Cedar Rapids, Iowa

WALT DISNEY FILMS
Bambi, 1942
Charlie, the Lonesome Cougar, 1967
Flash, the Teen-Aged Otter, 1961
Jungle Book, 1967.
Perri: The First True-Life Fantasy, 1957
True Life Adventures: The Vanishing Prairie, 1954
Walt Disney's True Life Adventures: The African Lion, 1955
Walt Disney's True Life Adventures: The Living Desert, 1953
Walt Disney's True Life Adventures: The Secrets of Life, 1955
Yellowstone Cubs, 1963

WEBSITES
California Roundtable on Recreation. Parks and Tourism. "California Children's Outdoor Bill of Rights." http://www.calroundtable.org/files/cobr_edit.pdf.

Forest Service. U.S. Department of Agriculture, "Woodsy Owl, A Short History," http:// www.fs.usda.gov/Internet/FSE_DOCUMENTS/stelprdb5193740.pdf.

Governor, State of Maryland. "Proclamation: Maryland Children's Outdoor Bill of Rights." www.governor.maryland.gov/documents/OutdoorBillOfRights.pdf.

Huffington Post.com.

Indiana Department of Natural Resources. "Indiana Children's Outdoor Bill of Rights." http://www.in.gov/dnr/7243.htm.

"McDonald's History." http://www.mcdonalds.ca/pdfs/history-final.pdf.

"Mutual of Omaha's Wild Kingdom." http://www.wildkingdom.com/nostalgia/history .html; http://www.wildkingdom.com/nostalgia/perkins_bio.html; http://www.wild kingdom.com/nostalgia/fowler_bio.html.

National Wildlife Federation. "About Green Hour." http://www.greenhour.org/section /about.

———. "'Green Hour' Parents' Guide," http://www.nwf.org/Get-Outside/Be-Out-There /Why-Be-Out-There/Parents-Guide.aspx.

———. "What Is a Green Hour." http://www.nwf.org/Get-Outside/Be-Out-There /Why-Be-Out-There/What-is-a-Green-Hour.aspx.

North Carolina Kids Outdoors. "NC Children's Outdoor Bill of Rights." http://www .nckidsoutdoors.org/.

Oregon Recreation and Park Association. "Oregon Children's Outdoor Bill of Rights." http://www.orpa.org/displaycommon.cfm?an=1&subarticlenbr=37.

Skenazy, Lenore. Free-Range Kids, http://freerangekids.wordpress.com/2011/07/13 /such-sadness-leiby-kletzky-r-i-p/.

Toys R Us. On-line catalog. http://www.toysrus.com/family/index.jsp?categoryId=225 6532&view=all.

SECONDARY SOURCES

Aitken, Stuart C. Geographies of Young People. New York: Routledge, 2001.

Allen, Thomas B. Guardian of the Wild: The Story of the National Wildlife Federation, 1936–1986. Bloomington: Indiana University Press, 1987.

Armitage, Kevin C. "Bird Day for Kids: Progressive Conservation in Theory and Practice." Environmental History 12, 3 (July 2007): 528–551.

———. The Nature Study Movement: The Forgotten Popularizer of America's Conservation Ethic. Lawrence: University Press of Kansas, 2009.

Arnold, Jeanne E., Anthony P. Graesch, Enzo Ragazzini, and Elinor Ochs. Life at Home in the Twenty-First Century: 32 Families Open Their Doors. Los Angeles: The Cotsen Institute of Archaeology, 2012.

Ayres, Leonard P. Open-Air Schools. New York: Doubleday, Page, 1910.

Banning, Evelyn I. "Social Influences on Children and Youth." Review of Educational Research 25, 1 (February 1955): 36–47.

Bederman, Gail. "'Teaching Our Sons to Do What We Have Been Teaching the Savages to Avoid': G. Stanley Hall, Racial Recapitulation, and the Neurasthenic Paradox." In Gail Bederman, ed., Manliness and Civilization: A Cultural History of Gender and Race in the United States, 1880–1917. Chicago: University of Chicago Press, 1995, 77–120.

Blackford, Holly. "Playground Panopticism: Ring-around-the-Children, a Pocketful of Women." *Childhood* (2004): 227–249.

Bouse, Derek. "Review of 'The Bear by Jean-Jacques Annaud.'" *Film Quarterly* 43, 3 (Spring 1990): 30–34.

Braus, Judy. "Environmental Education." *BioScience* 45, Supplement: Science and Biodiversity Policy (1995): S45–S51.

Bye, Clyde O. "A Study of the Sources of Material Available for Use in an Elementary Course in Nature-Study for Rural School Children, with Especial Reference to Animals, Birds, and Insects." M.S. thesis, Vocational Education, Iowa State College, Ames, Iowa, 1923.

Carpenter, Cheryl Lee. "The Social Production of Fresh Air Charity Work, 1870–1930," Ph.D. Dissertation, Syracuse University, 1994.

Cavallo, Dominick. *Muscles and Morals: Organized Playgrounds and Urban Reform, 1880–1920.* Philadelphia: University of Pennsylvania Press, 1981.

Charles, Cheryl. "The Ecology of Hope: Natural Guides to Building a Children and Nature Movement." *Journal of Science Education and Technology* 18, 6 (2009): 467–475.

Chatelet, Anne Marie. "A Breath of Fresh Air: Open-Air Schools in Europe." In Marta Gutman and Ning de Coninck-Smith. *Designing Modern Childhoods: History, Space and the Material Culture of Children.* New Brunswick, N.J.: Rutgers University Press, 2008, 107–127.

Chin, Tiffani, and Meredith Phillips. "Social Reproduction and Child-Rearing Practices: Social Class, Children's Agency, and the Summer Activity Gap." *Sociology of Education* 77, 3 (July 2004): 185–210.

Chudacoff, Howard P. *Children at Play: An American History.* New York: New York University Press, 2007.

Cialdini, Robert B. "Crafting Normative Messages to Protect the Environment." *Current Directions in Psychological Science* 12, 4 (August 2003): 105–109.

Clark, Clifford Edward, Jr. *The American Family Home, 1800–1960.* Chapel Hill: University of North Carolina Press, 1986.

Clements, Rhonda. "An Investigation of the Status of Outdoor Play." *Contemporary Issues in Early Childhood* 5, 1 (2004): 68–80.

Cohen, Lizabeth. *A Consumer's Republic: The Politics of Mass Consumption in Postwar America.* New York: Vintage Books, 2003.

Courtwright, Julie. *Prairie Fire: A Great Plains History.* Lawrence: University Press of Kansas, 2011.

———. "'When We First Come Here It All Looked Like Prairie Land Almost': Prairie Fire and Plains Settlement." *Western Historical Quarterly* 38, 2 (Summer 2007): 157–179.

Cowan, Ruth Schwartz. *More Work for Mother: The Ironies of Household Technology from the Open Hearth to the Microwave.* New York: Basic Books, 1983.

Danbom, David. *Born in the Country: A History of Rural America.* Baltimore: Johns Hopkins University Press, 1995.

Davis, Susan G. *Spectacular Nature: Corporate Culture and the Sea World Experience.* Berkeley: University of California Press, 1997.

Dods, Roberta Robin. "The Death of Smokey Bear: The Ecodisaster Myth and Forest

Management Practices in Prehistoric North America." *World Archaeology* 33, 3 Ancient Ecodisasters (February 2002): 475–487.

Downs, Laura Lee. *Childhood in the Promised Land: Working Class Movements and the Colonies de Vacances in France, 1880–1960.* Durham: Duke University Press, 2002.

Drake, St. Clair, and Horace C. Cayton. *Black Metropolis: A Study of Negro Life in a Northern City.* New York: Harcourt, Brace, 1945.

Ellison, David L. *Healing Tuberculosis in the Woods: Medicine and Science at the End of the Nineteenth Century.* Westport, Conn.: Greenwood Press, 1994.

English, Peter C. *Old Paint: A Medical History of Childhood Lead-Paint Poisoning in the United States to 1980.* New Brunswick, N.J.: Rutgers University Press, 2001.

Feldman, Roberta M., and Susan Stall. *The Dignity of Resistance: Women Residents' Activism in Chicago Public Housing.* Cambridge: Cambridge University Press, 2004.

Fiege, Mark. *Irrigated Eden: The Making of an Agricultural Landscape in the American West.* Seattle: University of Washington Press, 1999.

Fite, Gilbert C. "Some Farmers' Accounts of Hardship on the Frontier." *Minnesota History* 37, 5 (March 1961): 204–211.

Frost, Joe L. *Play and Playscapes.* Albany, N.Y.: Delmar Publishers, 1992.

Gagen, Elizabeth. "Too Good to Be True: Representing Children's Agency in the Archives of Playground Reform." *Historical Geography* 29 (2001): 53–64.

Gaster, Sanford. "Public Places of Childhood, 1915–1930." *Oral History Review* 22, 2 (1995): 1–31.

Gess, Denise, and William Lutz. *Firestorm at Peshtigo.* New York: Henry Holt and Company, 2002.

Gillis, John R. "The Islanding of Children—Reshaping the Mythical Landscapes of Childhood," in Marta Gutman and Ning de Coninck-Smith. *Designing Modern Childhoods: History, Space and the Material Culture of Children.* New Brunswick, N.J.: Rutgers University Press, 2008, 316–330.

Gutman, Marta, and Ning de Coninck-Smith. *Designing Modern Childhoods: History, Space and the Material Culture of Children.* New Brunswick, N.J.: Rutgers University Press, 2008.

Hays, Samuel P. *Beauty, Health, and Permanence: Environmental Politics in the United States, 1955–1985.* Cambridge: Cambridge University Press, 1987.

Hess, Robert D., and Harriett Goldman. "Parents' Views of the Effect of Television on Their Children." *Child Development* 33, 2 (June 1962): 411–426.

Hofferth, Sandra L., and John F. Sandberg, "How American Children Spend Their Time." *Journal of Marriage and Family* 63, 2 (May 2001): 295–308.

Holt, Marilyn Irvin. *The Orphan Trains: Placing Out in America.* Lincoln: Bison Books, 1992.

Horak, Jan-Christopher. "Wildlife Documentaries: From Classical Forms to Reality TV." *Film History* 18, 4 (2006): 459–475.

Hunt, D. Bradford. *Blueprint for Disaster: The Unraveling of Chicago Public Housing.* Chicago: University of Chicago Press, 2009.

———. "What Went Wrong with Public Housing in Chicago? A History of the Robert Taylor Homes." *Journal of the Illinois State Historical Society* 94, 1 (Spring 2001): 96–123.

Jackson, Kenneth T. "All the World's a Mall: Reflections on the Social and Economic Consequences of the American Shopping Center." *American Historical Review* 101, 4 (October 1996): 1111–1121.

———. *The Crabgrass Frontier: The Suburbanization of the United States.* New York: Oxford University Press, 1985.

Johnson, Richard H., ed. *Guide to the High Line Canal Trail.* Denver: Denver Water Board, 1999.

Jung, Raymond. "Leisure in Three Cultures." *Elementary School Journal* 67, 6 (March 1967): 285–295.

Kahn, Peter, H., Jr., and Stephen R. Kellert, eds. *Children and Nature: Psychological, Sociocultural, and Evolutionary Investigations.* Cambridge, Mass.: MIT Press, 2002.

King, Charles R. *Children's Health in America.* New York: Twayne Publishers, 1993.

Kirby, Jack Temple. *Rural Worlds Lost: The American South, 1920–1960.* Baton Rouge: Louisiana State University Press, 1987.

Kotlowitz, Alex. *There Are No Children Here: The Story of Two Boys Growing Up in the Other America.* New York: Anchor Books, 1991.

Lewis, David Rich. "Still Native: The Significance of Native Americans in the History of the Twentieth-Century American West," *Western Historical Quarterly* 24, 2 (May 1993): 203–227.

Link, William A. "Privies, Progressivism and Public Schools: Health Reform and Education in the Rural South, 1909–1920." *Journal of Southern History* 54, 4 (November 1988): 623–642.

Louv, Richard. *Childhood's Future.* Boston: Houghton-Mifflin, 1990.

Low, Setha M. "The Edge and the Center: Gated Communities and the Discourse of Urban Fear." *American Anthropologist,* New Series, 103, 1 (March 2001): 45–58.

Lukashok, Alvin K., and Kevin Lynch. "Some Childhood Memories of the City." *Journal of the American Institute of Planners* 22, 3 (Summer 1956): 142–152.

Lutts, Ralph H. "The Trouble with Bambi: Walt Disney's *Bambi* and the American Vision of Nature." *Forest & Conservation History* 36, 4 (October 1992): 160–171.

Lynd, Robert S., and Helen Merrell Lynd. *Middletown: A Study in Modern American Culture.* New York: Harcourt Brace Jovanovich, 1957.

MacLeod, David I. *Building Character in the American Boy: The Boy Scouts, YMCA, and Their Forerunners, 1870–1920.* Madison: University of Wisconsin Press, 1983.

Marten, James. *Childhood and Child Welfare in the Progressive Era: A Brief History with Documents.* Boston: Bedford/St. Martin's, 2005.

Matkin-Rawn, Story. "Afield with Ranger Mac: Conservation Education and School Radio during the Great Depression." *Wisconsin Magazine of History* 88, 1 (Autumn 2004): 2–15.

May, Elaine Tyler. *Homeward Bound: American Families in the Cold War Era.* New York: Basic Books, 1988.

McCullough, Constance M. "A Log of Children's Out-of-School Activities." *Elementary School Journal* 58, 3 (December 1957): 157–165.

McHale, Susan M., Ann C. Crouter, and Corinna J. Tucker. "Free Time Activities in Middle Childhood: Links with Adjustment in Early Adolescence." *Child Development* 72, 6 (November-December 2001): 1764–1778.

Mechling, Jay. *On My Honor: Boy Scouts and the Making of American Youth*. Chicago: University of Chicago Press, 2001.

Mergen, Bernard. "The Discovery of Children's Play." *American Quarterly* 27, 4 (October 1975): 399–420.

———. *Play and Playthings: A Reference Guide*. Westport, Conn.: Greenwood Press, 1982.

———. *Snow in America*. Washington, D.C.: Smithsonian Institution Press, 1997.

Miller, Susan A. *Growing Girls: The Natural Origins of Girls' Organizations in America*. New Brunswick, N.J.: Rutgers University Press, 2007.

Mintz, Steven. *Huck's Raft: A History of American Childhood*. Cambridge, Mass.: Belknap Press, 2004.

Mintz, Steven, and Susan Kellogg. *Domestic Revolutions: A Social History of American Family Life*. New York: Free Press, 1988.

Mitman, Gregg. "Cinematic Nature: Hollywood Technology, Popular Culture, and the American Museum of Natural History." *Isis* 84, 4 (December 1993): 637–661.

Morrison, Ellen Earnhardt. *Guardian of the Forest: A History of the Smokey Bear Program*. Alexandria, Va.: Morielle Press, 1989.

Nasaw, David. *Children of the City: At Work and at Play*. Garden City, N.Y.: Anchor Press/Doubleday, 1985.

Packard, Vance. *Our Endangered Children: Growing Up in a Changing World*. Boston: Little, Brown, 1983.

Paris, Leslie. "The Adventures of Peanut and Bo: Summer Camps and Early Twentieth Century American Girlhood." *Journal of Women's History* 12, 4 (2001): 47–76.

———. *Children's Nature: The Rise of the American Summer Camp*. New York: New York University Press, 2008.

Plevin, Arlene. "Still Putting out 'Fires': Ranger Rick and Animal/Human Stewardship." In Sidney Drobin and Kenneth B. Kidd, eds., *Wild Things: Children's Culture and EcoCriticism*. Detroit: Wayne State University Press, 2004, 168–182.

Pugh, Allison. *Longing and Belonging: Parents, Children, and Consumer Culture*. Berkeley: University of California Press, 2009.

Pyle, Robert Michael. "Eden in a Vacant Lot," in Peter H. Kahn, Jr., and Stephen R. Kellert. *Children and Nature: Psychological, Sociocultural, and Evolutionary Investigations*. Cambridge, Mass.: MIT Press, 2002.

Riney-Kehrberg, Pamela. *Childhood on the Farm: Work, Play and Coming of Age in the Midwest*. Lawrence: University Press of Kansas, 2005.

———. "Farm Youth and Progressive Agricultural Reform: Dexter D. Mayne and the Farm Boy Cavaliers of America." *Agricultural History* 85, 4 (Fall 2011): 437–459.

———. *Rooted in Dust: Surviving Drought and Depression in Southwestern Kansas*. Lawrence: University Press of Kansas, 1994.

Rivkin, Mary S. *Outdoor Experiences for Young Children*, ERIC Digest. Charleston, W.Va.: ERIC Clearinghouse on Rural Education and Small Schools, December 2000.

Robinson, Doan. *History of South Dakota*, vol. 1. Logansport, Ind.: B. F. Bowen, 1904.

Robinson, Reginald. "Leisure-Time Activities of the Children of New York's Lower West Side." *Journal of Educational Sociology* 9, 8 (April 1936): 484–493.

Rome, Adam. *The Bulldozer in the Countryside: Suburban Sprawl and the Rise of American Environmentalism.* New York: Cambridge University Press, 2001.

———. "William Whyte, Open Space, and Environmental Activism." *Geographical Review* 88, 2 (April 1998): 259–274.

Rosenzweig, Roy, and Elizabeth Blackmar. *The Park and the People: A History of Central Park.* Ithaca, N.Y.: Cornell University Press, 1992.

Rothman, Hal K. *Saving the Planet: The American Response to the Environment in the Twentieth Century.* Chicago: Ivan R. Dee, 2000.

———. *The Greening of a Nation? Environmentalism in the United States since 1945.* Fort Worth, Tex.: Harcourt Brace College Publishers, 1998.

Rugh, Susan Sessions. *Are We There Yet? The Golden Age of American Family Vacations.* Lawrence: University Press of Kansas, 2008.

Rutherford, Markella B. *Adult Supervision Required: Private Freedom and Public Constraints for Parents and Children.* New Brunswick, N.J.: Rutgers University Press, 2011.

Sallis, James F., and Karen Glanz. "The Role of Built Environments in Physical Activity, Eating and Obesity in Childhood." *Future of Children* 16, 1 (Spring 2006): 89–108.

Sammond, Nicholas. *Babes in Tomorrowland: Walt Disney and the Making of the American Child, 1930–1960.* Durham, N.C.: Duke University Press, 2005.

Schmidt, Charles W. "Obesity: A Weighty Issue for Children." *Environmental Health Perspectives* 111, 13 (October 2003): A700–A707.

Schmitt, Peter J. *Back to Nature: The Arcadian Myth in Urban America.* New York: Oxford University Press, 1969.

Shearer, Tobin Miller. "'Chickens, Crops and Tractors': The Use of Machines as a Sacred Resource in Mennonite Fresh Air Hosting Programs." *Journal for the Study of Religion, Nature and Culture* 4, 3 (Fall 2010): 153–181.

———. "More Than Fresh Air: African American Children's Influence on Mennonite Religious Practice, 1950–1979." *Journal of Race, Ethnicity and Religion* 2, 7 (May 2011), http://www.raceandreligion.com/JRER/Volume_2_%282011%29_files/Shearer%202%207.pdf.

Shefchik, Rick. "Kids Need New Anti-Litter Lesson." *Beaver County Times*, April 4, 2002, 81.

Skari, David. *High Line Canal: Meandering through Time.* Denver: C & M Press, 2003.

Smith, Michael B. "'The Ego Ideal of the Good Camper' and the Nature of Summer Camp." *Environmental History* 11, 1 (2006): 70–101.

Sobel, David. "A Place in the World: Adults' Memories of Childhood's Special Places." *Children's Environments Quarterly* 7, 4 (1990): 5–12.

Stearns, Peter. *Anxious Parents: A History of Modern Childrearing in America.* New York: New York University Press, 2003.

Strong, Melvin W. "A Study of the Sources of Material Available for Use in an Elementary Course in Nature Study for Rural School Children with Especial Reference to Inorganic Nature." M.S. thesis, Vocational Education, Iowa State College, Ames, Iowa, 1923.

Subrahmanyam, Kaveri, Robert E. Kraut, Patricia M. Greenfield, and Elisheva F. Gross. "The Impact of Home Computer Use on Children's Activities and Development." *Future of Children* 10, 2 (Autumn-Winter, 2000): 123–144.

Taylor, Joseph E., III. *Pilgrims of the Vertical: Yosemite Rock Climbers and Nature at Risk.* Cambridge, Mass.: Harvard University Press, 2010.

Taylor, Walter P. "Some Educational Activities of the National Wildlife Federation." *The American Biology Teacher* 15, 3 (March 1953): 81–84.

Thompson, Catherine Ward, Peter Aspinall, and Alicia Montarzino. "The Childhood Factor: Adult Visits to Green Places and the Significance of Childhood Experience." *Environment and Behavior* 40 (2008): 111–143.

Ufford, Walter S. *Fresh Air Charity in the United States.* New York: Bonnell, Silver, 1897.

Valderrama, A. L., et al. "Multiple Risk Factors Associated with a Large Statewide Increase in Cryptosporidiosis." *Epidemiology and Infectious Disease* 137 (2009): 1781–1788.

Vanderbeck, Robert M. "Inner-City Children, Country Summers: Narrating American Childhood and the Geographies of Whiteness." *Environment and Planning* 40 (2008): 1132–1150.

VanderWerf, Klasina. *High on Country: A Narrative History of Cherry Hills Village.* N.P.: The Cherry Hills Land Preserve.

Van Slyke, Abigail A. *A Manufactured Wilderness: Summer Camps and the Shaping of American Youth, 1890–1960.* Minneapolis: University of Minnesota Press, 2006.

Venkatesh, Sudhir Alladi. *American Project: The Rise and Fall of a Modern Ghetto.* Cambridge, Mass.: Harvard University Press, 2000.

Wals, Arjen E. J. "Nobody Planted It, It Just Grew! Young Adolescents' Perceptions and Experiences of Nature in the Context of Urban Environmental Education." *Children's Environments* 11, 3 (September 1994): 1–27.

Ward, Colin. *The Child in the City.* London: Architectural Press, 1978.

Wessel, Thomas, and Marilyn Wessell. *4-H: An American Idea, 1900–1980.* Chevy Chase, Md.: National 4-H Council, 1982.

West, Elliott. *Growing Up With the Country: Childhood on the Far Western Frontier.* Albuquerque: University of New Mexico Press, 1989.

Whyte, William H. *The Last Landscape.* Garden City, N.Y.: Doubleday, 1968.

Williams, Amrys O. "Head, Heart, Hands, and Health: 4-H, Ecology, and Conservation in Wisconsin, 1930–1950." Master's Research Essay, History of Science Department, University of Wisconsin–Madison, April 9, 2007.

Williams, Rhonda Y. *The Politics of Public Housing: Black Women's Struggles against Urban Inequality.* Oxford: Oxford University Press, 2004.

Wiltse, Jeff. *Contested Waters: A Social History of Swimming Pools in America.* Chapel Hill: University of North Carolina Press, 2007.

Wood, Richard E. *Survival of Rural America: Small Victories and Bitter Harvests.* Lawrence: University Press of Kansas, 2008.

Woolever, John D. "Animals and Why Children Fear Them." *American Biology Teacher* 15, 5 (May 1953): 121–123.

Wright, Lawrence. *City Children, Country Summer.* New York: Charles Scribner's Sons, 1979.

Zelizer, Viviana A. *Pricing the Priceless Child: The Changing Social Value of Children.* Princeton, N.J.: Princeton University Press, 1985.

INDEX